Imagining the Holy Land

Imagining the Holy Land

Maps, Models, and Fantasy Travels

BURKE O. LONG

INDIANA
University Press

BLOOMINGTON AND INDIANAPOLIS

This book is a publication of

Indiana University Press
601 North Morton Street
Bloomington, Indiana 47404-3797 USA

http://iupress.indiana.edu

Telephone orders   800-842-6796
Fax orders   812-855-7931
Orders by e-mail   iuporder@indiana.edu

© 2003 by Burke O. Long

All rights reserved

The paper used in this publication meets the minimum
requirements of American National Standard for Information
Sciences—Permanence of Paper for Printed Library
Materials, ANSI Z39.48-1984.

Manufactured in the United States of America

Library of Congress Cataloging-in-Publication Data

Long, Burke O.
Imagining the Holy Land : maps, models, and fantasy travels /
Burke O. Long.
p. cm.
Includes bibliographical references and index.
ISBN 0-253-34136-1 (alk. paper)
1. Palestine in popular culture—United States. 2. Palestine
—Foreign public opinion, American. 3. Chautauqua Institution.
4. Louisiana Purchase Exposition (1904 : Saint Louis, Mo.).
5. American School of Oriental Research in Jerusalem—Faculty
—Attitudes. 6. Stereoscopic views—Palestine—History.
7. Palestine—Maps—History.   I. Title.
E169.O4 L6572003
956.94—dc21
2002007976
1 2 3 4 5 08 07 06 05 04 03

For Sarita Gabriela

CONTENTS

Illustrations

Illustrations

Acknowledgments

I acknowledge with pleasure a few people and institutions whose support and encouragement were ample and generous as I gathered materials for this book. The American Council of Learned Societies and the William R. Kenan Charitable Trust awarded me research fellowships during 1997–98. The Dean for Academic Affairs at Bowdoin College provided crucial funds for preparing illustrations.

Leona Glidden Running and David Noel Freedman offered critical assistance some years ago as I plunged into the world of William Foxwell Albright. I still draw upon unpublished documents they graciously opened to me. The late Alfreda Irwin, historian at the Chautauqua Institution Archives, gave expert and friendly assistance in uncovering items related to Palestine Park. Lydia Chaverin McKenzie shared with me her enthusiasm for Chautauqua memorabilia and provided copies of rare historical material. Kay Schellhase, archivist at Lancaster Theological Seminary, made a special inventory of the unprocessed Chester McCown papers at the Pacific School of Religion, her place of former employment. This gift of volunteer effort proved critical to my research.

Other people, too many to name, unfailingly received my inquiries with interest and kindness. In this regard, I am especially indebted to staff members of the American Philosophical Society in Philadelphia; Great Passion Play in Eureka Springs, Arkansas; the Library of Congress, Washington, D.C.; the Missouri Historical Society, St. Louis; the Pacific School of Religion and the Badè Institute, Berkeley, California; Pitts Theological Library of Emory University, Atlanta; the library of Bowdoin College; and the public libraries of Lakeland, Florida; St. Louis; and Salt Lake City.

To all these colleagues and to others whom, but for lack of space or faulty memory, I would have mentioned, I offer heartfelt thanks. They have shown me countless examples of what "user friendly" means to a scholar on the hunt.

Imagining the Holy Land

Introduction
A Matter of Space

On a prominent hill from which one can see much of modern-day Jerusalem, the Holy Land Hotel stands like a sentinel, its east and west façades turned toward countless sunrises and sunsets. Since 1957, the hotel has offered luxurious accommodations and, as conditions permit, easy access to tours throughout Israel. Its signal feature, however, is that the mostly American and European clientele may stroll through a quarter-acre scale model of ancient Jerusalem and imagine "yesterday's scenes at today's city." A small sign, whose tone has now been surpassed by Internet hyperbole, decorously notes that the replica was built in consultation with historians and famous archaeologists.[1]

Such geopiety—that curious mix of romantic imagination, historical rectitude, and attachment to a physical place—is a vital aspect of contemporary Palestinian and Israeli experience.[2] It has long appealed to Anglo-Europeans and North Americans, mostly Christians, as well.

Indeed, from the very beginning of the American Republic, the *idea* of the Holy Land, as distinct from the physical place, was a flexible and powerful cultural myth. Biblical memory, romanticism, and thirst for the "real" land of revelation influenced many Americans' practical experiences of what they called Palestine, Canaan, Land of the Bible, or simply, the Holy Land. During the nineteenth and early twentieth centuries, increasing numbers of U.S. citizens—pilgrims, tourists, missionaries, preachers, settlers, explorers, archaeologists, Bible scholars, and diplomats—came into contact with Ottoman (later British Mandate)

1

FIG. 1. Spying the Promised Land, c. 1900.

Palestine. Middle-class tourism was becoming a new and fashionable industry. And concurrently, infatuation with the Holy Land had shifted from conceiving it as a non-earthly utopian space—imagined in poetry, song, and liturgy—to an idealized, touchable place—a fantasized reality on the ground.[3]

Most of the early travelers from North America were Protestant Christians. For them, the Holy Land was everlastingly the land of the Bible, a neglected backwater of the Turkish realm in need of reclamation by the West, wherein the drama of Christianity had begun. For American Jews of this period, affections for the Holy Land were tied to debates over Zionism and further complicated by the politics of marginality.[4] As Lester Vogel wrote, Palestine was

> both fetid Oriental wasteland and resplendent biblical garden. It was a tourist attraction and a place to see, a mission field and a place to evangelize, a Promised Land and a place to colonize, a wilderness, an outpost, a treasure chest of antiquity.[5]

Today, similar emotions tug at the heart, even if they are made vastly more complicated by the geopolitics of modern Israel and western Asia.

Romance enlivens tour brochures and claims column inches in the popular press. Cullen Murphy, a sophisticated observer of modern America, headlined an essay about a trip to Israel as though it were a memoir of youthful coming of age: "Hallowed Ground: A First Experience of the Holy Land."[6]

More than a hundred years ago, however, even though rising prosperity and expanding global awareness had stimulated tourism, many Americans could ill afford the rigors and costs of actual travel to Palestine. Quick to spot opportunity, entrepreneurs of religion and business brought the Holy Land to America. They presented its charms to a fee-paying public as nostalgia, exoticism, and edifying entertainment. People sang sentimental songs about Galilee and Jerusalem; they bought expensive wooden cabinets filled with Holy Land memorabilia; they attended elaborately staged fantasies of biblical story and custom. Others took surrogate tours by means of devices that turned dual photographic images of Ottoman Palestine into three-dimensional you-are-there experiences of Bible times. Still others found their Canaan in upstate New York, in a large model of biblical Palestine laid out along the shore of Lake Chautauqua. Bible scholars sought out, excavated, and mapped places of biblical piety, and then translated their enthusiasm into letters and essays of evocative discovery. Americans of means perused lavishly illustrated travel books, to which painters and photographers contributed—that is, when they were not busy exhibiting their work on their own. Everybody, it seems, added something to this vigorous discourse of Holy Land infatuation.[7]

The impulse to invent and visit a presentable Holy Land at home has hardly subsided. It thrives today in Internet virtual tours. And it fuels theme parks such as Arkansas-based "The New Holy Land Tour" and the high-tech "Holy Land Experience" alongside the extravaganzas of Disney World in Florida.

Nearly a century ago, one Madame Lydia Mamreoff von Finkelstein Mountford, an elocutionist and fantasist of biblical life, perfectly caught the spirit of Americanism, business acumen, and even scholarship that runs through all this activity. Speaking at groundbreaking ceremonies for the Jerusalem Exhibit planned for the 1904 St. Louis World's Fair, Madame Mountford meticulously explained various religious practices as they were performed for the occasion. Never one to miss a dramatic opportunity, she then swept her gloved hand toward the assembled dignitaries and proclaimed, "You cannot go to Jerusalem, so Jerusalem comes to you. To American energy all things are possible."[8]

The book you are about to read explores some of these imaginative representations of the Holy Land. You will enter elaborate, sometimes outlandish, always inventively constructed worlds of Holy Land attachments, spaces where desire enables fantasies of the "real" in representation or, in the case of models, in the absolute fake.

I have not attempted exhaustive coverage. However, the holy lands I have chosen strike me as typical and they exemplify a persistent tradition of representing the Holy Land to Americans. Each nurtured religion and geopiety as practiced at home rather than in actual travel to Palestine, although I am not convinced that very much ought to be made of the distinction.

One of these worlds, Palestine Park in upstate New York, began in the late 1870s, and stands at the headwaters of ideologically charged tourist spectacles found downstream in the Saint Louis World's Fair Jerusalem Exhibit of 1904 and the "New Holy Land" in the Ozark Hills of Arkansas today. From the 1920s to the 1940s, highly trained biblical scholars imagined holy lands theologically but also politically, in ways that joined the Holy Land to political debate of the time. Historical maps of the Bible, a subset of theological literature, conjured yet other holy lands while reinforcing certain values and assumptions identified with the United States. The various examples I have chosen advanced religious causes while speaking to cultural and political anxieties specific to the times of their popularity.

All of these real-imagined worlds allow me, as a historian and reader of Holy Land spaces, to transgress the borders usually drawn between elite and popular culture. It is commonly assumed, for example, that university-trained biblical scholars have long since outgrown the sentimental geopiety of earlier generations. Scholarship has matured, so the narrative of disciplinary identity goes. Scholars pursue increasingly objective, rational inquiries to gain more reliable descriptions of ancient biblical history and, where relevant, more adequate formulations of theological truth.

Yet Holy Land travels, actual or surrogate, have always been undertaken on the wings of imagination. Further, these journeys have usually involved Bible study, whether or not the travelers were tutored in the rules of increasingly technical scholarship. Professional Bible scholars—who form the guild to which I belong—have often addressed wider audiences. In such cases, and sometimes even within technical writings, they imagined holy lands in ways that were deeply congruent with vernacular travel diaries, photographic pilgrimages, and theme park models, though this is rarely acknowledged.

I reconstruct these many Holy Land worlds from artifacts and textual remains. In one case I have used material from direct witness and participation. As will become evident, I have tried to notice intellectual and emotional components in representations of the Holy Land. I have also looked for entanglements with ideology, that loose aggregate of lived personal or communal commitments to values and assumptions about what is real, what is accepted as naturally true and right in a given social order.[9] Each meticulously crafted model, photographic tour, theme park, or scholarly presentation purports to speak of things eternal, above the messiness of history. That is part of the mythic power of geopiety. Yet each of these holy lands is a creature of its time and is rooted in a particular, transient historical circumstance. Each involves problematic exclusions and inclusions, effaced histories and privileged scenarios, assemblages of nostalgic desire and fantasy, and embodied interpretations of the "true" Bible as well as claims to the truly American.

In a word, such holy lands are complex social spaces constructed out of physical place, socially shaped perceptions of that place, and human interactions in relation to that place—all at the same time. In my readings of holy lands I have thus drawn upon Edward Soja, who sees history, space, and the social order as dynamic and constantly interactive dimensions of human life.[10]

Soja argues that space is not merely background, an empty stage where events happen, or a container to be filled. Space is dynamic, like history and society. It is socially constructed; that is, constituted as value-laden lived experience in which social relations are represented in action and symbol, in structures of intellectual mapping, human interactions, and architecture.

There is perceived space, the material forms that can be directly observed, drawn and mapped, as for example the full-size model of Moses' wilderness tabernacle that visitors to the Arkansas New Holy Land may enter. Yet this tabernacle space is inseparable from conceptions of it, from a system of Christ symbolism that, when explicated to tourists, defines the "reality" of that space. Moreover, the tour guide and at least some visitors "live" that space. They perceive, conceive, and act, and thus internalize tabernacle space as Christ awareness.

Because official tour guides explain this tabernacle space, and because they offer little or no opportunity for dissent, they exercise a kind of power and authority over willing captives signed up for a tour. In action, costume, and symbolism, leaders articulate the "real" tabernacle, but obscure many alternative possibilities for imagining and living that space. However, some tourists to the tabernacle may have their independent experiences of this space, and hence may question, ignore, even reject the authoritative sense of spatiality provided by the tour guide and explanatory video tapes. Or an observer such as I can resist such impositions and stake out a place of counter-perspective.

For Soja, both actively participating in the dominant ethos of a socially constructed space and resisting that dominance are powerful modes of spatial practice. Both can be dynamic elements of any particular lived space. Thus, holy land spaces, whether constructed with artifacts of model, letter, scholarly text, or map, are social constructions in which, as Soja says, "all histories and geographies, all times and places, are immanently presented and represented, a strategic space of power and domination, empowerment, and resistance."[11]

For my purposes, the most important lesson to be taken from Soja is that the holy lands you are about to enter are complex, layered constructions. Physical place (which has to be imagined in some fashion), symbolically charged conceptuality (which imparts significance and value), and multiple perspectives (which allow for competing constructions and positioning inside of particular spaces) all overlap and bleed into one another in lived experience. There are many spaces, or rather many localized spatial practices for a given place, so to speak. With each holy land realized in America, whatever the medium, I try to be sensitive to such complexities.

I narrate selected episodes of heavily freighted holy lands conjured up by letters, photographs, maps, models, and fantasy travels. I have chosen episodes for their intrinsic interest and variety. I have also exposed cultural continuity, the threads of people and ideas which link holy lands in mingled streams of representation. My case studies are typical in a historical sense and mostly Protestant Christian, since these communities generated most of the action. Each example is rich in ideological entanglements and illustrative of the kinds of spatial practices through which people continually invent holy lands, even today. In short, I offer critical readings, what Soja calls affective geography, of those spaces. Others must judge how worthwhile the journey has been.

One

Lakeside at Chautauqua's Holy Land

East of Interstate 90, New York State Route 394 rises gently from Lake Erie's shoreline. Three miles past the small town of Mayville, a grandly colonnaded portico along the highway marks the main entry to the Chautauqua Institution, founded in 1874. Nodding to a security guard, some 7,500 summer residents every year pass through these gates into an irresistible lakeshore sanctuary.

Pastel-colored Victorian cottages set along shaded streets display American flags above filigreed balconies and flower gardens. Street names like Wythe, Vincent, Miller, Asbury, and Palestine recall founding patriarchs, Methodist connections, and a time when Bible and Holy Land study were uppermost in Chautauqua's programs. Today, the 750-acre enclave strikes a visitor as a meticulously curated college campus, summer resort, religious encampment, arts colony, American village square—and none of these wholly.

True to the vision of founders John Heyl Vincent, a Methodist minister, and industrialist Lewis Miller, a Methodist layman, the Chautauqua Institution remains dedicated to the cultivation of both spirit and intellect. A typical weekly program includes lectures by high-profile academics and public figures, organized courses of study, and performances by a professional symphony, opera company, and theater group. On Sundays there is community worship in the open-air auditorium located just off Bestor Plaza, a well-manicured center of village activities.

Fig. 2. Model of Palestine. Postcard view by George V. Miller & Co.
for the Chautauqua Press, c. 1910.

An easy walk from the site of the old steamer dock (long since taken away) where ships used to discharge Chautauqua-bound passengers is a scaled topographical replica of biblical Palestine laid out along about four hundred feet of sandy lakefront. More than a century ago, "Palestine," as the old maps called the model, was near and dear to the heart of Chautauqua's residents and a focus of their daily activities. It was a place for family recreation and a famous tourist destination, complete with landscape scenery and defining spectacle. It was a favored site for Bible study and religious devotion. Palestine Park and other Bible displays located nearby became well-trodden pathways in Chautauqua's landscape of Holy Land consciousness.

An 1877 map shows clearly the passion that imposed Bible-centered geography onto the shores of "Fair Point." Orderly rows of tent platforms or cottage lots, the earliest and lowest numbered locations, surround the main auditorium like ancient Israelite tribes encamped around God's wilderness tabernacle. Outward from this center and arranged along a rough ellipsis bounded by North and Palestine Avenues are landmarks in Chautauqua's re-created holy land. From Chapel Park, which by 1883 would be mostly given over to a museum of biblical archaeology, one could walk along Palestine Avenue to "Palestine," thence to Oriental House and a model of Jerusalem. Following North

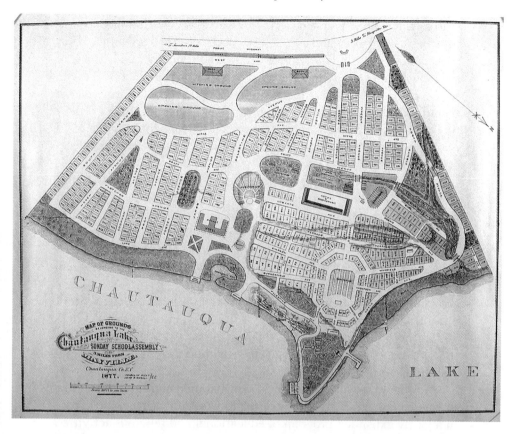

FIG. 3. Map of grounds. Chautauqua Lake Sunday School Assembly. Phoenix Letter Co., Buffalo, New York, 1877. Courtesy of Lydia Chaverin McKenzie.

Ave, one would curve back toward Chapel Park, passing along Morris Avenue to the Giza pyramid and the "Jewish Tabernacle," a scale model of the same Mosaic shrine already suggested by the main auditorium's placement. Beginning from a gated entry near the public highway (at the top of the map) and partly defining the southern and eastern boundaries of this concentration of Holy Land desire, Palestine Avenue looped through the assembly grounds toward its lakeside destination, Palestine Park.

Whether traveling from a nearby railhead by stage coach along the public way or arriving by steamship, Chautauqua's nineteenth-century visitors would have entered a territory signposted, at least in part, by Bible sites. Indeed, visitors using water transport would have had to pass Jerusalem and Oriental House, and "stumble over deceitful hillocks, treacherous brooks and pools, and great mounds of rugged rock," as one journalist imagined Palestine, on their way to their accommodations.[1] In this space of Holy Land consciousness, children and adults acted out their fantasies of biblical antiquity, nurtured romanticized notions of the Holy Land, and vivified the one story that mattered most to them, the revelation of God's redemption in Christ. According to a recent promotional brochure, some visitors to Chautauqua still think of Palestine Park as the "REAL Chautauqua . . . a deeply moving experience, a not-to-be-missed part of a summer vacation . . . [where] bits and pieces of the Bible story are put together."[2]

Today, Palestine Park and its power to nurture Holy Land consciousness have lost their spatial and programmatic prominence. Cut off from its originating gateway and destination, Palestine Avenue now goes nowhere in particular. The satellite biblical models have been replaced by "Miller Park," a tree-shaded memorial to co-founder Lewis Miller, whose cottage still stands near the site of the first auditorium, long since removed. The cottage is now a nostalgic stop on a tour of Chautauqua's origins. However, deprived of its location in the front rank of dwellings arrayed around the old auditorium-tabernacle, Miller's cottage no longer carries biblical associations. And of course, steamships no longer call at Chautauqua to send their passengers into a landscape of Holy Land awareness.

Nowadays, a walk among the somewhat unkempt hills and valleys of Palestine seems far less compelling to vacationers, who participate in a vastly expanded program of educational and religious activities. However, visitors may still read the signs, guidebook in hand, and take a self-guided tour. Although greatly attenuated from the lectures of an earlier day, twice-weekly presentations recount what brochures still call "Bible history." Within this space, both guidebook and lecturers recall biblical, not modern, Palestine, and visitors walk through a geographically materialized narrative of Christian redemption.[3]

By traveling to this surrogate holy land destination, as one sympathetic observer commented in 1879, an early Chautauquan was "enabled to secure a more vivid comprehension of Eastern life than is attainable without making a transatlantic voyage to the Orient himself."[4] In such a constructed space of tourism and religious devotion, fantasies of the Holy Land, entangled with ideologies of religion and national selfhood, were acted out.[5]

In its turn-of-the-century heyday, the Chautauqua Institution was one of America's most important centers of adult education outside the costly preserves of colleges and universities. Teachers included accomplished university-based biblical scholars as well as prominent church leaders, each of whom helped founders John Vincent and Lewis Miller to realize their purposes. All the more reason to pay close attention to this real-and-imagined Holy Land at home in America.

Chautauqua Beginnings

While the American civil war was raging, John Heyl Vincent left Paris for Ottoman Palestine. He would travel through Italy, thence by steamer to Egypt, and finally overland to Jerusalem. It was January 12, 1863, six weeks before his thirty-first birthday.[6] His itinerary was not unusual, but Vincent was no ordinary pilgrim-tourist. From the beginning of his ministry ten years earlier, he had devoted creative energies to instructing members of his congregation in the details of biblical history and geography. He had established an intensive "Palestine Class" for his congregation at Camptown, New Jersey, and had led study pilgrimages through a topographical map of Palestine laid out on the grounds near the church. He carried this interactive pedagogy to his other parishes, notably Galena, Illinois, in 1859.[7] About a decade after his trip to the Holy Land, Vincent would inspire construction of the much more ambitious "Park of Palestine," a part of his expansive vision for what was then called the Chautauqua Assembly.

Vincent entered Ottoman Palestine that winter of 1863 convinced that intimate knowledge of the topography of Palestine was basic to Christian morals, if not salvation. An intensely energetic man, Vincent was determined to observe, interrogate, sketch, record, pray, and talk his way beyond mere biblical literacy. He hungered for a lived familiarity with the land. "I resolved," Vincent wrote in his diary, "not to forget as I made my first step on shore that this was the Holy Land." The days that followed found him meticulously examining hundreds of spots "rightly or wrongly" associated with biblical events, evaluating as best he could the authenticity and condition of ruins, and recording his impressions of native peoples.[8]

Writing to one of his Sunday school pupils, Vincent recorded a stop along the route of the Israelites' escape from Egypt. He was exhausted, he wrote, after a sleepless night in a "dirty Arab house" disturbed by "fleas [that] crawled all over us and dogs outside . . . barking all night." But when he moved on to the Red Sea (note the biblical designation), such privations were quickly forgotten in the rush of feelings stirred by biblical memory and nature sublime. "Yesterday the three of us came to

Suez and went down to the Red Sea to the place where the Israelites crossed," he wrote. "The place is very wild and grand with scarcely a green thing to be seen. Among the wild, craggy cliffs, the deep gorges, the sandy and rocky plain, we kneeled down and prayed to the God of the Hebrews."[9]

Recalling scenes in the biblical drama, the literal truth of which he never doubted, profoundly moved Vincent. Living "the old life over again in Canaan," as he later wrote, undoubtedly reinforced his near obsession with biblical geography and history.[10] This same passion drove him to write many essays aimed at improving Sunday school instruction and the training of teachers, both of which were lifelong concerns he addressed with considerable success.[11]

Soon after returning from Palestine, Vincent met Lewis Miller, a wealthy inventor and industrialist. At the time, Vincent was Secretary of Sunday School Work for the Methodist-Episcopal Church, and Miller was an active Sunday school leader in the First Methodist-Episcopal Church of Akron, Ohio. Having worked together to establish standardized training courses for church school teachers, the two men began to envision gathering teachers in a woodsy setting to study the Bible and new methods of Sunday school instruction.[12]

Vincent was suspicious of the emotionalism connected with camp meetings, especially since they were enjoying renewed popularity after the Civil War.[13] Nevertheless he, along with many others at the time, believed that wilderness unspoiled by human artifice spoke of God and encouraged direct, authentic religious experience. To realize their vision of decorous, Bible-centered, out-of-doors Christian education, Vincent and Miller chose Fair Point, an existing Methodist camp meeting site in western New York State along the gently sloped shores of Lake Chautauqua. "What more appropriate," wrote Miller more than a decade later, "than to find some beautiful plateau of nature's own building for its [Chautauqua's] rostrum, with the sky for its frescoed ceiling . . . the camp-meeting spirit of prayer and praise for its rostrum exercises, the church-school for thought and development?"[14]

The first Chautauqua Assembly opened in 1874. The intense two-week session was filled with plenary lectures on practical Sunday school work and intense drills in biblical history, chronology, and geography. Teacher training, called "specimen meetings," included presentations of Sunday school lessons, sample recitations, and demonstrations on how to use new technology such as stereographs and lantern slides of the Holy Land.[15]

Determined that their assembly not be confused with rowdy camp meetings, and probably influenced by the resurgence of Methodist holiness meetings at the time, Vincent and Miller planned their own blend of wholesome recreation, worship, and study. There were in fact few recreational moments. Warned of the "usual discomforts of outdoor and camp life," people came anyway, taking on rules of decorum and suffering mosquitoes, heat, rain, crude nighttime illumination, rough cottages, and tent-platform accommodations. The gates were closed from Saturday evening until Monday morning. A Department of Order and its "police-page corps" strictly monitored activities. Recreations were banned "during lecture and institute hours," and those not willing to observe this "law" were admonished, "Please stay at home."[16]

From these austere beginnings, Chautauqua's educational activities very quickly expanded and spread through affiliates to many different locations in America. Leaders of the assembly, later to be named the Chautauqua Institution, took ambitious steps toward becoming a leading center of education for families as well as non-university students, a pioneering alternative to established colleges and universities. Early instruction included courses and competitive examinations during summer sessions and home study through the Chautauqua Literary and Scientific Circle, and a series of Chautauqua-published textbooks.[17] By the 1880s, the Chautauqua auditorium had become a main venue for public discussion of politics, economics, science, literature, religion, and topics of international concern to Americans who were just beginning to discover global awareness.

Although limited by social conditions of the time, such liberality of intellectual inquiry had at its core Vincent's populist vision of "universal culture," what a society in all its dimensions could become if imbued with certain broad, faith-based values. The theory was simple: "Life is one, and religion belongs everywhere." Vincent wanted to unify "people of all ages and conditions" around the "home idea of mutual love and tenderness; the church idea of reverence and conscientiousness; the school idea of personal culture; and the shop idea of diligence, economy, and mutual help."[18] Since they accepted Protestant religion and the Bible as fundamental to these goals, Chautauqua's leaders enlisted Christian clergy and university biblical scholars, visual aids, biblical displays, and instruction in biblical languages—all to build knowledge of the Bible among ever widening circles of students.

These efforts also nurtured a lively consciousness of the Holy Land, with which late-nineteenth-century Americans were already more or less infatuated.[19] Vincent did not pursue an earthly and heavenly Zion so assiduously as the Methodist founders of the camp meeting grounds at Ocean Grove, New Jersey.[20] Yet he valued a tactile, intellectual, and emotional at-homeness with the biblical land. Of course, the biblical land had to be imagined, and the ways of biblical people had to be summoned up with Bible in hand and desire in the heart. So land and its revelation-bearing heroes—an inner geography of religious devotion—became as familiar to Chautauquans as disciplined study, precious artifacts, photographs, costumed dramas (called "biblical entertainments"), scale models of biblical landscapes, and fantasy tours would permit. In the process, Chautauqua indulged a flair for ritual, celebrated unabashed patriotism, and read the Bible as the privileged book of American (Christian) civilization.

For Church and Nation

"We cannot separate Christianity from the history of human thought and progress," the Reverend A. D. Vail announced in August 1882. He was speaking to the first graduates of Chautauqua's home study courses, the Chautauqua Literary and Scientific Circle (C.L.S.C.).[21] Endorsing an ideology of cultural progress blessed by Christian uplift—not an uncommon sentiment of the time—Vail went on to encourage graduates to think of themselves as among the privileged cultural and spiritual, even racial, descendants of those Holy Land heroes who had first experienced God's revelation. Graduates would ceremonially enter space that had been civilized by high culture, that is, constructed of biblical ancestry, triumphant Christianity, and Protestant privilege.

Vail's message was partially encoded in a special ceremonial flag. Meant to symbolize the breadth of education John Heyl Vincent had mapped out for members of the C.L.S.C., the banner was emblazoned with three insignias (Chautauqua's Hall of Philosophy, a Bible, and the cross), and had been carried around the world on a pilgrimage to "famous places of literature, art, and religion."[22] The itinerary was not haphazardly chosen. As Mr. Vail, who had made the expensive silk flag, suggested, the banner memorialized the triumph of Christianity even as its plantings and raisings around the world mapped a geography of cultural progress. The Bible stood at the generative point of origin and provided the master narrative of the racially marked superior peoples of the world.[23]

Like most people of his social circles, Vail took as self-evident the superiority of Christianity among the world's religions. Nor did he question the patterns of white/black interactions that had marked American history, religion, and politics. For him, triumphant culture in the West was white and Caucasian, and stemmed from Greco-Roman (Aryan), Egyptian (Hamitic), and Jewish (Semitic) roots, "the three great divisions of the Caucasian race that sprang from the family of Noah." From these roots, Vail told his audience, Christian civilization of finer sensibilities and learning flowered, passing from the Bible and ancient Near Eastern societies, through the Greeks, and into European centers of intellectual activity. Impassioned with such missionary fervor, Chautauquans were about to be inducted into that good company and claim their patrimony in Christian-sponsored cultural progress.

As he made his pilgrimage, Vail said, he raised Chautauqua's banner at various centers of moral and intellectual wisdom. Cultural progress "seemed to burst, like the flames from a score of points at once, and in scores of places we saluted the rising, spreading, conquering spirit of the cross." He hoped for that "final triumph of Christianity that should betoken the speedy destruction of Mohammedanism." In the meantime, Vail concluded, the banner was entrusted to its "resting place in the ark of the C.L.S.C. that bears so much of precious freight and hope for the future of the Church and the Nation."[24]

In subsequent years, recollections of what came to be called Chautauqua's first "recognition ceremony" became regular parts of annual celebrations. Jesse Lyman Hurlbut, one of the Chautauqua Assembly's early and revered leaders, once rehearsed the banner's symbolic journey to what he, too, some forty years later, took to be the unquestioned roots of America's (Protestant) advanced culture. The flag had flown over monuments to Anglo-Saxon literary art (Shakespeare's tomb; the graves of Walter Scott and Robert Burns) and Anglo-Protestant religion (Westminster Abbey). Yet its finer raisings (and the longer, more lavishly noted points on the original itinerary) were in places central to Christian devotion to the Bible and to the Holy Land of biblical story.

> [The banner] had been waved from the summit of the Great Pyramid, of Mount Sinai in the Desert, and Mount Tabor in the Holy Land. It had been laid in the Manger at Bethlehem, and in the traditional tomb of Jesus in Holy Sepulcher Church. It had fluttered upon the Sea of Galilee, upon Mount Lebanon, in the house where Paul was converted at Damascus, and under the dome of St. Sophia in Constantinople . . . [and] the Acropolis and Mars' Hill in Athens.[25]

The excessive peroration is telling. American culture, presumed to be essentially Anglo-Protestant Caucasian, and the refined person whom Chautauqua programs aimed to cultivate could both trace a privileged pedigree to the Bible and the triumphant expansion of Christianity. Poised under this flag before marching through four arches representing "Faith, Science, Literature, and Art," members of each graduating class stood ready to be admitted to the fraternity of knowledge, "having wisdom and especially the highest wisdom of all, the knowledge of God."[26] Summoning up images of biblical exodus and entry into the promised land of unlimited possibility (at the time, both designations were thought apt descriptions of America's recent history), choristers sang,

> Arise and possess the land!
>   Not one shall fail in the march of life,
>   Not one shall fail in the hour of strife,
> Who trusts in the Lord's right hand?
> Arise and possess the land!
> The Lord shall sever the sea,
>   And open a way in the wilderness
>   To faith that follows, to feet that pass
> Forth into the great TO BE
> The Lord shall sever the sea![27]

Having ritually identified with biblical peoples and taken their position at the pinnacle of Christian-sponsored advancement, graduates of the C.L.S.C. then passed through Chautauqua's Golden Gate and walked up a slight incline to the Parthenon-like Hall of Philosophy. Mapping a territory of aspiration and achievement, they entered a realm of superior wisdom rooted in knowledge of God. Like the Israelites of old, they took possession of a land. Was it the Holy Land? The American continent? Or knowledge's terra firma, where spirit and intellect meet in cultured refinement? Perhaps they could lay claim to all of these while entering that ideational space, a holy land which had given form to the Bible, led them to higher wisdom, and defined their own privileged place in American, Protestant, Christian civilization.

At Home in Palestine

Even before such elaborate ceremonies had been devised, other occasions promoted value-laden identification with biblical peoples and the

Holy Land. During the Assembly's first season, Chautauquans could imagine themselves journeying to biblical Palestine while viewing a 13' × 30' panoramic landscape painting on display in the main auditorium. Created by William Henry Perrine, a Methodist minister, sometime traveler to Ottoman Palestine, professor at Albion College in Michigan, and amateur painter, the huge canvas presented a fantasy tour of the Holy Land with biblical locations clearly marked.

Like other artists who traveled the country giving lectures on their work,[28] Perrine regularly stood before Chautauquans and took them on vivid walks through the countryside of biblical narrative. According to one report, he held his audience for two hours on one warm August night. The performance was surely a testament to fervent geopiety and the success of Vincent's plan to discourage camp meeting riffraff. The "best judges" praised these "excellent works of art," wrote the Assembly's official chronicler. What is more, the writer added, the paintings added to Chautauqua's already intense Bible study the enriching benefits of actual travel, making Perrine's "full and accurate knowledge of the topography of Palestine" very valuable to the audience.[29]

Five years later, in a smooth blend of reportage and promotion, an *Assembly Daily Herald* essayist suggested that because electricity had recently come to Chautauqua, the Perrine paintings conveyed the Holy Land more dramatically than was possible in the early days of dim and flickering pine-fire illuminations. The wondrously rendered and illuminated "Holy Land from Lebanon on the north, to the great desert in the south" was not precisely a map, or a fanciful bird's-eye view of the land. Perrine's paintings and lectures, something like an oversized illustrated travelogue, proved far more captivating. As one Chautauquan put the matter, "It presents exactly what a traveler sees in journeying through the Holy Land." Landscape and points of interest combined with such unity of effect, the reporter continued, that "one easily looses [sic] himself, and forgets that he is gazing upon a painting and imagines himself suspended high over the Mediterranean and looking upon a veritable landscape."

Of course, the visually represented faraway space was inert and had to be imagined as holy geography. Guided by Perrine's interpretive comments, at least some of the Chautauquans who gazed upon the panorama may have imagined themselves as pilgrims to that place of textual memory and religious desire. Artificial light and shadows, supplemented with didacticism and geography, supplied the necessary "sentiment of history" which, for the reporter, made Perrine's work come

FIG. 4. Chautauquans at the Pyramid of Gizeh.
Harper's New Monthly Magazine 59 (1879).

alive. Shadows over Samaria added perspective and suggested "the contempt" that the Jews felt for that region. A glowing sunset threw "most gorgeous hues on Carmel and lower Galilee in honor of the miracles of Elijah and Jesus." Beyond the Jordan River, the heights of Gilead and Bashan were lit up "in commemoration of the fact that two and one-half tribes of Israel lived there." The Mediterranean Sea was rendered in subdued colors so that "the landscape, which is the chief object of interest, may stand out the more boldly." Completing the illusion of actual travel to the Holy Land, the writer noted, a "reduced view in chromo is on sale at the Oriental House" for souvenir hunters.

This newly electrified exhibition elicited praise for a fellow Chautauquan, Thomas Edison, along with a self-congratulatory reaffirmation of Chautauqua's (and America's) place in the narrative of cultural progress. It could not have hurt that co-founder Lewis Miller was a son-in-law to Edison. "Distinguished scholars and divines," continued the reporter, "frequently stood around discussing the painting's merits." They blessed "the inventive genius of him who discovered and harnessed ... the powerful light which, beyond the light of the moon at full orb, sheds such luster on the canvas."[30]

During the Assembly's second season, residents of Fair Point added fantasy reenactments of biblical events to their educative recreation. Following that elliptical way through the assembly grounds, Chautauquans could journey with the ancient Israelites in Egypt, past the pyramids and Moses' wilderness tabernacle, toward the Promised Land. In those early years, J. S. Ostrander, a clergyman from Brooklyn, New York, dressed up as a biblical priest and gave daily lectures explaining the Christian symbolism found in the tabernacle model.[31] A few years later, one Reverend Mr. Hill assumed this duty, regularly answering, as one reporter stated, "a thousand questions pertaining to the Old Tabernacle and its furniture."[32] Apparently mapping that modeled biblical space with landmarks of Christ equivalence, Hill made clear that the old Jewish ways, inadequate as to salvation but prophetic of things to come, had been perfected by Christianity. God's new promise took fleshly form in Jesus, who was at once tabernacle-temple, high priest, and sacrificial offering.

The tabernacle and pyramid models had been built under the direction of the Reverend Dr. W. W. Wythe, then Superintendent of the Department of Recreation, who, as the Chautauqua Institution grew, became responsible for many of Chautauqua's facilities.[33] A medical doctor and Methodist minister, Wythe was remembered as a spry and portly, versatile genius whose mechanical skills and store of knowledge not only made enormous contributions toward transforming the grounds "into the beautiful city in the woods," but added greatly to Chautauqua's religious programming. In about 1877, Wythe traveled to Palestine, one account stated, in search of "treasures of Biblical interest." In what may be an indication of the era's fascination with exotic, "Oriental" (and biblical) peoples, Wythe was praised for his facility with Oriental languages and effortless familiarity with Palestine. As one reporter wrote in 1876, "if Wythe could be suddenly dropped down in Palestine or any other part of the Orient, he would be quite as at home as in any other place."[34]

Being at home in Palestine, that is, in the physical and ideational spaces of Chautauqua's holy lands, might be an apt way to describe Chautauqua's preoccupation with Holy Land geography and Bible study. Leaders sought not only to make the Bible a text of intimate acquaintance, but to make Chautauquans into a biblical people who lived the geography and topography of the Bible narratives, what was called sacred history, as immediate *Christian* experience. The exotic "Orient," much in fashion in Victorian America but often experienced by actual travelers as disappointingly unhygienic and backward, could thus be summoned up as an energizing fantasy that was both remote and familiar, imported from distant places but made to fit American expectations.

Holy Land theater offered one popular means. Chautauquans frequently dressed in biblical costume and wandered the grounds, participating in staged performances of biblical customs led by Reverend Ostrander.[35] One evening, as reported in Chautauqua's newspaper, the "Orientals" staged a "Mohammedan prayer meeting," demonstrated wedding and funeral rites, and exhibited "Oriental hospitality" with striking displays of "salutations, embracing, and [foot] washing." Not quite able to condone the primitive paganism he saw in such ceremonials, even if merely simulated by fellow Chautauquans, the reporter nonetheless allowed that "at the bottom of such uncouth performances there has, no doubt, been much sincerity."[36]

Such patronizing tolerance shows just how authentic Ostrander's performances were taken to be, at least by the Chautauquans, who found them quite irresistible. Actors and observers could immerse themselves in a fantasy world of contemporary Palestine—the illusion of actual travel into the Bible's world—without having to endure the fleas and barking dogs that awaited John Heyl Vincent as he made his own pilgrimage. Chautauquans did not have to directly confront the social

FIG. 5. Group of "Orientals" in Palestine Park, c. 1880.
Ostrander is in the front row, far right.
Courtesy of the Chautauqua Institution
Archives, Chautauqua, New York.

conditions of contemporary Catholic and Greek Orthodox Christians, Jews, and Muslims that many travelers found to be deeply troubling aspects of their pilgrimages.[37] Instead, by assuming, as many did at the time, that the "Orient" had remained culturally stagnant for thousands of years, having missed European advancement, Chautauquans believed they could encounter the primitive and the biblical, while emotionally reaffirming their own place in a narrative of cultural progress. Safely approaching that fictionalized "biblical" world, they apparently believed that they saw the Bible with the eyes of those who wrote it. And yet they could remain at a distance from its uncouth, if captivating, ways.

Such sentiments, when mixed with fascination with world exotica, probably contributed to the popularity of one Madame Lydia Mamreoff von Finkelstein Mountford. A modestly famous elocutionist and repeat visitor to nineteenth- and early-twentieth-century Christian assemblies, Mountford brought her own theatrical realizations of holy land to Chautauqua's stage.[38]

The "Madame" was quite as imposing in appearance as in speech. Her title and string of names were not simply *dramatis personae*. Madame Mountford laid claim to impressive paternal lineage through Russian (Mamreoff), Austrian (Finkelstein), and British (Mountford) respectability, all the way back to the biblical tribes of Mamre (the supposed genealogical origin of Mamreoff) and Ephraim. By her own account, Madame Mountford (née Lydia [Mary Olive] von Finkelstein in 1855) was born in Jerusalem of non-denominational Protestant parents, was baptized in the English Episcopal Church of Palestine, and much later, during a performance tour in India, married a man of British and Indian parents. Convinced that she was, contrary to expectations for women, called to become a "messenger of the Word," Miss von Finkelstein immigrated to the United States in about 1875. Shortly thereafter, she (and for a time her brother, Peter) gave dramatic presentations of Bible story and custom to spellbound audiences in England, North America, India, Australia, and New Zealand. Described by one Australian reporter as "a blonde of Amazonian proportions with a gait and manner that any tragedy queen might envy," she excelled in restless operatic melodrama.[39] Sitting, lying, walking, singing, evoking cries of the desert and city streets, and donning elaborate native dress, she portrayed biblical patriarchs, kings, prophets, and humble biblical folk. Lydia von Finkelstein illustrated biblical stories, psalms, parables, and scenes in Jesus' life. She presented on stage the legends and traditions she knew from Palestine,

FIG. 6. Lydia Mamreoff von Finkelstein in costume.
Photo by Ray D. Chapman, New York, c. 1885.

and realized her fantasies of the Palestine Jesus had known. Not incidentally, she proclaimed her version of the one true Christian message.[40]

As early as 1883, apparently still known as Miss von Finkelstein,
she and her brother Peter turned up at Ocean Grove, New Jersey, in
connection with a second model of biblical Jerusalem built by W. W.
Wythe. In this seaside Zion, a utopian village rooted in the Methodist
holiness movement, the von Finkelstein company portrayed Arab life
and, as a contemporary report noted, made the biblical text come
thrillingly alive.

> Peter, her handsome brother, with other attendants, formed the back-
> ground, and frequently participated in the graphic details which the
> lecturer gave of Arab life, from early Bible times down to the period
> when these delightful personages themselves roamed the hills and
> valleys "beyond Jordan." Peter frequently flourished a dangerous look-
> ing scimitar, to the admiration of the small boys, and terror of nervous
> old ladies who, in what they saw and heard, had a realistic illustration
> of many passages familiar to them from the Scriptures.[41]

The von Finkelsteins were a curious blend of cultural affectations—
children of Austrian-Russian-biblical nobility, born and raised Protestant in Jerusalem, but presented as "natives" of Palestine, a "living
Bible" (as she loved to say), living in America and following the circuits
of religious spectacle. Their performances made it easy for Christian
audiences to appropriate a theatrically rendered contemporary Palestine for its imagined relevance to ancient "Jewish" or biblical life. In
receiving this act of "performed ethnology," as Troy Messenger argued,
Christians could figuratively identify with a theatrical amalgam of nineteenth-century evangelists, contemporary Arabs and Jews of Palestine,
and fictionalized biblical Jews who, curiously, spoke some stage Arabic.[42]

As one of her published solo lectures makes clear, Lydia Mamreoff
von Finkelstein presented herself as a native of Jerusalem, "Jewish" in
knowledge and custom, but perfected in Christianity. This status assured her incomparability among peripatetic elocutionists and transformed her theatrical Bible and Holy Land into a unique reaffirmation
of Christian authenticity. "There is one name that binds us together,"
she customarily proclaimed at the opening of each performance. In that
name of Christ she then greeted her audience, and added,

> Coming as I do from the same land that gave Him birth, the same
> mountains and hills and valleys that greeted his eyes when He was
> incarnated into this world greeted mine when I was born into this

world. So I do not speak to you as one who has simply traveled in Palestine as tourist or explorer, or who has lived there a few years as a missionary, but as one of the people of the country; for that is the . . . rock out of which I was hewn.[43]

At Chautauqua in 1891, Madame Mountford presented "Village Life in Palestine" along with incidents in the life of Jesus. A local cast of eleven men, women, and children, possibly Chautauquans, supported her performance. A news report emphasized the costumes of "fine linen and silk, all hand woven in beautiful rich designs."[44] Lovingly displayed and explained in her lectures, this biblical finery, like her own assertions of noble Russian and priestly biblical lineage, helped Madame Mountford appeal to upwardly aspiring members of America's middle class. The Holy Land that counted for salvation was an aristocratic place, inhabited by a savior of King David's lineage, whose parents "owned property" in Nazareth and Bethlehem, and whose mother, Mary, was a direct descendant of King Solomon through her mother, Anna.[45]

One of Chautauqua's resident "Orientals," August O. Van Lennep, playacted every day, both on- and off-stage. A native of Turkey, a peddler of Holy Land stereographs, possibly a convert to Christianity, Van Lennep "was always clad in a costume of the far East," according to an early admirer. He was credited with being the "animating spirit among the Orientals at public entertainments and in giving the whole Assembly its flavor of life from the people of Bible lands."[46] Van Lennep regularly staged an "oriental funeral service"[47] and wandered about giving "peripatetic lectures on the Park of Palestine."[48] Under trees and beside the lake, he attracted curious, sometimes bemused, Chautauquans who reveled in being close to this bit of Holy Land drama. Using the title of honor, one reporter described the "Effendi" and a finely costumed young girl settling down one afternoon, shaded from the intense summer sun. He sat "Turkish fashion . . . enjoying the breeze of the Lake, smoking his narghile, with the little child sitting near him." Enamored Chautauquans gathered round to see this exotic creature on his outdoor stage. "A crowd of Yankees soon surrounded them," wrote the reporter, perhaps with a trace of skepticism, "plying him with questions, to which he always responded in the language of the Orient, apparently to their entire satisfaction."[49]

In these early years, Van Lennep presided over the Oriental House, a two-thousand-square-foot two-story replica of a dwelling, with a large inner courtyard "such as one would enter in the Far East."[50] From the

FIG. 7. August O. Van Lennep, c. 1880.
Courtesy of the Chautauqua Institution Archives,
Chautauqua, New York.

parapet on its roof, each morning and afternoon, Van Lennep issued the Arabic call to prayer.[51] Within, Chautauquans could purchase souvenirs and wander through a room filled with replicas and artifacts.

Not all Chautauquans were enamored with such studied theatricality, however. Jesse Lyman Hurlbut wryly noted that he never saw any Chautauquans prostrating themselves at Van Lennep's summons to prayer. Indeed, some assembly goers "actually mocked the make-believe *muezzin* before his face."[52]

What, then, was the appeal of these orientalizing cross-dressers, these modelers of Holy Land ethnography? Were they versions of parlor entertainment, otherwise available to the wealthy through booking agents?[53] Did Chautauqua's "Orientals" cater to America's emergent imperial sense and attendant fascination with peoples perceived as primitive and exotic?[54] Did they, like pressed flowers, satisfy a desire for tactile intimacy with a holy land whose very materiality—its people, land, flora, and fauna—spoke as the prophets of old?[55]

Perhaps all of the above. And more. These outlandish pretensions to an authentic biblical Palestine were staged before members of a church and a nation, each of whom was presumed to be heir to the redemptive promises of the Bible. Those who dressed up, playacted, and lived the imagined atmosphere and defining experiences of the land seemed to want to become those whom they impersonated. Chautauqua's "Orientals" made available not contemporary Ottoman Palestine but a fantasy of what could not be had, a land and people that had flourished in countless retellings of biblical stories, or perhaps in telling the singularly important narrative of redemption in Christ. Those who participated perhaps found a kind of religious assurance through the artificial realism of fantasy. Intensely pursued conflation of peoples, cultures, and times offered Chautauquans—at least those who did not deride the whole show—a space in which to "move, if only temporarily, from their American status as a metaphorical chosen race in the New World, to the actual favored nation of the Old."[56]

Yet, while impersonating non-Christian others and asserting a certain kinship with them, the "Orientals" could recall to the missionary-minded that the matter at hand was, after all, Christianity triumphant. Van Lennep, it was reported, ended one of his talks on Palestine shepherd life with "My sheep hear my voice, but a stranger's voice will they not hear." Transforming his vaguely Semitic, Jew/Muslim/biblical persona into the archetypal shepherd Jesus, Van Lennep seemed to nudge his audience, those specially chosen, toward renewed Christian devotion.[57]

About a century later, Noel A. Calhoun, a Presbyterian minister with a flair for the dramatic, continued in Van Lennep's tradition. Wearing a striped shepherd's robe and Arab head covering, he seemed perfectly at home pacing about the diminutive hills of Palestine, shepherd's crook in hand, and addressing crowds assembled near the River Jordan. An artificial lamb his only prop and the hills of recollected biblical Palestine his only stage, Dr. Calhoun created a real-imagined place of materialized biblical interpretation.[58] Old Testament narratives and the sacrifice of the lamb all received their redemptive finality in the New Testament Christ. Throughout, Christian witness mapped a territory of Christian fulfillment and, as in Van Lennep's playacting, displaced the pre-Christian otherness of the shepherd *dramatis persona*. "You try to give a bird's eye view of the whole and get into the history, prophecy and fulfillment of the Old Testament," Calhoun told a news reporter, who added comments by repeat visitor Beverly Dabelle. "It is kind of unbelievable in this day and age," Dabelle said of Calhoun's Christianized biblical space, "that this is so close and so true to the nature of the Holy Land."[59] Evidently she preferred an idealized essence of Holy Land to the contentious particulars of modern Palestine.

Our Tiny Bit of Holy Land

W. W. Wythe, who, it will be recalled, built models of the biblical tabernacle and an Egyptian pyramid, also assembled a replica of Palestine in time for the first Sunday School Assembly of 1874. Tiny villages set on hilltops, valleys of biblical association, the Jordan River, the Sea of Galilee and the Dead Sea, Mount Hermon in the north—all were laid out to scale. Lake Chautauqua made a convenient Mediterranean Sea. About one hundred feet from the Dead Sea, on the point of land leading to Chautauqua's steamship dock, the Oriental House and Van Lennep guarded the approaches to Palestine as well as Wythe's model of Jerusalem.[60]

Later enlarged and reconstructed, Palestine Park soon became a tourist attraction at the center of this small assemblage of Holy Land longing. A favored locale for Sunday school lessons, "Oriental" performances, and ritual pilgrimages, the walk-through model became a richly constituted symbol of Chautauqua itself. Children searched the Dead Sea for polliwogs or sailed their toy boats on the Sea of Galilee. Friends and soon-to-be-wed couples gathered for discreet socializing near Bethlehem. Eulogists intoned praise for departed Chautauquans

FIG. 8. Chautauqua's founding "patriarchs," c. 1880. John Heyl Vincent is in the center, facing to his right. Jesse Lyman Hurlbut is at the far right.
Courtesy of the Chautauqua Institution Archives,
Chautauqua, New York.

along the banks of the Jordan River. Photographers peddled stereo-graphs of the miniature landscape and made souvenir photos for summer residents. Graduating classes of Sunday school teachers posed amidst the hills of Judea. One stereograph even memorialized Chautauqua's founding patriarchs as they posed for the camera on the descents of Mount Hermon, arranged around John Heyl Vincent like Victorian gentlemen on holiday.

As will be recalled, John Heyl Vincent had led study pilgrimages through topographical models of Palestine marked out on the grounds of churches he served.[61] One eyewitness from Galena, Illinois, wrote that nearly everybody "undertook a trip to Palestine"—girls, boys, mothers, grandmothers—even fathers, she said with pleased surprise. Along the way pupils mastered geographical songs and other mnemonic devices, eagerly seeking achievement certificates awarded for their knowledge of the Bible. As students in the class progressed from pilgrim to resident, then explorer, dweller, and finally templar in the Holy Land, they received identity cards marking their status as stewards of the land of Jesus. All of Galena seemed absorbed in Holy Land consciousness. Townspeople contributed "maps, pictures, relics, and other curiosities from the far East, models of the Tabernacle and the Temple, [and] stereoscopic views" to an exhibition set up at the church. *"Dwellers in Jerusalem"* wearing tiny badges served as guides, while others agitated for a *bona fide* Biblical Museum in town.[62]

Realism was the driving aim, fantasy the enabling impulse. In one parish, members of a similar Palestine Class sent letters to the local newspaper, describing in detail their pilgrimage to the Holy Land. Somewhat apologetic, Vincent later wrote that "through no fault" his pupils found themselves "deceiving more than one simple-hearted reader in the community."[63]

Vincent believed that such intense study of geography and promotion of surrogate pilgrimage could only reaffirm the truth of the Bible for those troubled by skepticism. He was especially concerned about those children who, perhaps falling under the influence of the newly emerging historical analysis of the Bible, might reach adulthood with weakened acceptance of Scripture as trustworthy history and religious teaching. Alongside commitment to biblical orthodoxy was allegiance to a widely shared ideological construction. Time had stood still in the East. The "Orient" of exotic degradation, relative to the "Occident" of Christian civilization, had been providentially preserved in its backwardness so as to confound the skeptics. Or, as the irrepressible Madame Mountford would put it before a group of Mormons in 1898, "God the Father (through the agency of the Turkish Empire) had so preserved the Holy Land . . . that the land of the Apostles might retain its purity and holiness as in days of old."[64]

Vincent agreed fully. "There are those," he wrote in an 1884 textbook,

> who believe with firm faith, that, for these days of skepticism and of merciless and conscienceless historic criticism, the [Bible] lands have been kept almost in their original condition, that the testimony of the modern skeptical traveler might (though unintentionally on his part, but necessarily) corroborate the teachings of the Bible.

Indeed, the conditions of society had been so little modified that

> one may live the old life over again in Canaan. Soil and scenery, the seasons of the year, Jacob's well and the Jordan, Ebal and Gerizim, the plain, the wilderness and the city, all give witness to the words of the Book. . . . [The land] that presents itself is the memorial presentation in concrete form of what the Book says was true there thousands of years ago.

Knowing the land, if not through actual travel, then in diligent study and fantasies of a "Palestine Class," is critical to maintaining the Bible's status as Holy Book.

> Once give [the Bible's] wonderful transactions an actual locality among the hills, valleys, and cities which may still be found and visited, connecting and comparing them with the records of our present history, and our youth will readily distinguish the miraculous from the mythical, and discover not only clear illustrations of many portions of the Bible, but strong and irresistible evidence in favor of its divinity.[65]

Grounding the real in the fantasy of a scaled replica was exactly what Vincent was after when he commissioned Wythe to build a model of Palestine. As an early chronicler wrote, Vincent dreamed of "a complete reproduction on a small scale of all the characteristics of Canaan, as shall render a visit to it second only to a vision of the land itself."[66] The sense of "holy land" that Vincent took as self-evident encompassed a mental geography of narrated events and, like the Bible, a gendered genealogy of divine promise. Palestine Park would present salient features of the sacred land, where lived and flourished Abraham, Isaac, Jacob, Joseph, Samuel, Saul, David, Solomon, and above all and greater than all, the Lord Jesus, who became man and lived on our earth and died for our sins. He lived and died and rose in Palestine. From Palestine he ascended to heaven. No wonder we call it the "Holy Land."[67]

Published guides to Palestine Park tried to assure that visitors indeed would see what Vincent saw. A guidebook of 1920, authored by educator and longtime park lecturer Jesse Lyman Hurlbut, described in great detail the main geographical features of Palestine (not the model) and its inhabitants.[68] Hurlbut anchored everything in what he called sacred history, that is, the Bible rehearsed straightforwardly as a historical record aimed at divulging the revelation of God in Christ. Occasionally he would remark that an ancient prophecy had even been fulfilled in a contemporary fact of geography. To wander through this Chautauqua space filled with Christ awareness (Hurlbut called the guide a "travel book") was to be figuratively transported to the actual Holy Land, or rather to a mental place that energized and reaffirmed Christian belief. It was to feel connected to a chain of biblical events leading to Christ and the early triumphs of Christianity. Even maps, unlike those printed in the later *Guidebook* of 1936, did not distinguish the biblically configured model from Palestine of the Ottoman Empire.

Yet the "holy land" of such fantasy journeys was not simply packed away in some assemblage of Christian memory. It connected to something of political consequence. "Here journeyed Abraham and the patriarchs," Hurlbut wrote in 1920.

> Here Joshua fought the battles of the conquest . . . here David wandered, and afterwards reigned; here the prophets preached; and here Jesus Christ lived his thirty-three years on earth.

Since that heroic age, however, a rightful inheritance had been fought over, lost, regained, and was about to be reclaimed. First the Crusaders, Hurlbut averred, then the Jews for eighteen centuries longed to possess the land. And now, since World War I, "all the nations have been centered on this land with a new interest."[69] Why? "On December 8, 1918," Hurlbut told his readers, "the city [Jerusalem] was taken without siege by the British Army under General Allenby, and it now remains under the control of Great Britain."[70] He apparently felt no need to add that these were Christian forces reclaiming their patrimony.

Indeed, press accounts imbued with colonialist prerogatives often pressed the analogy with Christian crusades.[71]

If we take the hint seriously, we might suppose that some Chautauquans wandered the hills of Palestine, *Guide Book* in hand, not only to enact a pedagogy of spiritual enrichment, but also to claim what was deemed rightfully theirs, spiritually, culturally, politically. By knowing the minutiae of geography, topography, and biblical narrative, indeed by becoming those biblical people, Chautauquans could claim their rightful Christian inheritance, even without leaving the United States.[72]

This collapse of the actual Palestine into the manageable experience of its scaled replica is one of the more interesting aspects of Chautauqua's "holy land" in America.[73] One stereograph photo from 1875 shows the "Valley of the Jordan from the Summit of Mount Hermon," with the Sea of Galilee visible in the lower center, the "Mediterranean" to the upper right.[74] The woods, people, and tent platforms of the campground have been crudely removed from the image so that one gazes into a background expanse of horizon and sky, as though standing in Palestine itself. Another photo from the same set depicts a costumed lecturer, probably Van Lennep, standing before men, women, and children who have been arranged behind him across the hills of Palestine. The caption melds geographical artifice with faraway Palestine: "Taken from the Dead Sea. Mt. Hermon at a Distance. A Crowd is assembled in the Land of Moab for the Afternoon Lecture."[75]

Wythe's model of Jerusalem reached for a similar illusion. It was originally displayed underneath a canopy, which at some point resembled the famous Dome of the Rock (called the Mosque of Omar by nineteenth-century Western travelers), a shrine that had long dominated old Jerusalem's skyline.[76] The Palestine site had also focused the passions of Jews, Christians, and Muslims, who saw Jerusalem as central to both religion and imperial ambition. For some two and one-half millennia the site had received the offerings of pious devotion as well as suffering the indignities of claim and counter-claim, triumph and defeat, holiness and sacrilege. In Wythe's time, the golden domed structure was a Muslim shrine, traditionally considered the site of Mohammed's departure from earthly life. Earlier the building had been a Crusader church, and before that, the location had held at least two Jewish temples. It was probably the most widely recognized visual icon of the Holy City itself.

FIG. 9. Valley of the Jordan from the heights of Mt. Hermon,
Palestine Park, c. 1880. Courtesy of the
Chautauqua Institution Archives,
Chautauqua, New York.

To view Wythe's model of Jerusalem under its Dome of the Rock
canopy, then, was to stand figuratively within a particular Holy Land
space heavily vested with potent memory and religious passion. Yet it was
also to stand outside that space and possess the whole city and its hilly
environs in one sweeping glance. Encircling rows of chairs, though facing
the model, marked the boundaries of yet another ideational space defined
by backdrop scenes of Ottoman Jerusalem. Facing inward, Chautauquans
could listen to lectures and master the Holy City. Facing outward, they
would be reduced to a human scale of partialness, as if gazing upon
selected portions of the contemporary city from a colonnaded balcony.

FIG. 10. Wythe's model of Jerusalem, c. 1885.

This laminate of altered scales and historical association nonetheless served the realism of fantasy. One early photograph removed evidence of the viewing platform and simulated horizon and sky as a distant backdrop for the city.[77] A reporter, stressing verisimilitude, noted in 1879 that artist W. H. Perrine enhanced the model by supplying "form and tint to the valleys, plains and mountains roundabout Jerusalem . . . [making] a very perfect transition from the topographical contour and colors in cement to the perspective continuation in the lines and tints of the landscape on the environing canvas." The writer added that this "literal panorama" was based on sketches and photographs taken by "the Doctor [Wythe] himself from the roof of the Casa Nuova Convent . . . during his two month stay in the city." (Perhaps that bit of authenticating origin lingered in the cityscape paintings encircling the assembled chairs.) Perrine's work, the reporter continued, gave "vast enlargement to the scene, in fact lifting the environment out of the artificial narrowness of limit and expanding it to the natural horizons of the holy city."[78]

Thus imagining Jerusalem's entire "natural horizons," a Chautau-quan would gaze upon a landscape kept precious in the heart but con-figured by miniaturized topographical markers, which in commentary mapped the territory as biblical and thereby significant. Yet the model, the simulacrum, was empirically precise, *real*, for Wythe had preserved it in sketches and photographs. Like Palestine Park, Jerusalem's dimen-sional and visual verisimilitude materialized the factuality of Christian-ized biblical history. Or so it seemed to the reporter:

> To the eastward, the eye takes in the Mt. of Olives, the Mts. of Offence, a few summits of the desert of Judea, glimpses of the Dead Sea and the Mts. of Moab, extending seventy miles away to the southwest. To the south and southwest immediately above the val-ley of Hinnom are the Aceldama, Hill of Evil Council, Plain of Rephaim, Mar Elyas, Mts. of Judea and the mountains that shut out Bethlehem. . . . The city is seen on its throne of hills in the amphi-theater of mountains. On this hill of vision doubtless David stood when he said, "Beautiful for situation, the joy of the whole earth is Mt. Zion, on the sides of the north, the city of the Great King." Read this beside the Model and all will be plain.

The attempt at such illusions, rather than their technical successes by contemporary standards, is the important point. On the one hand, the articulated spaces of the fake Holy Land (Palestine Park; Jerusalem; the Oriental House; the Biblical Museum; costumed "Orientals"), in-deed the realism of what Vincent called "our tiny bit of 'Holy Land,'"[79] enabled a fantasy of the actual, yet unattainable, Bible land of antiquity. On the other hand, desire—or perhaps need—for fantasy produced the effect of a "real" Holy Land and enlivened it with emotional intensity. It is as though fantasy and reality, which are by convention held to be opposites, cling to one another in dynamic embrace, each desiring, jus-tifying, and enabling the other.[80]

Perhaps Chautauqua's simulations of the Holy Land may be seen as a scrupulous and upright precursor to America's twentieth-century wax museums, roadside grottos, theme parks, and modern pretensions to Old World art and culture. Under Umberto Eco's astute gaze, these flavorful extracts of American nostalgia are "instances where the American imagination demands the real thing and, to attain it, must fabricate the absolute fake."[81]

One early account gives some indication of how thoroughly Ottoman Palestine's actual landscape was conflated with its miniaturized representation. Taking "a journey through the Holy Land," the Chautauqua daily newspaper noted, children marched

> from the [Children's] Temple down through the Auditorium making a beautiful appearance with flags and banners flying. They sang "Shall we gather at the River" with all the sweetness of children's voices. They then proceeded to Palestine, where they formed a semi-circle extending from the Mediterranean Sea to the Valley of Jordan. Rev. Vincent ascended Mount Hermon and explained to his young, but attentive, hearers the places most prominently connected with Bible history.[82]

Hurlbut recalled that among Bible students wandering over Palestine, "notebooks in their hands, studying the sacred places," a few might "pluck and preserve a spear of grass, carefully enshrining it in an envelope duly marked." Others repeated rumors—untrue, Hurlbut declared—that soil from the Holy Land itself had been spread about Palestine Park, "constituting it a sort of *Campo Santo*."[83] If holy soil had not been spread about, then at least some of Palestine's water was imported. Mary Frances Bestor, daughter of the president of the Chautauqua Institution in the 1920s, once carried a small vial of Palestine Park water all the way to the actual Dead Sea. There, having carefully protected the precious relic during the family's pilgrimage, she exchanged its contents for the real thing, which she subsequently emptied into the Dead Sea of Palestine Park.[84]

Vincent himself may have encouraged such fervor. On at least one occasion he rhetorically imagined all of Chautauqua as a place of biblical resonance. Frank Bray's *Reading Journey through Chautauqua*, Vincent wrote, was a "complete handbook for a pilgrim who would 'see the spot' and understand its significance, the value of each part, and its relation to the whole." Indeed, Chautauqua, like Jerusalem in verse 2 of Psalm 48, "is a place 'beautiful for situation' where Nature and Art unite to bless all who land on its shores."[85]

Even sailing toy boats in Palestine Park could be wistfully recalled, at least on celebratory occasions, as playfulness in a space that opened onto divinity. "Amongst the most precious things of my life was a little tin boat that you could wind up at the smoke stack," wrote Edwin Booth, speaking of his summers at Chautauqua around 1905.

> You could put it on the Dead Sea and it would run to the other end. ... But when I watched my little boat on the Dead Sea I was unconsciously conscious all the time that I was in Jesus' land. The little villages down there where He lived, where He talked, where He touched His comrades in the long ago made Him come alive to talk to me in the living present.[86]

Of course, Chautauqua's grown-ups also wandered the grassy hills and rocky valleys of Palestine and visited Jerusalem. Perhaps they, like Edwin Booth, were mentally transported to the land where all the events of importance to their sense of Christian civilization had taken place. In John Davis's view, not only the playacting in Palestine Park but the "disruption of scale between viewer and viewed" and the "artificially panoramic gaze ... rendered [the tiny landscape] easily graspable and digestible," something to be understood and possessed.[87]

It could be not only possessed, but absorbed into Chautauqua's heroic mythology. Soon after Jesse Lyman Hurlbut's death, a poet eulogized him and Palestine Park, with which he was often associated. Both were keepsakes of the heart, like the Holy Land of Christian imagination. Rachel Dithridge conflated, but never confused, Hurlbut with faraway Palestine, perhaps even with Christ, and with Chautauqua's "tiny bit of 'Holy Land,'" which lay within easy sight and hearing of her family's lakefront cottage.

> Upon the little hills of Palestine
> Erect, and full of life, we see him stand,—
> A dear familiar figure, year by year.
>
> His voice rings clear,
> Above the rustle of the singing trees
> Above the murmur of the whispering waves;
> They are words of wisdom that we hear,
> Made potent by that life of graciousness.
>
> What though he comes no more!
> We, who have loved him never can forget;

For us he walks beside the lake today,
We hear the benediction of his voice
Across the little hills of Palestine.[88]

The Voice of Jesus Freed

The material piety of early Chautauquans aimed at what traditional Protestant theology demanded as the mark of salvation—a personal, unmediated experience of God (Christ) in the heart. An object of fantasy that could be acquired through the fictions and meticulous realism of Chautauqua's holy land seemed, at least for some, to foster such a confirming experience as much as to satisfy longings for it. If skepticism could be set aside, or left on the steamer ship; if flaccid belief could be stiffened by worship and lectures in the outdoors; if the "real" Holy Land could be approached in fantasies enabled by replica, then perhaps the assurances of faith could grow stronger.

Rudyard Kipling for one was not convinced, however. On a visit late in the 1880s, he poked fun at what were for him the ambitious pretensions of Palestine Park. Flirtatious young people strolled irreverently about a peak that overlooked holy Jerusalem, he said. Where some saw the biblical land, he saw "artificial hillocks surrounding a mud puddle and a wormy streak of slime connecting it to another mud puddle."[89]

Perhaps for many others, though, Chautauqua's lakeside Holy Land truly helped them fight the skeptics. Vincent surely believed it would. In effect, the "real" as reproduced and encountered within the absolute fake took on a quality that religious travelers and explorers frequently gave the actual land of Palestine. The perduring landscape, even in miniature, was a direct and reliable witness to divine revelation of long ago. As geoscripture, Palestine's geography attested to the truths of biblical prophecy and Christianity. Chautauqua's miniaturized holy land could do likewise.

Perhaps more than any other writer, William M. Thomson, a missionary to Ottoman Syria and Palestine, gave popular currency to this ancient Christian idea about the biblical land. In a lavishly illustrated study-travelogue, which sold more than two hundred thousand copies, Thomson presented the Holy Land as a "vast tablet whereupon God's messages to men have been drawn." In such a place of readable topography, heroic carriers of the message were important, too. For God's messages had been graven deep in living characters by the Great Publisher of glad tidings, to be seen and read by all to the end of time. The Land and the Book—with reverence be it said—constitutes the ENTIRE and ALL-PERFECT TEXT, and should be studied together.[90]

At least some visitors to the assembly grounds thought that biblical models and diversions, joined with Vincent's intense concern to get the facts of geography and sacred story right, did the work of Thomson's "all-perfect text." It was to do the work of the Protestant Reformation as well. The fantasy of desire and projection could rescue a human, intimate Jesus from the aloof icons of dogmatists and the cold interiors of institutional religion.

Methodist theologian Edwin Booth hinted at such as he reminisced many years later about Vincent's "tiny bit of 'Holy Land.'" Yale biblical scholar Charles Foster Kent and Chautauqua's Jesse Lyman Hurlbut, both of whom were active churchmen and passionate about biblical geography, had worked closely together on perfecting the model, as Booth recalled. They wanted to assure that the topography of Chautauqua's Palestine and its biblical reference points reflected the very latest scholarship about the land and its persistent witness to biblical revelation. "Hurlbut never moved out on a fact that he could not sustain," Booth once declared to a crowd gathered in Chautauqua's amphitheater.

> He got the greatest thinkers of our world and of our church to gather for him the facts. Then he put them into popularization for my consumption and my father's consumption. . . . Jesus . . . was set out again in a real incarnation in a real humanity so we could understand him. . . . Charles Foster Kent and Jesse Lyman Hurlbut were doing it for us here in America in trips through the Holy Land with stereoptica. I have studied these all my life until now I seem to know how high Mount Hermon is. I seem to know how deep the Sea of Galilee is. . . . All of Judea's hills come alive for us and we can hear the voice of Jesus freed from all dogma and freed from all churches speaking to us.[91]

Palestine Park and its related artifacts and affectations were material-ideational icons in an iconoclastic Protestant culture. As ideologically charged images, they defined real and imagined places to be entered and studied, invested with ultimate truths, and purchased with religious and patriotic passion. These iconic spaces were also successful projects of industrious piety directed toward edifying ends.

It was perhaps inevitable that such entrepreneurial energy, and its success, would soon catch the attention of more ambitious, better funded, and less scrupulous propagators of Holy Land consciousness. Why not import the Holy Land to the ultimate site of public spectacles, a World's Fair utopian cityscape that announces in every street and monument, every flag and display, the wondrous progress of Christian civilization?

Two

Starred and Striped Holy Lands

Forest Park is a roughly rectangular sanctuary of green in west central St. Louis. Grassy hills articulated with clumps of shade trees and landscaped shallow lagoons roll outward toward busy thoroughfares along all four of the park's boundaries. A golf course is set in the dips and rises of the park's western reach. Here, pedestrian pathways wind along the fairways and eventually meet a single road climbing up to the Saint Louis Art Museum, a magnificent neoclassical building complex that commands the heights on the northeastern side of the park.

The fine arts first took up residence in this grandly proportioned palace as part of the Louisiana Purchase Exposition, the St. Louis World's Fair of 1904. Like so many Old World aristocrats, royal or nearly so, the arts conveyed their privileged social position through architecture. Set in a utopian, monumental city of fountains, waterways, grand promenades, formal gardens, and displays of cultural achievement, the Palace of Fine Arts testified to America's turn-of-the-century aspirations to be counted among the world's most powerful and yet civilized nations.

From the palace's "Terrace of States," a system of formal gardens and paved walkways fell gently down the slope, past the Grand Lagoon and the open Plaza of St. Louis to the Fair's main entrance at the huge Wabash Railroad terminal. Set lower on the hill and radiating downward along parallel axes from the Palace of Fine Arts were huge Halls of Education and Social Economy, Electricity and Machinery, Manufacturers, Liberal Arts, and Varied Industries.

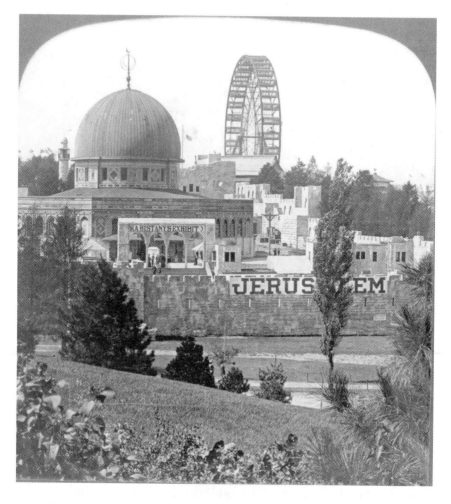

FIG. 11. Jerusalem at the Louisiana Purchase Exposition, St. Louis, 1904.
Stereograph by the H. C. White Company.
Courtesy of the Prints and Photographs Division
of the Library of Congress.

The upsweep of grandeur toward the Fine Arts building would have almost immediately enchanted visitors disembarking the train. Formal, controlled, and unified, the idealized urban space evoked the seemingly timeless ideals of ancient Greece or Rome—republican yet imperial, powerful yet refined. The "Pike," an avenue of popular diversions, stretched along the bottom of the hill as though a quarantined concession to vulgar curiosity.

Adjacent to the Palace of Fine Arts, set on about eleven acres of prime real estate, was a nearly full-sized replica of Ottoman Jerusalem as it appeared around 1900. The Jerusalem Exhibit was as large as most of the Fair's main exhibition palaces. Its location lent additional prominence. Holy Land and Fine Arts, as co-regents, flew the Stars and Stripes over an empire of industrial prowess, international standing, and cultural might.

About three hundred miles southwest of St. Louis, traveling on Interstate 44 and then over perilously winding roads into the Ozark Mountains, travelers come across The Great Passion Play™, a modern re-creation of the Holy Land set in the northwest corner of Arkansas. On the park's western edge, a seven-story-high Christ of the Ozarks faces the forested valley and hills, which are home to Eureka Springs, population 1,900. Once a thriving spa community (a few healing-waters hotels survive), the town has now been quaintly restored as a somewhat quirky in-gatherer of Americana, tourists, artists, and assorted eccentricities. Its gallery shops, Victorian cottages, cafés, and small inns cling to a slope that in 1885 was clear-cut near the top to build the gabled and massively chimneyed Crescent Hotel.

Nowadays, guests on the elegant veranda of the dowager Crescent gaze eastward toward the Christ of the Ozarks, who, with outstretched arms, offers patient invitation to all who would come near. Eureka Springs has prospered in part because of that statue and its nearby subdivision of Christian nostalgia. The park includes more than fifty acres of sights and sites of biblical Palestine, the Church in the Grove, a Bible Museum beneath the Smith Memorial Chapel, and a Center for the Sacred Arts. Since the late 1960s, tours of the New Holy Land and nightly performances of The Great Passion Play in the huge amphitheater have attracted more than six million visitors and plenty of Christian entrepreneurs. Motels proclaim "Christ Is Lord" or display the works of Bible-belt authors in their lobbies. Nearby are the Covenant Gardens (biblical plants) and the Promised Land Animal Park (biblical animals). The Statue Road Inn, which advertises "Hospitality our Motto, Christ our Leader, Cleanliness our Rule," serves meals and after-the-show desserts at the "Daily Bread Deli." Christian T-shirts and other implements of apparel politics are available at the foot of Passion Play Road.

The park's founder, Gerald L. K. Smith, came close to matching the ambitions of the promoters of Jerusalem at the St. Louis World's Fair. He certainly matched their zeal for carving at-home holy land territory out

FIG. 12. Christ of the Ozarks. c. 1990.
Used by permission of the Elna M. Smith
Foundation, Eureka Springs, Arkansas.

of native topography. Like the "New Jerusalem" of St. Louis, or the "tiny bit of 'Holy Land'" at Chautauqua, Smith's "New Holy Land" in Arkansas is wrapped in Bible-centered religious devotion and fervent nationalism. Unlike its forebears, however, Smith's sacred project, like his patriotic ardor, was marked by the virulent prejudice and wrenching social upheavals that afflicted America before and after World War II. To include St. Louis and Eureka Springs among Chautauqua's descendants is to consider the enduring interplay of Holy Land spectacle, artifice, and fantasy. It is also to draw maps of malleable holy land spaces, well funded and charged anew with twentieth-century, not nineteenth-century, social and ideological friction.

A Dream and a Vision in St. Louis

Respected businessmen and clergy of St. Louis set out to replicate Jerusalem and fill it with their idea of an Oriental city—plus a little piety and entertainment. They planned noisy comings and goings of resident "natives" of Palestine, employed to bustle about just as they did under Turkish rule. They envisioned pilgrimages to New Testament locales and a sensational panorama of Jesus' death on the cross. And of course, as at the actual tourist destination, natives in colorful costumes would hawk camel rides, guided tours, and trinkets.

Supporters thought that the Jerusalem Exhibit would tastefully amuse as well as edify. Properly vetted guides would teach visitors about the full significance of the Bible and its holy places. Moreover, as a destination of moral uplift, Jerusalem would be a desirable presence at the Fair, as one testimonial suggested, among the rather unseemly titillation all too familiar in large expositions.[1]

Faithfulness to the original was key. As with Chautauqua's Palestine Park, great pains were taken to assure that Bible scholarship, observations and measurements by trusted observers, and genuine artifacts would create authentic realism in the midst of fantasy. Indeed, E. Morris Ferguson, general secretary of the New Jersey Sunday School Association, enthusiastically proclaimed that those who were not able to attend the world's Fourth Sunday School Convention in the real Jerusalem that year might just as well make the pilgrimage to St. Louis.[2]

Yet, even if most of its executives and planners thought of their holy land in terms of Christian moral uplift, the new Jerusalem was inevitably circumscribed by other ideologies. One official guidebook embodied a notion of Western progress by explaining the World's Fair

FIG. 13. "The Whole Family at Jerusalem."
Louisiana Purchase Exposition, 1904.
Photo by B. W. Kilburn, published by James M. Davis, New York.

as a comprehensive celebration of worldwide (mainly Euro–North American) artistic, industrial, and technological advancement.[3] The "universal exhibition" also lauded what were widely accepted as America's righteous (and progressive) achievements: westward territorial expansion, energetic capitalism, controlled democracy, business competition, entrepreneurial invention, and populist education. The Fair offered staged but nevertheless reassuring images of a vigorous United States enthroned as the vanguard of civilization, democratic liberty, and cultural progress. And she was heir to God's blessings bestowed on the world through ancient Jerusalem.[4]

The elaborate fantasy of Jerusalem as Holy Land thus lent moral and religious authority to the exclusions, celebrations, and paradoxical aspirations to universality that were embedded in a particular vision of America and her limitless future. In things that mattered most in politics and symbol, the Fair presented the United States as a Protestant, democratic empire free to spread its creeds of liberty. And free, it was mistakenly thought, of the long shadows of aristocratic Europe.

Official publications repeatedly stated that in addition to exhibiting worldwide cultural advancement, the Fair commemorated "the greatest real estate transaction history records, the sale of France's Louisiana territory to the United States Government."[5] Not only did commissioned writers treat expansion across the continent as a self-evident sign of America's ordained destiny, they sanctified the Fair's core values by enshrining President William McKinley's words on the frontispiece of its official history.

> Expositions are the time-keepers of progress. They record the world's advancement. They stimulate the energy, enterprise and intellect of the people. . . . Every exposition, great or small, has helped to some onward step. Comparison of ideas is always educational. . . . Friendly rivalry follows, which is the spur to industrial improvement, the inspiration to useful invention, and to high endeavor in all departments of human activity. It exacts a study of the wants, comforts, and even the whims of the people, and recognizes the efficacy of high quality and low prices to win their favor. . . . Without competition we would be clinging to the clumsy and antiquated processes of farming and manufacture, and the methods of business of long ago, and the twentieth century would be no further advanced than the eighteenth century.[6]

Consumerist competition, individualism, entrepreneurial invention, mass education, progressivism—these were the genetic codes which defined the United States, that fittest among the civilized nations embarked on a Darwinian climb from barbarity.

In all ways possible, the Exposition proclaimed its idealization of America before more than nineteen and a half million increasingly affluent and educated visitors, mostly American.[7] As Martha Clevenger noted, the architectural and artistic schema of the Fair

> reinforced the concept of unilinear progress, traceable as it was from Greece and Rome, via the Enlightenment, the Age of Reason, and the French Revolution, to the American Revolution, and finally, at the Louisiana Purchase Exposition, to the Louisiana Purchase itself.[8]

The Fair's official hymn reaffirmed God's hand in this achievement while crowning the young nation as a "land of a new and lordlier race."

> Eternal Light,
> Fill with thy might
> These domes that in Thy purpose grew,
> And lift a nation's heart anew!
>
> Illumine Thou each pathway here
> To show the marvels God hath wrought
> Since first Thy people's chief and seer
> Looked up with prophetic thought,
>
> Bade Time unroll
> The Fateful scroll,
> And empire unto Freedom gave
> From cloudland heights to tropic wave. . . .
>
> Thou, whose high archways shine most clear
> Above the plenteous western plain,
> Thine ancient tribes from round the sphere
> To breathe its quickening air are fain;
> And smiles the sun
> To see made one
> Their brood throughout Earth's greenest space,
> Land of the new and lordlier race![9]

The Fair was organized into two main segments, large halls housing the main exhibits and the "Pike," a street of commercial amusements. Although Jerusalem was classified by management as one of the Pike concessions (souvenir booklets of the Pike included photographs of it), its position on the brow of the hill next to the Fine Arts building suggested a more ambiguous status. Despite its central location, the model was not deemed a major exposition, such as the Hall of Electricity. Nor was it likened exactly to other amusements on the Pike, such as Dante's Inferno, the Hereafter, the Magic Whirlpool, Mysterious Asia, or Cummins's Wild West and Indian Congress. Jerusalem was kept apart, near the center of monumental utopia, on gently sloped land that Fair president David Francis found, in a moment of sheer fancy, "happily suggestive of the Palestine original."[10]

Supporters of the Jerusalem Exhibit in fact tried actively to maintain distance from the Pike's more gaudy and morally doubtful attractions. For them, Jerusalem was to be a religious educator and witness to

Fig. 14. Cyclorama of the Crucifixion.
Jerusalem Exhibit, Louisiana Purchase Exhibition, 1904.
Courtesy of Special Collections, St. Louis Public Library.

the triumph of Christian civilization.[11] President Theodore Roosevelt hoped that the Exhibit would "secure prominence to the religious side of the world's development."[12] More forthcoming about his practical concerns, a clergyman testified that it would bring "great benefit to the cause of Christianity." Moreover, said another, Jerusalem would be a "wonderful money-maker" of great appeal to every investor "interested in the advancement of Christianity."[13] The fair ship Cultural Progress would carry heavy and mixed cargo in her hold: an ecumenically wrapped evangelizing Christian Holy Land to be off-loaded as curiosity and tourist amusement, religious educator, witness to Christ, pilgrimage destination, and money-maker.

Inside the city's walls, as well as riding camels and having their fortunes told, visitors could take a tour through familiar landscapes of Christian piety. Like many tours of the Holy Land, including those pilgrimages of imagination induced by illustrated travel books, the

Jerusalem Exhibit was organized in Protestant fashion to retrace the steps of Jesus where the land itself was the shrine, not a relic-laden church. One advertising leaflet proclaimed that "native" guides would take fairgoers from the Jaffa Gate along winding streets, stopping at the "Towers of David" and the "wailing wall of the Jews . . . [and the] Mosque of Omar," built on the site of the "temple where Jesus taught." From there, a pilgrim could travel the Via Dolorosa to the Church of the Holy Sepulcher, where every hour a "Sheik of Jerusalem" would deliver a lecture. As a dramatic climax, the tour included a visit to a fortress-like building whose narrative murals and wax figures, the "Cyclorama of the Crucifixion," melded Gospel events with their Jerusalem locations. This alone was "worth the whole price of admission to Jerusalem," the leaflet averred.[14]

Inside the city's castellated walls, all these attractions were free, including operatic dramatizations of biblical stories and a diorama of the Mount of Olives. Near the Jaffa Gate, "Raphael" of London hawked revelations of world events—past, present, and future—through the new "science" of earthology. One Reverend David Heagle delivered illustrated lectures—unrivaled entertainment, proclaimed one promotional brochure—on Moses' wilderness tabernacle (enhanced by night and sunrise light shows), Solomon's temple, and a ten-square-foot replica of the holy city itself.[15] A guttural hubbub of foreign tongues, bright Middle Eastern garb, animals, and shouting merchants supplied a flavor of authenticity to the fantasy.[16]

One skeptical journalist assayed the bizarrely concocted New Jerusalem and noted, "There is nothing like this at Coney Island."[17] A more reverent St. Louis Mirror editor assured readers that the Exhibit would "vitalize for everyone the story that has wrought the world into what it is to-day . . . [and] recall to all the actuality of the history upon which Christianity has been builded to its present mighty influence."[18]

The company formed to finance and build Jerusalem was headed by Alexander Konta, a St. Louis banker. Investors were breezily assured that Mr. Konta would use experience gained from frequent trips to Jerusalem to help him manage the exhibit and bring to it "features as could only be obtained by official sanction . . . never heretofore . . . part of Oriental displays."[19] Lending support was an advisory board consisting mostly of local clergymen, some of them fairly prominent, drawn from a broad spectrum of Protestant, Catholic, and Jewish organizations. However, like those of the Exhibit itself, the Protestant proclivities of the board were unabashed, and so engrained that no effort was made to adjust appeals for money and endorsements to suit Jewish, or for that matter, Catholic sensibilities.[20]

The board's first president, William Beverly Palmore, Methodist Episcopal Church South, was the well-known editor and publisher of the *St. Louis Christian Advocate*. Among several vice-presidents was fellow Southern Methodist James Wideman Lee, who had successfully led churches in Georgia before taking up duties at St. John's Church, St. Louis, in 1893.[21] In great demand as a speaker, Lee had preached and taught at Chautauqua in the 1880s. By the time he joined the advisory board, he was widely known for the unusually successful *Earthly Footsteps of the Man of Galilee*.[22]

With stunning half-tone reproductions of photos by the famous Robert E. M. Bain and commentary by Lee, the folio-size, expensively produced book enticed readers into a richly visual pilgrimage to the land of Jesus. The volume confirmed Lee as a master homilist, biblical student, and propagator of specifically Protestant Christian renderings of the Holy Land. Readers, like the photo expedition itself, could invade the land with "harmless, scientific instruments," Lee wrote in his introduction. They could map conquered territory, often represented as drearily empty, with recollections of Christian beginnings. From the comfort of heavily draped Victorian parlors (the analog to Lee's luxurious expedition tent, flying the U.S. flag), pilgrims might imagine the simpler lives and wanderings of Jesus and Paul. This romanticized geography, in Lee's words, traced the "footsteps of Christ and his Apostles . . . the places made sacred by their lives." Like many others at the time, including the founders of Chautauqua, Lee thought of his readers as members of a Christian civilization that was destined to triumph in the world and, most pointedly, to recover Palestine from the hands of its Ottoman rulers.[23]

The pilgrimage-invasion, a winning alliance of commercial interests and missionary piety, was a stunning success. The publisher secured a preface by John Heyl Vincent, who was by then chancellor of the Chautauqua Institution and a bishop in the Methodist Church. The book was skillfully marketed, and daily newspapers in England and America offered it as a premium. *Earthly Footsteps* sold over a million copies.[24]

Organizers of the Jerusalem Exhibit must have been pleased to have the added prestige of Mr. Lee's support. *Footsteps* had installed him by plebiscite as a Bible expert who spoke authoritatively to Christians from experience in the land itself. He was no stranger to grand expositions, either, having spoken at the 1893 World's Parliament of Religions.[25] Moreover, Lee's reputation for being "patriotic and broadly catholic, generous and sympathetic"[26] fit the ideals espoused by leaders of the Louisiana Purchase Exposition, despite their presumption of Protestant Christian privilege. Not surprisingly, organizers invited him to write a guidebook for the exhibition.[27] In turn, Lee and another member of the Exhibit's advisory board, Napthali Luccock, saw to it that the *American Illustrated Methodist Magazine*, which they edited, indefatigably publicized the moral and educational promise of the New Jerusalem in St. Louis.[28]

Lee's endorsement of the project was the longest and most extravagant testimony prepared for potential investors. More than any other's, his recommendation counted on American Protestants' sense of belonging to a chosen nation and their utterly extravagant affection for the Holy Land which piety imagined. Indeed, like Chautauqua's company of the godly urged to "arise and possess the land," fairgoers and investors were urged to enter the Holy Land in St. Louis. They would penetrate a space invested with particular (Christian) yet universal (eternally spiritual in human nature) meanings that were presumed to be the essence of faraway Jerusalem transferred to its replica. Simultaneously, they could assure for themselves and the United States a role in the providential advance of Christian civilization, which began on the street of Jesus' suffering.

> [Jerusalem] has always voiced man's undying belief in God and the necessity he was under to love and serve Him. . . . It is an unworldly city; it is without a theater, or a barroom or a dance house. Jerusalem ministers to the lofty and great and holy in man, and stands for the eternal in human nature. . . . The Via Dolorosa, or the Pathway of Pain . . . It is strange that this short way should mark the beginning of western civilization. Here the world learned a new secret of strength and a new method of life. Here began the street which has extended through the ages, and along which healthy, heroic, triumphant human life has walked ever since.[29]

With great expense and prodigal consumption of land, the parent company would build its cathedral, a "dream and a vision" at the apex of the Fair, potential investors were told. Organizers would populate the city with authentic Jerusalemites, and fill its spaces with contemporary buildings as well as historic sites of biblical memory. "The display will, in short, be Jerusalem itself," replete with biblical reference and an

Fig. 15. Jaffa Gate, Jerusalem. Postcard view of an actual Jerusalem scene
sold at the Jerusalem Exhibit, Louisiana Purchase Exposition, 1904.

exotic mix of Bedouin, peasants, merchants, native Christians, Copts,
Muslims, Turks, rabbis, and priests going about their business.[30] Indeed,
some postcards and souvenirs depicted scenes of the actual Jerusalem
labeled simply as "Jerusalem, the St. Louis World's Fair."

The city was to be carefully constructed, investors were assured,
not only to achieve a realistic illusion but to encourage an experience
of what planners thought to be the "real" Jerusalem. The "hills, valleys, pools, and streams" of the New Jerusalem would conform to
biblical accounts. Sites favored by Christian pilgrims would be readily
available, free of the annoying distractions and confusing disputes
over holy sites often disdained by Protestant travelers to Ottoman
Jerusalem. There would be the Church of the Holy Sepulcher, for
example, "a vast collection of churches, chapels and shrines" contain-
ing "thirty seven alleged holy places." This is "the spot to which most
of the tourist pilgrims wend their way immediately." A visitor would
see the "Temple area," acknowledged as "one of the four holy places of
the Mohammedans" but, as commentary made clear, primarily important for its association with Abraham, Jacob, and the temples of

Solomon, Zerubbabel, and Jesus. The Via Dolorosa would be "of supreme interest" because it had been made sacred "with the tears of many generations of pilgrims, who, according to their faiths, strove to follow in the footsteps of the Lord."

A prospective visit to the Mount of Olives, however, elicited a less carefully ecumenical tone. That iconic place of betrayal and submission would offer pilgrims a "pleasant refuge" from the "multiplicity of more or less fictitious 'holy sites,' mechanical ritual, and ecclesiastical strife." Christians of Protestant persuasion who are, it is implied, justifiably impatient with the religious practices of sibling Christianities in Ottoman Jerusalem could find true nourishment for the soul at this spot where Jesus withdrew from the tumultuous city streets. There—as often reported by actual travelers—they could forsake the external trappings of religion for a melding of geography and memory. They could simply follow "in the actual footsteps of our Lord" down a mountain "scarcely changed at all since the time of Christ."

Similarly, a visit to the "Jews' Wailing Place" would confirm not Jewish spirituality but the persistent Christian theology of displacement. The sight of "pale, deformed and sad Jews," investors were assured, would be "reproduced in all its picturesqueness." For the thoughtful visitor, the writer added, such a display will be "touching and prophetic."[31]

The scene was familiar from countless travel books—it was even reproduced for a World's Fair postcard—and was typically described with the sort of patronizing pity reserved for the misguided. The hunched and sorrowful Jews, wrapped in shawls of prayer, suggested "their sins and the sins of their nation" and their doleful petitions that the "once holy and beloved House . . . may be quickly rebuilt." However, as "prophecy" the faux ethnography of abjection intimated to many a tourist-pilgrim that reconciliation with God was available to the forlorn Jews if they would but accept Jesus Messiah as the rebuilt temple.

Besides giving such interpretive frameworks to pilgrimage, the *Prospectus* went on to announce that daily on-site lectures by Madame Lydia Mamreoff von Finkelstein Mountford would insure that visitors to the New Jerusalem would be properly instructed. As discussed earlier, Madame Mountford was widely admired for her performances of biblical drama before American, English, and Australian audiences. "Born and brought up in Jerusalem," famous as an "eloquent speaker . . . [and] marvelous word painter," she was deemed a thrilling and trustworthy guide to the realities of Jesus' Jerusalem.

COOK'S PALES-
TINE EXHIBIT.
Opposite the Temple
of Fraternity.

COOK'S EGYP-
TIAN EXHIBIT.
Section 149, Trans-
portation Building.

THOS. COOK & SON
NEW YORK, LONDON,
JERUSALEM, ETC.

ONE OF COOK'S PALESTINE DRAGOMANS. *K. S. Gandour*
Jaffa Palestine 1904

FIG. 16. A Thomas Cook dragoman. Postcard.
Thomas Cook's Palestine Exhibit, Louisiana Purchase Exhibition, 1904.
Courtesy of Special Collections, St. Louis Public Library.

FIG. 17. Cover of *World's Fair Souvenir Album of Jerusalem*.

Most travelers to Ottoman Jerusalem miss the true significance of what they see, added the *Prospectus*. That will not happen in St. Louis with the likes of Madame Mountford as escort. She will avoid the misrepresentations and diversions perpetrated by an ill-prepared (and non-Christian) "dragoman" who imperfectly understands English. Even if well disposed, he is not "fitted by nature, education or religious training to comprehend the full significance of the scenes which to him have grown ordinary."

Fortunately (the relief is almost audible), in the new Jerusalem, "lecturers and guides . . . men and women of education and experience" will explain the features of the holy city "not only from the standpoint of their history and construction, but also . . . their traditional and scriptural significance." A visitor will not be a mystified "onlooker, as he is in the [actual] city of Jerusalem, with only a vague conception of what

BIRD'S-EYE VIEW JERUSALEM EXHIBIT,
LOUISIANA PURCHASE EXPOSITION, ST. LOUIS, MO., 1904
WATSON & HAZELTON, ARCHITECTS, CHICAGO.

Fig. 18. "Bird's-eye view of Jerusalem," from
World's Fair Souvenir Album of Jerusalem.

it all means." Rather, with the help of Madame Mountford and others, he will be able to lay hold of the essential Jerusalem and the immediacy of Christian Scripture in its pure blush of inspiration. All "will be thoroughly explained to him, enabling him to grasp its full significance in every respect" far more vividly than classroom study could ever provide, investors were assured.[32] Ironically, not too far from the Jerusalem Exhibit, the Thomas Cook Company sold tours to Palestine, apparently without any suspicion that their famed "dragomen" would in any way compromise the Christian visitor's experience.

An official souvenir album reinforced these gestures of imperial dominance and, like all such books, displaced complexly layered individual experiences with pre-packaged memory.[33] Simulating heavy gold-stamped binding, the cover was designed as an opening in Jerusalem's wall through which one glimpsed the city itself. Actually it was a frontispiece rendering of an architect's drawing of Jerusalem poised on a wooded rise, open to the sun and removed from anything unseemly. Victorian-garbed people flowed through its gates, as though approaching their heaven-on-earth home. On the cover, a superimposed Crusader Cross radiated beatific light onto this neatly packaged illusion and defined the viewer's commanding perspective. The souvenir was of the eternal, "real" Jerusalem, the biblical city of God held fast by triumphal Christian imagination.

The album contained photographs of Ottoman Jerusalem—not the St. Louis replica—with textual commentary. All was organized like a pilgrimage to the places where Jesus walked and taught, and where the Christian church arose. Pen and ink drawings framed each photograph and depicted associated biblical incidents. Presented as embracing images, the drawings overpowered the photographs and assured prominence to timeless Christian understandings of place, pilgrimage, and Bible.

Nine of fifteen photos, for example, documented "Stations of the Cross" along the Via Dolorosa and illustrated New Testament scenes of Jesus' suffering thought to have occurred there. The Dome of the Rock, although acknowledged as sacred to Muslims, appears as part of a decorative cartouche that foregrounds King Solomon directing construction of the first divinely authorized house of God. An interior close-up shows the massive outcropping of rock inside the domed structure. The photographic image floats within the embrace of a drawing depicting Abraham's near sacrifice of Isaac on this rock, the traditional Mount Moriah. Perhaps pious Isaac prophetically contemplates the ram shown in cameo nearby, the Old Testament surrogate victim, which in later Christian exegesis symbolized Jesus' sacrificial death.

Or again, photographs of two Jerusalem gates, identified in the accompanying text by their historic Muslim, Jewish, and Christian names, are printed in overlapping shield-like cameos. The superimposed drawing depicts angry townspeople stoning a man and thus effectively transforms the photographic references to ancient history into a specific space which invokes a timeless paradigm of Christian identity. Saint Stephen fearlessly witnesses to the Gospel, and dies for it, outside the city of rejection (Acts 7:57–60).

Nowhere was such zeal for Christian evangelism (and its cousin, capitalist expansion) more evident than at the ceremonies which broke ground for the Jerusalem Exhibit. The "dream and a vision" arrived on a hot summer day in 1903, and with great style.

Richly caparisoned horses, donkeys, and camels paraded women, high officials, politicians, and other guests to the cleared hilltop where Jerusalem was to be erected. Almost everyone was decorously overdressed and perspiring. At the center was a large open platform and altar-like structure, the sacred "rock of Moriah" that would be incorpo-

Fig. 19. Dome of the Rock, from *World's Fair Souvenir Album of Jerusalem*.

rated into the Exhibit's "Mosque of Omar" or Dome of the Rock. People waved banners of Judaism, Christianity, and Islam. National flags of Turkey and the United States jumbled the perimeters like rival but tolerant claimants to sovereignty over Holy Land territory. Some fifty men and women said to represent "almost every type of Oriental people" living in Jerusalem milled about, costumed in colorful gabardines, turbans, embroidered dresses, blousey trousers, and Bedouin robes. One hundred and fifty songsters provided music, while the "natives" on display offered a prepared program of speeches, prayers, biblical readings, chants, and specially designed ceremonies.

Officials and notable dignitaries, including a senator from Kansas, offered celebratory speeches.[34] Always attuned to the theatrical moment, Madame Mountford, director of exhibits and displays, spoke grandiloquently "in the name of the inhabitants of the City of Jerusalem." She perfectly sensed the flavor of Holy Land infatuation and

Fig. 20. Gates of Jerusalem, from *World's Fair Souvenir Album of Jerusalem.*

Christian, America-first mercantile nationalism that infused the day. "You cannot go to Jerusalem," she told the crowd, "so Jerusalem comes to you. To American energy all things are possible."

Dr. Palmore, president of the Jerusalem Exhibit Advisory Board, added learned and historical sweep to the occasion which, as nothing else, codified New Jerusalem's privileged location in World's Fair geography and the triumphant claims of Christianized civilization. Gesturing toward the made-to-scale great rock of sacrifice, he assessed its fitness for solemn duty. Having remained "untouched by a chisel through all its thousands of years of history," the rock was, in the end, a reliable witness to Christian truth. "The blood of the slain lamb, which will be sprinkled on this stone," he told the audience,

> points back over 2000 years to Calvary, as Abraham's offering of Isaac pointed forward across 2000 years to that goal of prophecy and keynote, or golden text of history . . . the world's greatest tragedy and

sacrifice, where incarnate love surrendered his life that the world might have life more abundantly.

Trying to counter tawdry amusement with the primacy of both Christianity and cultural progress, Palmore added,

> The meeting of all nations at this Fair in the interchange of the highest thoughts and products of human genius will much promote the brotherhood of man, but this Jerusalem exhibit will lift the thought of the multitude to the fatherhood of God.

Indeed, for Palmore the exotica that had been carefully collected to exemplify the "real life of the city as it is to-day" signified little outside this sweeping Christian framework. He imagined the city limned with New Testament allusions (the most direct are indicated by my italics in the quotation below) which effectively suppressed any interpretive potential other than his own.

> In our streets will be seen the *money changers, scribes and lawyers, and they who love to be seen of men praying at the street corners*, with their broad phylacteries; street vendors will cry to *everyone that thirsteth and supply living waters*. Heralds will proclaim official news, the advent of notable visitors, royal edicts, the rise and fall of values of native and foreign coin; criers will make known the lost and found, with the offered reward. *Laborers will stand idle in the market place, because no man hath hired them*, and they love greetings and salutations in public places. . . . *The lame, halt, and the blind will ask alms by the wayside.* . . . The weird and thrilling call of the muezzin from the mosque of Omar will be heard at all the regular hours calling the faithful to prayer.

In the New Jerusalem, Islamic practice would be ornamental, part of the realistic theatricality of reproduction, but alive religiously only in Christian imagination. The Dome of the Rock would be consecrated, Palmore noted, by a symbolic reenactment of the sacrificial death of the Lamb of God. The nearby El-Aksar mosque had no biblical associations, he added, and besides, it was "originally used as a Christian church." When completed, the building would host "educational, denominational, and philanthropic conferences." Daily visitors could attend "lectures and elaborate illustrations of Bible history, lands, costumes, and customs" that would furnish, as Madame Mountford would soon say in her own speech, a "living commentary" on the Christian Scriptures.

Moreover, Palmore concluded, Jerusalem—the actual city and its replica—represents the generative source of Christian triumph. "The glad tidings proclaimed from Jerusalem nineteen centuries ago," he told his audience, "are now sung in 400 languages and dialects and, like the reveille of the British drum, never cease their roll around the world." That Christian army, aligned now with British imperial might, would consummate its victory at the end of days, Palmore implied, as he gathered lines from a familiar carol into one last rhetorical flourish:

> For lo the days are hastening on,
>   By prophet bards foretold,
> When with the ever-circling years,
>   Comes back the age of gold:
> When peace shall over all the earth
>   Its blessed banner fling
> And the whole world send back the song,
>   Which now the angels sing.[35]

David R. Francis, president of the Louisiana Purchase Exposition, added a gloss of cultural advancement. The Fair's effort to present an encapsulated narrative of the "progress of civilization from the inception of history," he said, would lack completeness if it did not present to fairgoers a replica of that city

> where were enacted deeds, where were uttered sayings and where were occurrences whose effect has been felt for twenty centuries past, and whose effect will continue to produce upon civilization an inestimable impression until the end of time.

All civilized nations are drawn to Jerusalem, Francis added. Just as all nations come to St. Louis to celebrate progress toward what Palmore had called the "universal Brotherhood of Man," so too they will come to the replica of the "wonderful city" which first gave voice to that worthy goal—brotherhood in the name of Christ, of course.

Madame Mountford, the final speaker of the day, provided commentary on the many staged ceremonies. She explained Holy Land theater as ethnography, commenting on the simulated sacrifice of the lamb, the laying of the city's cornerstone, the planting of a tree of life, songs, Muslim, Jewish, and Greek Christian prayers, and Bible readings. Despite the display of diversity, she assured members of the assembled company that the Holy Land was, thanks to God, really in the hands of stalwart Christian militants, no matter the indignities of world politics.

Bible believers and students not only possessed the keys to heaven, but by right enjoyed free access to the gates of Jerusalem as well. All teachers of Sunday schools and their pupils would feel afresh the ancient biblical exhortation "They that love the Lord are as Mount Zion that cannot be moved, but abideth forever." There could hardly be a more appropriate sign of such resolute love, she added, than the New Jerusalem, whose patron Saint Louis had "crossed the seas to defend Jerusalem in the days of the Crusades." Then, dramatically addressing the Exposition officials, Madame Mountford likened them to medieval crusaders helping to reclaim Jerusalem for a world still in need of the one true faith. "By granting this concession," she told them, they were fulfilling a prophecy of Isaiah. "Many nations shall come up and say, 'Come up, and let us go up to the mountain of the Lord, for out of Zion shall go forth the instruction and the word of the Lord from Jerusalem'" (Isaiah 2:3).

Rise up and build this holy city in America, Mountford seemed to suggest. Put it at the epicenter of the Exposition, and at the generative core of human progress. It is God's work, and a vocation of shimmering brightness emboldened by the song of American destiny, ever marching toward the messianic kingdom for which Christians wait. "Rejoice ye with Jerusalem, and be glad with her all ye who love her," she concluded. "Prepare ye the way! Cast up the highway! Gather up the stones. Lift up a standard over Jerusalem!"

Edmund Philibert, an unmarried Roman Catholic carpenter, was about thirty years old when he visited the Jerusalem that Madame Mountford had so extravagantly welcomed to St. Louis. He attended the World's Fair twenty-eight times during the summer and fall of 1904, and kept a diary of each of his visits. Philibert systematically worked his way through the neoclassical cityscape and recorded his impressions of each area, often in exceptional detail, while meticulously accounting for every penny spent. On the twenty-second excursion, he went directly to Jerusalem, paid his fifty cents (about one hour's wage for a union carpenter employed by the Exposition at the time), and entered the Jaffa Gate.[36]

It is difficult to say whether Philibert shared, or even could have articulated, what organizers of the Jerusalem Exhibit had deposited in their fantasies of Jerusalem. His musings are impressionistic, not philosophical. And he does not mention numerous troubles that disturbed the city and which, along with upbeat publicity, were often featured in local newspapers. On some days, the utopian "dream and a vision" seemed flawless. On other days, well, it seemed like a traumatic visitation.

The Exhibit's opening was delayed because of uncompleted work. Under pressure from Exhibition officials, the Jerusalem managers staged a hastily planned dedication just inside the Jaffa Gate. Very few first-day fairgoers attended, and so it was announced that the ceremony would be made a regular feature of each day's activities.

Participants made the most of the diminished ceremonial space anyway. Under American and Turkish flags, "residents" performed bits and pieces of religious observances according to the rites of Greek Christian, Jewish, and Muslim communities, all explained by Madame Mountford. A thin crowd of onlookers gazed upon costumed "natives," heard Greek, Hebrew, and Arabic, and witnessed exotic evocations of customs associated with the Bible. Clearly feeling connected to the primal babble and color of antiquity, one reporter noted that a ram's horn, a *shofar,* was blown by a "native of Jerusalem" who was "a descendant of a family that was never carried into captivity."[37]

The delayed opening may have been an omen that circumstances would conspire against the desire of Jerusalem's Christian promoters. Fewer fairgoers than expected attended the exhibit, and revenues apparently were small in relation to those of other concessions at the Fair.[38] A disastrous fire caused after-insurance losses of about $15,000, around $300,000 in today's dollars. Rivalry among two residents for the title "King of the Gamblers" ended in the murder of one of the claimants. Biblical strongman Samson died from gunshot wounds arising out of a personal quarrel. Then there were labor troubles. Three members of the Biblical Historical Opera Company resigned toward the end of the year and sued the Jerusalem Exhibit Company for unpaid wages.

Worried stockholders and creditors had already sued the Jerusalem Exhibit Company in mid-summer, alleging insolvency because expenses exceeded receipts. Later, the Louisiana Purchase Exposition threatened to shut off utilities to Jerusalem because of past-due accounts. In response, the company filed suit against the Exposition, alleging financial harm because infrastructure—utilities, roads, walkways to Jerusalem—had not been completed on time as contractually promised.[39]

Even Madame Mountford grew disenchanted. Her plan for an exhibit of Holy Land photographs taken by Mormon artist Charles Ellis Johnson was abandoned by a new management team just before the Fair opened.[40] Nevertheless, she attended to her duties as director of exhibits and presented almost daily dramatizations of Palestine life in performances of "Two Thousand Years Ago." But she eventually resigned, possibly because of multiplying financial difficulties, claiming later in a moralistic display of self-pity that officials had made "a burlesque show of the most sacred scenes and localities of the Holy City of Jerusalem."[41]

Adversity had its opportunities, however. Amidst increasingly desperate circumstances, publicists promoted Jerusalem's educational programs and its success at bringing religious uplift to her visitors. Unpleasant incidents were just so much confirming evidence of the "Oriental" reality of Jerusalem, reality which made flights to biblical memory even more pertinent. One account reported the birth of a Syrian baby "in a manger of which the Savior was born" (unfortunately for the analogy, it was a girl). A merchant licensed to peddle curios inside the Dome of the Rock was accused by another resident of desecrating the Mosque. The ensuing "riot in Jerusalem . . . recalled the purging of the Temple of Herod of money-changers." A writer of headlines dubbed a late-night, gun-waving fracas between the Exhibit's manager and disgruntled merchants as a demonstration of the "superior bravery of Caucasians."[42] Despite offending the sensibilities of fairgoers and tourists, such events of urban tension showed the authenticity of the replica and its lived biblical reference. They also could justify the attitudes of, as the World's Fair hymn intoned, a "lordlier race" toward the exotic, but backward "Orient."

Although Edmund Philibert mentioned none of these matters in his diary, he left us precious evidence of how one visitor experienced this Holy Land at home in America. Was the biblical fantasy enabled for him? Did he share, or live out, the American political values and perspectives embedded in the space? Was he amused, educated, uplifted?

Philibert noted the novelty of a camel ride. "Riding at a trot is nicer than at a walk," he wrote. "The camels kneel to receive their burden and as they rise you are thrown first one way and then another." He seemed more absorbed, however, by the realistic diorama of Christ's crucifixion:

> Judas with a rope going to a solitary place . . . the Soldiers repulsing the crowd and shooting dice for Christ's garments. The figures stood out and looked very natural.[43]

Philibert lingered at David's Tower, "the oldest and most interesting parts of Jerusalem." Did he perhaps purchase a photograph? A World's Fair photo such as "Moorish Street" would have encouraged such a tilt toward biblical antiquities. Jerusalem's glorious biblical history, the caption asserted, had "little in common with the narrow, tortuous, and dirty" streets of modern Jerusalem depicted in the photographic image.[44]

FIG. 21. Camel ride. Jerusalem Exhibit, Louisiana Purchase Exposition, 1904.
Stereograph by the Keystone View Company, 1904.
Courtesy of the Missouri Historical Society, St. Louis.

In any case, Philibert allowed himself at least a little skepticism about the claims of biblical antiquity pressed by the Exhibit. He noted that the massive tower was "the place where David is supposed to have written most of the Psalms."

Philibert commented on the system of regulating rights to commerce outside the "Mosque of Omar," apparently finding it a curious ethnographical marker. Inside, he viewed the great sacred rock that had figured so prominently in the Exhibit's groundbreaking ceremonies.

Mentioning none of its biblical and Christian associations, however, Philibert paraphrased Muslim traditions he had received, perhaps from a guide, while registering his own sense of self-satisfied superiority. "Mohammedans believe," he wrote, that the rock from which Mohammed ascended into heaven is

> so holy that it went up with Mohammed but was not quite holy enough to enter heaven, so it remained suspended in the air, with no connection whatever with the earth.

Furthermore, they all believe that "on judgment day the Valley of Hebron will be spanned by a keen edged sword about the width of a hair." Those who can cross will enter paradise, "as a rule the Mohammedans," he noted wryly. And those who fall off, all Jews and Christians, will "go down to destruction."

Matters that were closer to his Roman Catholic Christianity, however, Philibert rendered with utter credulity, as though blurring, but not confusing, the distinction between the model and the devotional reality. Looking upon a despondent Judas, the "House of Joseph of Aramethea, with the tomb of Christ in his garden," and the "crucifixion itself," he retraced the path of Jesus' suffering.

> We went along the Via Dolorosa or Way of Sorrow, a narrow street along which Christ bore the cross. The next stop was at the barracks where Christ was tried while His Mother waited with friends in a building on the opposite corner. The next I think was the Church of the Holy Sepulchre.

None of this is very surprising in context. The Jerusalem Exhibit amused Philibert, but at the same time its geography of devotion enabled a lively sense of Christian beginnings. The displays and lectures did little to challenge either the privileged status of biblical literalism or the sense that Christian truth conveyed superior status relative to those who believed legends about holy rocks and sword bridges. Philibert did not comment on the heavily Protestant ethos pervading the Exhibit. In the end, perhaps the Holy Land he experienced was a vaguely Christian space constructed of Bible- and Jesus-centered devotion, that nondenominational source of generative energy which defined barely articulated, comfortably familiar truths.

Clevenger argued that fairgoers generally identified with the "worldview that underlay and informed the intellectual structures, the exhibits, the architecture, the use of space, and the entertainment they encountered at the World's Fair."⁴⁵ Reinforcement of the customary and accepted is often the essence of entertainment, and loss of this habitat resides at the core of nostalgia. We shall never know whether Philibert matched Clevenger's model fairgoer. Nothing in his diary suggests that he dissented from the Fair's embedded hierarchy of race, imperialism, and moral imperatives for Christian and territorial expansion. But he was surely nostalgic at the end of his visits—and poorer. His $1.95 daily outlay was the pay for about three and a half hours of union-scale carpentry work at the Louisiana Purchase Exposition.⁴⁶

Philibert's yearning may have had something to do with the impending demise of what he knew to be the transitory pleasures of the utopian cityscape and its Holy City within. On closing night, his twenty-eighth visit, he recorded impressions in lingering prose, each comma refusing inevitable loss.

> I walked through the Sunken Garden and along the Government Terrace and over the Plateau of States. . . . I walked up to the Grand Basin and sat watching the Cascades awhile, then I ascended to the Terrace of States and as this was my last opportunity I spent some time in viewing the Cascades and illumination in all directions, then descending the east steps I walked along by the Grand Basin and Plaza of St. Louis taking a farewell look at everything as I went, and it made me feel a little sad to think that it would soon be all over forever, for I had spent many pleasant days there.

Christian Nostalgia in Arkansas

Edmund Philibert wistfully looked back upon New Jerusalem and the lordlier race's utopia, about to be dismantled. Some sixty years later, Gerald L. K. Smith looked back, too, longing for an intact, purebred Christian America. And he had the means to convert private nostalgia into public works. Beginning with a massive statue of Christ, and building steadily, he created his "sacred projects" and New Holy Land in Eureka Springs, Arkansas.

At the time, Smith was a controversial old war-horse of far-right Christian nationalist politics. Since his death in 1976, the heated controversies surrounding his political activities and visionary plans for Eureka Springs have been largely forgotten. Control of the sacred projects created by the Elna M. Smith Foundation, named for Gerald's wife, remains in the family. Marvin Peterson, son-in-law to Smith's trusted lieutenant Charles F. Robertson, now oversees the sprawling enterprise of Christian nostalgia. Despite this connection, Smith's strident politics are no longer in evidence (he always claimed he wanted them kept out of the sacred projects anyway). The exhibits hardly give much offense, as long as one accepts the cultural coordinates that define the space as Christian, patriotic, and evangelical. One glossy color brochure presents a reverential account of Mr. and Mrs. Smith's endeavors, noting that their projects were "gifts to humanity" to enable visitors to "vividly remember God's great gift to man on the cross at Calvary."[47]

Yet the spectacles of Christian testimony do not quite cover traces of the America-first, segregationist, anti-Semitic political gospel that Smith preached from the 1930s to the 1970s.[48] For one thing, some of the park's start-up funds came from Smith's ultra-conservative political arm, the Christian Nationalist Crusade, a cause he promoted in a sharp-tongued and bigoted newsletter, *The Cross and Flag*.[49] For another, Smith's virulent jingoism lives on, though much subdued, in the vocal Americanism and Bible-centered Christianity that pervade the sacred projects today.

Within a landscaped enclosure on the shoulder of Magnetic Mountain stands Christ of the Ozarks. A visitor passes Mr. and Mrs. Smith's enclosed sarcophagi just inside the gateway. At the far end, a colonnaded viewing area allows full view of the statue and surrounding countryside. With his sixty-five-foot arms outstretched, Christ looks out over Eureka Springs in a pose of regal compassion. (See figure 12.) Symphonic arrangements of Christian hymns wafting from tastefully disguised high-fidelity speakers urge respectful quiet. The space seems to honor Christ the heavenly King and the belief in the resurrection of the saved as much as it distills Gerald and Elna Smith's lives to an epitaph-like essence: devoted servants of the Lord, awaiting their final reward.

A plaque near the statue provides a signature quote from the Gospel of John: "And I, if I be lifted up from the earth, will draw all men unto me" (John 12:32). Offering one version of Christ's post-resurrection work, the words of John at the same time underwrite the evangelical impulse embedded in all of the park's exhibits and performances. Jesus' words are paradigmatic for the tour guides, who actively witness to their Christian convictions and ask participatory assent of their audience. Smith himself, at least in authorized accounts, set the example. The many activities of the Elna M. Smith Foundation, wrote Charles Robertson, editor of *The Cross and Flag*, would create an expanding memorial to Smith's "desire to bear witness to the world of their love of God."[50] Indeed, posthumously published accounts present him as an embattled Christian patriot, a despised defender of Christian orthodoxy who determinedly lifted up Christ in all his endeavors.[51]

At its inception, however, Christ of the Ozarks quickly became controversial. Smith's reputation and penchant for outrageous effrontery had not escaped the notice of year-round residents of Eureka Springs and the Little Rock *Arkansas Gazette*. Many citizens were ambivalent toward this infamous orator, whose locally ingratiating ways and grand vision of Christian exhibits seemed to portend much-needed economic prosperity for their town. Surviving resistance, the statue was dedicated in 1966. That did not end the controversy, however. Some four years later, a federally financed road improvement project that would have included a scenic loop around the monument drew spirited opposition. Though finally approved by planners in Eureka Springs, it was vetoed by Treasury Secretary John Volpe, after which Smith complained that a "little handful of Jews had blocked construction." His foes had actually done him a favor anyway, he averred, because the new road, which he had supported, would have interfered with his plans for building the New Holy Land.[52]

Visitors today are probably oblivious to the furor that once charged these events. Facing Eureka Springs, his back turned to the park's many exhibits, Jesus makes, with his outspread arms, a supremely apolitical gesture. He offers mute benediction and invitation to all comers who seek private religious inspiration. Except perhaps those leather-sheathed bikers who, as one employee told me, once made loud fun of the place. From parkside, inside the amphitheater where the Great Passion Play is performed, the back of Christ's massive head appears like a sentient marker dominating the distant tree-lined horizon. Like God, Christ of the Ozarks requires no eyes or turning of the head to keep all in view, to invite adoration, and to suppress political entanglements of privatized piety.

Leaving the Christ memorial and heading back toward the park's central exhibits, visitors pass the single-room Church in the Grove, a white clapboard building moved intact from a nearby Arkansas location. Inside a fenced area and to one side of the church is a bronze-colored, badly weathered Styrofoam replica of the Liberty Bell. A flyer available on site invites visitors to fill the space with their own cultural experiences, listening "to the walls as they tell the history of the country church and its important role in building our nation."

Fig. 22. Church in the Grove and Berlin Wall. Eureka Springs, Arkansas.
Photo by Burke Long.

To approach the muse of the chapel walls, however, most tourists walk past a memorialized fragment of the Berlin Wall. They can hardly ignore the striking art (touched up every year because of sun fade) or forget the anonymous East Berliner's allusion to the Twenty-Third Psalm, crudely scrawled in German: "Though I walk through a dark valley, I have no fear." The Smith Foundation Web page urges visitors to admire "the spirit of the person who risked his or her life to make this declaration of faith." An on-site sign, the printed voice of anonymous facticity, fills the space with testimony: "In darkness this artist saw light; in despair, the Word of God; in repression, hope for freedom." That hope was realized on November 9, 1989, an event that leads naturally, it seems, to Scriptural association: "So if the Son sets you free, you will be free indeed" (John 8:36).

One can well imagine tourists—I saw mostly evangelical, charismatic Christians when I visited—traversing this mapped space of baptized nationalism. Proximity of artifact and recollection urged them to enact unexamined verities of rural American (Protestant) Christianity and unredeemable Communism's justified demise. Smith's nostalgia for a simple America and his virulent anti-Communist crusades haunt the space, though their ugliest excesses, like the hysteria of America's Mc-Carthyism, have faded from view. And the political edge given the memorial's dedication in 1991, which featured veteran crusader for conservative causes Anita Bryant singing "God Bless America," is probably unknown to most visitors today.[53] The chapel and grounds now evoke an appealing fantasy enshrined in the old-time hymn "The Church in the Wild Wood." The chapel in fact once carried that name, and is a popular site for weddings, a guide mentioned to me. Perhaps, in addition, voices from Smith's nationalist crusades, or from a Protestantism that still guards its fictions of a traditional America, stir the heart. Self-Exculpatory Conscience celebrates Christian-American Democracy Triumphant. Destroyed is that anti-Christ regime which erected, as a leaflet reminds visitors, a blood-spattered "edifice of godless leaders' defiance of Holy God Himself."

Some three hundred yards from the little church is a 4100-seat amphitheater where casts of about 250 townspeople give weeknight performances of "The Great Passion Play." Inside the landscaped enclosure, faraway biblical Jerusalem and her environs have been reduced to an intimate geography of melodrama, the pinpointed sites of Jesus' suffering now imposed on Arkansas topography. From the bottom of the natural bowl, one's eye travels from street level, upward and farther out, to cut-away buildings, then to the Mount of Olives, Golgotha, the garden tomb, and to the place of Jesus' ascension. Finally, at the uppermost reach, oak trees mark the theater's boundary and, in the drama, the limit of Jesus' visible presence on earth. In the far distance presides the panoptic Christ of the Ozarks.

Connected low-profile buildings, California-styled suggestions of Spanish mission architecture, separate and protect this expectant space from outside distractions (a sign prohibits photographs and video recordings after 5:30 P.M.). Visitors stream through the grandly colonnaded main entry. Here, as one leaflet states, patrons Gerald and Elna Smith used to greet their fee-paying guests before each performance. Flags of Arkansas and the United States fly nearby.

The amphitheater enclosure mediates myth, memorial, and amnesia. Folklore, leaflets, and official publications honor Smith's Christian witness and personal largesse, not his political notoriety. Flags suggest the fervor of (Christian) patriotism. Jesus' passion played out against a geography of melodrama fills the amphitheater with nightly reaffirmations of the only story that matters, Christ's one-time and eternal subjugation of Satan.[54]

FIG. 23. Amphitheater. The Great Passion Play, Eureka Springs,
Arkansas. Photo by Burke Long.

Awareness of Gerald Smith's anti-Semitic ravings disturbed the
opening season of the Passion play. The script, as Calvin Trillin wrote,
contained most of what the Council of Bishops had listed as "ways in
which a Passion Play might be subverted into an exercise in anti-Semitism."[55] With stubborn insensitivity to public feeling at the time, the
Smith Foundation named the project "Mount Oberammergau Passion
Play" in honor of its Bavarian counterpart, which was then being widely
criticized for perpetuating anti-Jewish stereotypes.

Despite fading memory of these controversies and a recently stream-
lined script, the nightly performances have yet to escape the ethical
consequences of Hollywood-like conventions and a narrowly exclusive
Christianity. Duplicitous Pharisees and priests, an evilly sneering King
Herod, and gratuitously vicious Roman soldiers still strut through the
Jerusalem streets and cut-away buildings. Pontius Pilate, who regrets his
role in Jesus' death and is disdainful of trouble-making Jews, belabors
the innocence of Jesus while magnifying the guilt of Jewish leaders and
the bloodthirsty mob. In a video recording still on sale in gift shops, the
rabid crowd screams the line from Matthew 27:25 that has so often
justified anti-Semitic frenzy: "Let his blood be upon us and upon our

children."[56] This aspect of the play was criticized by the Arkansas Interfaith Conference as recently as 1991, and has now been dropped in live performance.[57] Yet an announcer still opens each performance with, "Welcome to Mount Oberammergau and the Great Passion Play." On the night I attended, a performer dressed as a high priest, brandishing a fist full of money, cried out, "I've run out of programs. Who'll give me three dollars for a dollar bill? I *am* a Jewish high priest, after all." Jesus and some of his followers, it seems, continue to wage a version of Smith's war against those he targeted as enemies of Christ.[58]

Across an open plaza from the amphitheater, visitors pass through a full-size replica of Jerusalem's Golden Gate. Of course, the actual gate has been bricked up for centuries awaiting, as tradition has it, the Messiah's return to reclaim the earth as his own. So, might this open gate anticipate the expected Messiah's passage? Or does it yet bespeak a sublimated desire to (re)conquer Jerusalem and make it wholly Christian space? In the early 1970s, embarking on fundraising efforts for his New Holy Land, Smith urged potential supporters,

> IMPORTANT: The enemies of Christ are in possession of the original Holy Land. They are desecrating the shrines. They are building housing projects on the holy sites. . . . We are faced with a situation where the enemies of Christ in the Holy Land will use the despoiled areas to glorify the antichrist instead of our Savior.[59]

In capital letters, contributors were asked to help create "THE MOST SENSATIONAL PROJECT OF THE CENTURY" by sending in one thousand dollars. It was to be, apparently, a Jew-free surrogate for the despoiled sacred Holy Land.

The replicated gate now effaces these ugly beginnings. It leads, not to Jerusalem (that is still in the offing, I was told), but to some fifty acres of hillside dubbed the "New Holy Land." Traveling in a tram or bus, tourists are asked to imagine themselves in a landscape of Christianized biblical memory as they pass thirty-seven "authentic Old and New Testament Exhibits." Incarcerated by the format of the tour and its loosely scripted commentary, tourists do not, indeed may not, wander independently of the driver or on-site guides. At places deemed especially important to proclaiming and reaffirming an approved version of salvation, guides in fantasy biblical dress recall incidents in the New Testament narrative of Christ's ministry and work of blood atonement.[60] As part-time lay ministers, the guides witness to the gospel's power to convert indifferent hearts. Sometimes they lead a song or offer closing prayer.

FIG. 24. Tabernacle model.
The New Holy Land Tour, Eureka Springs, Arkansas.
Photo by Burke Long.

Given pride of place, the first stop in the New Holy Land is the
Israelites' wilderness shrine, Moses' tabernacle. It is surely the most
elaborate display and has better claim than most to embodying the
essence of the Smith Foundation's version of gospel truth. "The tabernacle contains God's entire plan of salvation," Paul Shaw, maintenance
and construction supervisor of the New Holy Land, told me.

Shaw is a burly Texan, an engineer who favors open-necked shirts,
hard hats, and gospel songs (he gives regular performances in the Smith
Memorial Chapel). He carries a Bible in his contractor's briefcase. "The
tabernacle overwhelms *you*, rather than you overwhelming *it*," Shaw
said with sudden intensity when I asked him why a full-size model was
important. "You discover untold meanings as you actually try to construct it. And imagine yourself inside the very space that contains every
detail of God's eternal plan for saving us!"[61] A mystery as inexhaustible
as the Scriptures, one might add.

Mr. Shaw's enthusiasm suggests something of the stake he and other
evangelical Christians have in the tabernacle. It is not simply important
theologically or conceptually. It is a material reservoir of desire and

Fig. 25. Moses' Tabernacle in the Wilderness.
The Reverend Dick Ludig, tour guide, is at the right.
Used by permission of the Elna M. Smith Foundation,
Eureka Springs, Arkansas.

fantasy, each inextricably linked to the nearly perfectly simulated and unattainable real thing. The model is a full-scale replica that purports to conform in every detail to the "real" shrine as described in the Bible. In on-site and video versions of regular tours, guides costumed as priests, themselves inventive constructions of a textually imagined biblical reality, perform tourist theater that enables, or at least encourages, visitors to fantasize about biblical peoples and the youth of (biblical) Christian authenticity. As will be evident below, a filmmaker used special cinematic techniques to enhance this relational complex of desire, fantasy, and the "real."

Playacting within this meticulously constructed space, even if not expertly done, heaps representation upon representation. The model simulates biblical history where there is none (that is, in Eureka Springs) and replicates a historical structure (where presumably there was history somewhere in the desert near ancient Egypt). But that, too, comes to us only as representation, a shrine fulsomely imagined in a biblical text whose details of design are sometimes ambiguous or incomplete. Oriented strongly toward reaffirming fundamental evangelical doctrines, the modeled space constructs a layered geography of Christ equivalence, the represented "real" that, like many other New Holy Land exhibits, seems calculated to engender an experiential analogue to the concept of God's incarnation in Jesus. In the guise of historical representation, the journey through the modeled tabernacle thus maps the time-bound space of the ancient biblical Holy Land as a timeless territory of Christian possession.

Or so it seemed to me as the Reverend Dick Ludig invited tourists to accompany him on a video journey through Moses' tabernacle.

"Are you ready for the tabernacle?" he called out. "All right, then, set your calendars to fifteen hundred B.C." Lifting a burnished Moses-like staff, Ludig strode toward heavy curtains that marked the outer boundary of the shrine and quickly set the coordinates that would plot visitors' movements through this real-and-imagined space.

"Our journey today is from the world of sin to the throne of God. I hope you'll remember this journey and I hope that as you walk in your own life, you'll know where you're headed."[62]

Reverend Ludig is a large man with ruddy skin, thinning white hair, and a full beard. Lively blue eyes punctuate folksy idiom, corny humor, and dramatic flair. He was born of Jewish parents in Indiana, but later converted to Messianic Christianity and served churches in east Texas until, after retiring, he began to lead tours at the New Holy Land. Now probably well into his seventies, Ludig moves more slowly than in the 1994 video recording. Nowadays, he offers only special hour-long study tours, leaving others to handle the daily crowds who are guided through the tabernacle every fifteen minutes, nine to five, six days a week, from May to October every year. His passion for the tabernacle seems not to have diminished one whit, however. The day I visited, the journey through meticulous details of tabernacle symbolism stretched far beyond its scheduled one hour.

From beginning to end, Ludig deployed the first premise of traditional typological exegesis: everything about the ancient tabernacle corresponds in some way to Christ.[63] In this way, theater and commentary collapsed temporal perspectives into an encompassing experience of all-time, or no-time.

Perhaps on one level of purpose, demarcated time was actually irrelevant, even in a space ostensibly produced and mapped by historical recollection. While discussing priestly rites, Ludig explained that he wore white linen trousers, tunic, and head covering just as the high priest wore on the Day of Atonement when he alone entered the Holy of Holies. "God gives him the garments to wear," Ludig explained, turning to his audience. "And you'll have them too," he said, alluding to that judgment day when survivors of the great tribulation stand before Christ-God (Rev 6:9–17). "I am dressed in those garments today," he added. "The garments of a sinner."[64]

In such ways, Ludig made sure that simple lessons drawn from a journey through the tabernacle could replenish and sustain devotion to a personal savior. His fervent message at times resembled an evangelist's call for recommitment by the faithful, even while Ludig undermined the institutional settings in which such (re)conversions typically occur. "I don't care about religion," he noted toward the end of the video tour, his blue eyes darting over the audience. "I care about the Lord Jesus Christ and his people. Don't you? And I care that every sinner would meet him."

Such evangelistic urgings began as the tour group moved just inside the tabernacle's perimeter curtain. Encouraged to imagine themselves as Israelites approaching the wilderness shrine, visitors viewed a reenacted "sin" offering. While Ludig effortlessly blended explanation with homily, attending priests silently led a lamb (clearly a visual and material metaphor for Christ) to the place of slaughter.[65]

The action followed a conflated biblical text. In Exodus 29:42, God establishes as part of the law governing the wilderness shrine that Israelites should make a "regular burnt offering throughout [their] generations." Leviticus 4:3–7 adds further details of purification ritual and the idea that burnt offerings purge the guilt of transgression. There God's instruction to Moses directs that a priest bring an unblemished bull "before the Lord as a sin offering," to be slaughtered in a carefully prescribed manner and ultimately consumed in the fire of burnt offering.

In the video, tourists (and viewers at home) watched all this action as simulacra—the lamb (more resonant for Christians than the textually prescribed bull), the slaughter, the sprinkling of blood around the horned altar, the burning of the carcass. Action and commentary produced a space of typological equivalence, a dramatization of Christ the Lamb of God as the singularly important "burnt offering" and the consistent focal point for the tour.

As members of the audience shuffled inside the perimeter curtain, Ludig noted a rough-hewn wooden structure that would hold fast the animal destined for slaughter. "The lamb is brought here and led into the hand of God," he explained, pointing to the five pieces of wood that framed the enclosure, three on one side, two on the other. The logs were angled to form an open "V" shape as though, if one were looking from above, the interlocked fingers of two hands had nearly closed. There's an ancient Jewish teaching about the hand, Ludig averred. "Give God something. Put it into his hand. Let him have control. Stop trying to run God's business for him. Even from the cross, remember, Jesus lifted up his eyes to heaven and said, 'Into your hands I commit my spirit.'"

Meanwhile, other costumed attendants gently pushed the sides of the enclosure together, like five fingers of two hands closing, and the lamb was held fast, enclosed by the "hand of God." The video camera closed in with intimate immediacy. A priest drew a knife; another placed a small bowl under the animal's neck to catch the blood. Moving in still closer, with softening focus and slowing action, the camera framed the hand that held the knife, which was deftly drawn under the lamb's neck. The animal's head dropped gently, as though it were dying quickly and, incidentally, sparing viewers the sight of flowing blood and muscular twitches. Later, a priest sprinkled blood on four corners of the altar as other attendants carried the slaughtered lamb to its place of immolation.

It is impossible to assess how the tourists assembled for the video responded to this reenacted ritual. Some actions were less meticulously choreographed than claims to authenticity and faithfulness to the underlying biblical text might have demanded. Furthermore, the simulated sacrifice was apparently done only for the filmed version of the tabernacle lecture. On the daily fifteen-minute tours, visitors must imagine the ritual of animal sacrifice from the guide's brief description. In any case, perfect understanding, not replication, of Old Testament practice is the important goal, for in theological concept and within this Christianized space, the old order has given way to the new. So the past, or rather one's imperfect representation of the past, can never be the decisive point. Ludig proudly explained,

> When we built the tabernacle we did everything we could to make it as authentic appearing as possible. A lot of work and research here. Everything you see here is the right size, the right shape, the right color, the right function, the right location, the right design. But the laver, huh, we were in trouble before we started here.

Ludig admitted that the Bible gave no instruction on how to build these large washbasins. However, even this insurmountable barrier to authenticity was overcome. "I know something that I think is more important," he commented. When associated with Christian baptism, ritual washing in the laver (here the video recording depicts a priest ritually cleansing his hands) prepares one to walk with and serve God.

> Notice how close the water is to the altar? To me that tells me something about Christian baptism. We need to keep 'em together, don't we? And you're baptized believers. But listen. It teaches you something we don't do very well. We don't teach our people that they're supposed to be walking closer to God after they're a baptized believer. Am I right?

Similarly, as priests carried out the sin offering, filming techniques enhanced the illusion of realism even as Ludig's commentary mitigated its shortcomings. My students gasped when they saw the lamb's head drop. And I had to check my own first impressions by repeatedly hitting the pause and slow-motion buttons. Of course, the fake was ultimately discoverable. And in any case, interpretive overlay rendered moot the imperfection, even its imperfectability. By their occurrence together, commentary and illusion suppressed a clash of values that might have threatened the whole enterprise of making tabernacle simulacra.

Actually slaughtering a lamb, even for reasons of historical verisimilitude, would probably have shocked those tourists who adore pets, and who do so in a country where criminal laws protect animals from abuse. Just beyond this potential discord run the unstable fault lines between environmentalists and large corporations whose clashing interests frequently come down to a fight over protecting a single species of wildlife.

The filmmakers seem to have anticipated this arena of resistance, while ever so dimly acknowledging the larger horizon of political struggle. Softened focus; slowed motion; soothing strains of new-age Muzak; a lamb cradled gently on the way to immolation; a burnt offering that dissolves into sanitized, computer-generated flames. All these techniques lent a dream-like quality to the lamb's demise, which, as my students' reactions attest, seemed at first anything but a dream. The video editing took account of squeamishness, undertook to mollify its outbreak, and at the same time enabled the desire for "the real" to be satisfied, at least provisionally, in realistic simulation.

Yet the shock that threatened to destroy this Christian space seems to have demanded even more direct containment. "Kosher killing is painless," Ludig stated, authoritatively invoking a familiar defense of a rule that is felt to be alien and barbaric. Yet the fantasy-enabling reality of tabernacle space had within it the recollection of Jesus' sacrificial death, too. The raw horror of that might have pressed upon some of the tourists, had it been given the least encouragement to surface. If there was any discomfort, Ludig quickly overcame it. Jesus' death—real, painful, and not kosher—vitiates the old ways of Judaism. "Jesus' death certainly wasn't kosher, was it?" he asked. "Absolutely awful? You're right. And there's a reason. Your sins and my sins are absolutely awful in God's sight."

Thus, at this spot just inside the tabernacle's perimeter, the first reenactments embodied the whole tour space—a journey from the world of sin to the throne of (Christ) God. By juxtaposing the ancient "sin offering" with Jesus' eternal atoning sacrifice, Ludig produced Christian supersessionist space that subsumed and neutralized what purported to be authentic biblical (Jewish) practice and law. God instigated the death of the one sacrificed lamb that counts, not according to the laws of *kashrut* (Jesus' death was painful, not kosher, said Ludig), but according to some qualitatively different, non-Jewish rule and redemptive purpose.

Not surprisingly, the tabernacle's other features were also made to generate layered dimensions in the space of Christ awareness. Standing alongside the inner reaches of the tabernacle, tourists gazed upon the shewbread—unleavened, not puffed up, Ludig explained, signifying Jesus' humble, sinless state. They saw the ark of the covenant with golden cherubim wings enclosing a space for God's "glory," which, though lost to history like the old tabernacle, will appear again when Jesus returns (the film shows a pulsing glow). Six hundred and thirteen laws filled the ark, Ludig said. "That's a lot of law. Don't let it bother you. God's mercy seat is above every bit of it. Thank you, God."

At the end of the tour, Ludig summed up his presentation and once again announced the interpretive coordinates that mapped the space he, or the Smith Foundation, regularly seeks to construct for its visitors. "Well, that's a Jewish understanding of this journey from the world of sin to the throne of God," he said with a shrug. He signaled an ever so slight dismissal and ignored the Christian ideas that had suffused and animated the tour. "But I know you're not Jewish. Now the question is, are you still Christians, or have you been backsliding on me?" Following a joke about backsliding in churches, Ludig continued,

> The fact is, you do have to walk from the world of sin to the throne of God. And we lifted up Christ at the altar, didn't we? And you understood that. We talked about baptism, and you guys understood that.

This walking closer to God is where we have the breakdown. And I'd like you to remember some of these things because back home you're gonna have some sleeping beauties and I'd like you to wake 'em up and get them back to walking with God.

That opportunity to follow God was decisively presented in Jesus, and is continually available only to Christians, Ludig explained in a post-tour question and answer period. Someone had asked about King Herod's temple and the sanctuary's inner curtain that was torn asunder at the moment of Jesus' death. Ludig launched into a favorite topic, one which he occasionally reiterates on the special study tours. The Jewish temple had long since taken the place, religiously speaking, of the more ancient, but lost, wilderness tabernacle. "A sad day," he said during the live tour. On camera, claiming "Messianic Jewish" authority for his teaching,[66] Ludig asserted that Herod's temple had been corrupted by the king himself, a "great fornicator, a great murderer, a great adulterer."

Like a return of Gerald Smith's forgotten crusades, the video recording at this point cut to a moralizing scene from the "Great Passion Play." King Herod, resplendent and pompously playing to the crowds, clattered by in a Roman-style chariot. At his side was Salomé—gossamered, bejeweled, seductively decadent, the gendered and sexualized archetype of Everyman's downfall.[67] The Sadducees, Ludig's voice-over continues, were just as corrupt as Herod, for they "purchased the right of priesthood from the government in Rome." Then, too, the "shekinah glory cloud" no longer stood over the inner Holy of Holies. (Here the film reverted to the pulsating light hovering in the tabernacle.) Nor was the Ark of the Covenant there. But the temple's inner curtain, the one that split from top to bottom at the moment of Jesus' death—"D'you know what they saw? Darkness." He pauses for emphasis. "Just darkness."

These Jewish violators of ancient holy space had deceived the people, Ludig explained, allowing the vestiges of Smith's triumphal anti-Jewish crusades and the tradition of exclusive Christianity to go unchallenged. The true "glory" of God had already passed from the Jewish temple to its new location. Inserting himself into the space conjured up by this language, and merging his own voice with God's, Ludig cried out with indignation,

Do you want to see my glory? It's on the center cross. That's my beloved son. And you do need to have a priest to come to God. His name is Jesus. *Yashuah Hammashiah*. And we need to follow him, don't we?

That question, aimed at every member of the audience, suggests once again the evangelizing drive that lies at the heart of this Christianized tabernacle, and more broadly, of the New Holy Land tour in its entirety. The tour aims to generate lived space, a socially constructed realm of experience that will be familiar to those used to Protestant worship services. A minister preaches the word, offers prayers and homilies, and urges congregants to (re)commit their lives to Christ.

This experiential aspect became evident soon after the reenacted sin offering. Commenting on the incense that would have been used in ancient priestly rites, Ludig explained that even though not widely practiced in churches today, burning incense teaches good "Christ lessons." For one, as the smoke rises up to God it says, "Let your prayer and praise reach up to God, let your prayer and praise reach up to God—" (Ludig was speaking faster now and waving his arms like an orchestra conductor) "—let your prayer and praise reach up to God." Perhaps a little startled, the assembled tourists timidly joined in.

The attempt at creating an experience of congregational praise, rather than its success, is the important point. The constructed geography of the wilderness tabernacle involved not simply imagined ancient space and enacted lessons of Christ equivalence, but also immediate religious experience. As a lived space of embodied typology, it encouraged worship. The realism of material substance (the model, its costumed attendants and implements, its reenacted sacrifices), along with commentary, enabled a fantasy of authentic encounter with the "old" but, for Christians, discarded ways. At the same time, one could embrace the "new" ways of Christ alive, the Word-made-flesh among believers.

Read as affective geography, the tabernacle produces Christian social space, a lived journey of symbolically encoded experience (the accumulated livings of many Christian communities) that is decoded as commentary unfolds. Christians are presumably meant to reaffirm assent to the referential system of Christ equivalence so as to experience Christ's presence in moments of lapse and in anticipation of eschatological closure. If this fantasy is realized, believers might internalize a grandly spatialized theological possibility, that God became flesh in the body of a human being, Jesus (and does so again in the body of the modern believer).

Indeed, at the conclusion of a special hour-long study tour that I attended, Ludig reverted to his talk of the unleavened shewbread, unpuffed-up and sinless, like the piece of Passover *matzah* he held up for display. It is like Christ, he said, transforming the artifact of biblical and Jewish ritual into Christ awareness. "Without sin, and pierced in body," Ludig continued, "as *matzah* has been pierced to allow steam to escape." Then, with dramatic suddenness he crumbled the *matzah* in his hands and passed the pieces around, saying, "Take, eat—all of it." Caught by surprise, we willing captives of Ludig's powerful scenarios indeed took, and ate. And commuted tabernacle, if briefly, into generational solidarity, into participation in the age-old lived space of the Eucharist.

In retrospect, the constructed geography of the New Holy Land Tour and its related sacred projects seem powerful productions of nostalgic desire, devotion, and fantasy. Yet the mapping of Arkansas topography as Holy Land signposted with Christ equivalence cannot claim to be final. Other readings uncover counter-perspectives and counter-geographies—the layered assemblage of exclusions and inclusions, alternative histories and politics effaced by privileged scenarios of desire.

So, too, creators of Jerusalem–Holy Land in St. Louis assembled a complicated space of Christian uplift and nationalistic celebration in a time when America was asserting its destined place to dominate those in need of uplift. But alternative histories and geographies could not be entirely suppressed. A material-ideational landscape that illustrated the advancement of Christian civilization at the same time evoked resistance. Perhaps errant Jerusalem residents and bowdlerized displays got out of hand and for some, like Madame Mountford, threatened the sanitized space of Christian fantasy. Or lawsuits and job actions belied the scenarios of untroubled religious devotion. Or, today, a critical perspective can make visible the arrogance of privilege that, like nationalism and unrestrained capitalism, had been built into this holy land at home.

The holy lands of St. Louis and Eureka Springs, like Chautauqua, were malleable spaces produced for and made available to Americans. They enabled travelers disinclined or unable to travel abroad to experience ready-made fantasies of the "real" Holy Land, and reaffirmed the cultural identities of a fairly specific band of middle-class Americans. Holy Lands were good for business and good for religion.

The missionary impulse, however, demands ever more converts, or if not converts, at least ever widening territories of conquest. What if actual travel to holy lands at home could be eliminated altogether? Photographic technology, so useful for transforming constructed displays into memorabilia or enlivening diaries of Holy Land travel, could potentially bring the Holy Land—or someone's idea of it—to every school, library, church, synagogue, and living room in America. If the price were right, that is, and the resources for developing markets and distribution networks were sufficient.

Stereographs were a key means to this end in turn-of-the-century America. Invented in the mid-nineteenth century, these relatively cheap systems of three-dimensional imaging had become quite ubiquitous and fashionable by about 1900. They were particularly successful in providing vicarious experiences of faraway places and satisfying voyeuristic tastes for the exotic. Even further removed from actual Palestine than the materialized fantasies of theme parks and World's Fair models, specially packaged stereographic tours of the Holy Land paradoxically seemed at the time less artificial than any of those other extravagant surrogate holy lands. Such photo tours were crucial in the evolving commodification of desire, fantasy, and the "real" enshrined in the fake. And the Chautauqua Institution, with its network of biblical study, would play its part.

Three

Parlor Tours of the Holy Land

Longtime Chautauquan Edwin Booth once recalled that Charles Foster Kent, a noted biblical scholar from Yale University, had helped assure the accuracy of Palestine Park. In addition, he and Jesse Lyman Hurlbut, among the most revered of Chautauqua's early leaders, took countless Americans on stereographic pilgrimages to the Holy Land. "They went to Palestine to look at the sacred sights . . . they sold these viewers and they made these stereopticon slides," declared Booth to an appreciative crowd of fellow Chautauquans in 1965. "All over America the whole land of Palestine came alive. We seem to have lived there."[1]

Booth is to be forgiven if his remarks were a little exaggerated. He canonized Hurlbut at a time when the Chautauqua Institution was preparing for its centennial celebration. However, the association of Kent with Hurlbut and three-dimensional photographs of the Holy Land is entirely accurate. And his enthusiastic recollection of their power to create a fully realized sense of place is wholly believable.

Charles Foster Kent was an expert in biblical geography and he enhanced his turn-of-the-century studies with a set of specially commissioned stereographs. As a student in 1892, Kent made a study pilgrimage to Palestine. He returned in 1910 to further his geographical researches. In 1914, the year he gave his first lectures at Chautauqua, Kent and Hurlbut published *Palestine through the Stereoscope*, a revised edition of a photographic tour that Hurlbut had authored about a decade earlier. The photographs and commentary were carefully arranged, the authors wrote for the new edition, to help readers "know intimately the places that are magical in their power to give us a vivid realization of actuality in the Biblical narrative."[2] Readers became pilgrims, willing captives of the ideologically charged spaces of Christian devotion created between printed image and explanation.

The stereoscope, a hand-held device which gave a three-dimensional effect to dual-image photographs, was at the time approaching the summit of its popularity. Mass-produced and relatively cheap, the integrated system of mechanical viewer and photograph became fashionable for classroom pedagogy, tourist mementos, and parlor travel to exotic places of the world.[3] Holy Land stereographs were among the earliest to be produced, and in 1897 Underwood & Underwood, soon to become the premier publisher of such items, began aggressively marketing a boxed set of seventy-two Palestine views, *Journeys in the Holy Land*.[4] The first of many country-specific tours, this collection of Palestine photographs was followed by many others packaged variously to appeal to different segments of the market. Such Holy Land tours remained enormously popular well into the 1920s.[5]

Together and singly, Hurlbut and Kent took full advantage of the fashion—the one to reach a Christian public with results of his research on biblical geography, and the other to advance the cause of Sunday school instruction and Christian missions. As scholars, they made the results of historically oriented scholarship (the biblical "facts" which Booth said guided Hurlbut's lectures at Palestine Park) available for evangelical purposes. As tour guides, Hurlbut and Kent negotiated paths between the confusing experiences that Ottoman Palestine presented to many pilgrims and the unambiguous reinforcements of faith and cultural identities that theologians, politicians, missionaries, World's Fair promoters, and other pilgrims wished to find there. Like Palestine Park, or New Jerusalem in St. Louis, or the Holy Land of Eureka Springs, these parlor tours of Palestine produced ideational spaces fraught with tension. Desire for the "real" Holy Land enabled fantasies of "the actuality of biblical narrative," while the illusions mediated socially rooted cultural assumptions and discomforts, as well as ideological convictions.

No one claimed that such entertaining and edifying armchair expeditions were superior to actual travel in Palestine. However, as many gave high marks to Chautauqua's Palestine Park or to the New Jerusalem in St. Louis, Hurlbut and Kent (and their publishers) praised stereographs as very satisfactory surrogates for what was to them a singular reality of the Holy Land. The essence of that reality was now easily accessible, affordable, assembled and sold at home in America.

The Tour Guides

Charles Foster Kent was about eighteen years old when he left his rural home near the Erie Canal in Palmyra, New York, about twenty miles east of Rochester. He enrolled in the Sheffield Scientific School in New Haven, Connecticut. The following year, shifting his interests from science toward the humanities, he transferred to Yale College, and subsequently graduated in 1889. He had intended to study law, but, under the spell of William Rainey Harper, the first Woolsey Professor of Biblical Literature at Yale, Kent took up graduate work in Semitic languages and Bible. He had just passed his twenty-second birthday. In two years he collected his Ph.D., and like most young biblical scholars of the day, pursued postgraduate studies in Germany, including four months of travel in Egypt, Palestine, and Greece. By then, his teacher and mentor had been elected president of the newly reorganized University of Chicago.

As Kent headed for what he referred to as his "much talked of Palestinian trip" early in 1892, he was worried about the frenzied pace Harper had set for himself. In bold-stroked handwriting, Kent issued a playfully urgent plea for Harper to heed the romantic siren of the East.

> You are cordially invited to let the cares of Chicago University go, buy a *Reise-Decke* and rough it as a son of the way in the lands where all is purely Semitic.[6]

Apparently Harper took the joke, and did not abandon his duties in Chicago. Kent kept writing, seeking his teacher's advice, sharing impressions of Ottoman Palestine, discussing plans for Chicago lectures, and shaping essays to be published in journals founded by Harper.[7] The long-distance discussions bore fruit, for on his return Kent taught for three years as a member of Harper's faculty. He subsequently moved to Brown University, and in 1901 succeeded his teacher and mentor as the Woolsey Professor of Biblical Literature at Yale College, a post he held until his death in 1925, just months before his fifty-eighth birthday.[8]

Throughout his career, Kent maintained cordial relations with his Chicago colleagues. Through the Chicago-based American Institute of

Fig. 26. Charles Foster Kent, c. 1910.
Courtesy of the Archives of Yale University.

Sacred Literature, Kent joined Harper, Shailer Mathews, and many other university-based scholars of the day in promoting historical, as opposed to ecclesiastically submissive, study of the Bible. They carried its results to wider audiences, especially through correspondence courses and intensive summer programs at Chautauqua.[9] Eulogized as a man of "buoyant enthusiasm, tireless energy, and surprising versatility,"[10] Kent fashioned his career as active churchman, biblical historian, and geographer. He wrote and lectured widely for professional and popular audiences, including those at Chautauqua in 1914 and 1924.[11] One biographer thought that Kent did "more than any other American scholar of his day to make accessible to the public the significant results of biblical study."[12]

While a student in New Haven, Kent longed to travel to that land where, as he later wrote to Harper, all was purely Semitic. Well, not quite all. For sure, Kent saw biblical names and people everywhere. But a muscular ideology of religious heroism equally animated his experiences. By identifying with—and enduring—the unspoiled harshness of the land, Kent believed that he could touch something authentically spiritual. So believed many travelers to Palestine, as well as many whose grand schemes brought versions of the Holy Land to America. Edgar Goodspeed, a New Testament scholar at the University of Chicago from 1898 to 1937, gave clear expression to the idea when he recalled, some fifty years later, his own 1899 study-pilgrimage to Palestine.

> Thinly populated and almost desolate as we saw it, it brought us all the closer to its ancient story, for there was nobody to come between us and it, and to distract our minds from what had been. Such a detachment is impossible for the traveler of today, who sees a land seething with unrest, and hurries over it, as far as he is allowed to go, with a speed that makes any real identification with its ancient life and condition impossible. So we were fortunate in the very primitiveness of our tour of Palestine. There was nothing to interrupt our communion with its great past, and this perhaps makes it worthwhile to record it in some detail.[13]

In his version of Goodspeed's naïve sentiments, Kent told Harper that most of the men in his traveling group were experienced, independent, and adventuresome. "The motto of the crowd from the start is 'roughing it,'" Kent wrote, certain that Harper, and for that matter James Breasted, the great University of Chicago explorer of Egypt, would approve.[14] Refusing comforts, however, had a touch of the imperiously easeful in it. The little band of travelers, "six students with common purpose," used no tents and hired local horses tended by "a hasheesh-eating fiend of an Arab . . . fully as wily as the ordinary son of Ishmael." They also took on a Maltese "capital cook" and a "faithful coal black son of Ham" to carry what little baggage they had.

Kent and friends avoided the very few hotel accommodations that were available and loftily refused to submit to the "galling dragoman-serfdom common to the majority of travelers." They were their own dragoman, Kent told Harper, and like free men of a lordlier race born to rule, "we went just when and where we pleased."[15]

Their journey included at least one stopover at an outpost of civilization, at Tell el-Hesi, an archaeological site about thirty miles southwest of Jerusalem. The excavator was Frederick Bliss, an American employed by the British-governed Palestine Exploration Fund. Bliss recalled Kent's unannounced arrival. "A gentleman rode up saying, 'I am Kent of Yale, are you an Alpha Delta?' I said yes and took his hand, squeezing it in different ways hoping they would include the forgotten grip." Apparently satisfied, Kent was then shown round the site. As Bliss wrote, they later enjoyed a sumptuous repast of soup, salmon and rice, leg of lamb, roasted potatoes, peas, and dessert, followed by tea and chocolate.[16]

Compared to many tourists who demanded and could afford luxurious tenting arrangements, Kent and company were rather abstemious trekkers. They didn't usually dine on salmon or lamb, and they often slept in huts or under the open sky. Nonetheless, they traveled with the aid of a servant underclass entourage, which did not lessen their confidence that they were in fact gaining the "truest impressions" of life and ruins. If only his teacher had joined this "outing in Palestine" to enjoy "the experiences and scenes which this land of ancient story offers," Kent wrote.[17] He did not mind sixteen-hour days in the saddle, or sleeping "hat and shoes on" in flea-infested huts with little biting creatures "promenading along our spines." One morning-after body count certified one hundred and nine "dead and wounded." Like an Odysseus stranded on Flea Island, Kent endured and triumphed. He was amused in retrospect and found comfort in the thought that he was living in the land as the ancient biblical peoples had done. Through such self-enforced primitiveness, he surmounted repeated troubles, escaped "dangerous episodes," and enjoyed "opportunities for getting ideas of the land through our contact with the natives and missionaries."[18]

Kent was in thrall. As though taking his cue from William Thomson's *The Land and the Book*, he found that virtually every step and tent stake in the soil of Egypt and Palestine evoked a glorious biblical past. "Every experience is a commentary on some of the Biblical passages," Kent wrote, "and as we begin to get into this life we begin to feel those things which before were only intellectually intelligible."[19]

Even visceral pleasure at lordly dominance evoked biblical proto-types. He could shout just as loudly as "these howling begging Orientals" in Egypt, Kent told Harper at the beginning of May. Besides, coming to "enjoy having twenty or thirty of the black fellows climbing all over me, howling 'Gut donkey' at the top of their voices," Kent pressed his will against theirs and prevailed. He took great care not to appear in a hurry, and though tried in patience, he was willing to walk away when disputes arose—even in the desert wastelands. And he would "generally succeed in getting his will and rates." Recalling Bible stories of wily patriarchs, Kent mused, "We can well understand the narrative which records that Laban seven times revised his contract with Jacob" (Genesis 29–30).[20]

Ottoman Palestine in 1892 was as entangled with such romantic notions and attitudes of superiority as it was troublesome and dangerous for travelers. Kent's experience was not exceptional in this regard. Nor was he unusual among Anglo-Europeans in recoiling from, as he wrote that May, the "Oriental World which inverts most of our Occidental ideas of custom and propriety." Offense was easily transformed into reassuring patterns of biblical narrative. Traveling through the sparsely populated and barren Galilee, for example, seemed "a fascinating northern ride through New Testament scenes." Not only was he traversing a real-imagined Bible landscape, the little band of five were mapping an inner terrain of religious belief. With three companions to represent a conservative theological position, Kent wrote, and a man from Andover Seminary to help him argue more progressive ideas, the trekkers filled those sixteen-hour days with energetic talk. "This giving of reasons for the faith within us," he declared, "has been invaluable in fixing our opinions, and these old questions become intensely real when considered in this land that gave them birth."

The Holy Land was not only imagined as biblical and generative of religious faith. It was open territory, ripe for inroads by missionaries of freedom and pliant to the will of American explorers. Palestine was just one more place for young America, guardian of enterprise and freedom, to flex its world-power biceps. As the Holy Land, it quickened Kent's desire for excavative conquest. "We longed to get hold of a shovel and go to excavating," he wrote to Harper. "American capital and enterprise ought to be at work opening up some of these treasures."

Although the ancient treasure chest held God's revelation, contemporary Ottoman Palestine was quite another matter. Pitiable and repellant, unproductive and nearly untouched by cultural advancement, the "Orient" set in relief what Kent thought admirable about his own kind. "The barriers between East and West are fast crumbling," Kent would tell Chautauquans in 1914, but the "Orient" still shows its ancient, not so happy character. It is "dreamy, introspective, emotional, the West alert, aggressive, and logical. The West is individualistic and jealous of the rights of men, but such an idea never entered the head of the Eastern man."[21]

It was fairly common to demean Palestine as a cultural backwater. In fact it was a neglected province of the declining Turkish Empire, and easy to characterize as left behind by the industrial and social developments that Anglo-Europeans so extravagantly celebrated in world's fairs. Such a portrayal did ideological work, however. A contemporary "Oriental" (and exotically primitive) Palestine, devalued in the present but revered in its antiquity, confirmed emotional attachments to notions of "Occidental" progress and helped justify political and religious attitudes, if not actions, of dominance. Pilgrims sought to skim the dross and extract the purely biblical, the "real" Holy Land, from its distasteful contemporary trappings. This mental space of obsession, of antiquity and devotion, was to be entered and possessed.

Yet why should the "real" be so obscured, seemingly forgotten even by God? In one remarkable comment in that remarkable May 1st letter, Kent grappled with the dissonance between lionized past and degraded present, but without disrupting the underlying ideological framework. "Why, when other lands are making such progress," he reflected, "is this country with such demonstrated possibilities still held back to the life and customs of an antiquated past?" The answer invoked both religious devotion and scientific empiricism, and while easing Kent's discomfort, defended historical scholarship against its detractors, who accused it of weakening confidence in the Bible.

In the backwardness of Palestine, Kent wrote to Harper, "is to be seen the latest manifestation of the Divine guidance in the history of this land chosen to teach the world." Because the Holy Land had hardly changed since ancient times, it could witness directly to the Bible and confound the skeptics. Divine providence made it so.

This life, such a picture of that reflected in the Bible, has thus been preserved that travelers and students might picture it by pen and camera so that no one can arise in future ages and say that it was not true.

Kent went on to impose onto this geography of biblical realities something like Christian purpose, which justified the presumed right of superior "Occidental" civilization to lift Palestine from her degradation. The backwardness Kent noted, and which travelers from Europe and America frequently lamented, had persisted for a purpose. However, once that purpose was satisfied, that is, when skepticism toward the Bible had been put to rest, then the less than fully civilized would receive the revolutions of modernity.

Now that this life has been, as it were, crystallized, the land is ready for that foreign civilization which is already beginning to come in and change much of the old. The railroad from Damascus to Beirut, which now bids fair to be put through in the near future, will soon revolutionize many things.

Yet antiquity retained its appeal, for Kent wanted to live close to the land and inhabit those imagined spaces of biblical Palestine. He returned in 1910 to further his research on ancient geography. By then he was the Woolsey Professor at Yale College. A decade earlier, he had published *Biblical Geography and History*[22] to such acclaim that, following revisions incorporated after this second trip, it would be reprinted six times. Success was assured because Kent correlated his study with separately published illustrative stereographs.[23]

In the preface, Kent stated more fully the theological convictions that continued to shape his idea of the Holy Land. Standing fully in the shadow of William Thomson's *The Land and the Book*, Kent saw the truths of the Bible etched in the topography, peoples, and crumbling ruins of the land. The science of geography, now his fully established academic specialty, gave unique access to those truths.

Biblical geography is a description of the divine character and purpose expressing itself through natural forces, in the physical contour of the earth, in the animate world, and, above all, in the life and activities of man.

Geography is the first chapter in that long story of revelation, Kent believed. For "through the plains and mountains, the rivers and seas, the climate and flora of the biblical world, the Almighty spoke to men as plainly and unmistakably as he did through the voices of his inspired seers and sages." How much more vividly, then, might God's words be grasped by means of those stereographs that Kent had assembled to "illustrate the most important events of biblical geography and history."[24] Some features of the land, such as ruins along the seacoast at Tyre (in modern-day south Lebanon), even attested to the truth of the Bible's prophecies (Ezekiel 26).[25]

When dealing with sites associated with the New Testament, Kent invoked geoscripture to summon up a then popular notion of Jesus as the Great Prophet who quietly, in bucolic moments apart, brought a distinctive voice of God into the world. The land is holy witness, for the heights around Nazareth are exactly those hills which "spread out before the young boy of Nazareth" and for this reason offer "one of the most beautiful and significant views in all of Palestine."[26] Inside the town itself, comings and goings at the village fountain, an image that was tirelessly replicated in magazines and souvenir postcards of the day, elicited a scholarly reverie on what the Gospel writers neglected to report about Jesus' youthful awakening.

> In imagination we see the boy of Nazareth, in close touch with the life of his home and neighbors, by experience and keen sympathetic insight learning what was in the heart of man, amidst these simple surroundings laying the foundations for a work which was to influence all mankind.[27]

Similarly, baptism in the muddy Jordan River spoke through clarifying Christian homily. As the river wound through a "thicket of bushes and overhanging trees," Kent wrote, it defined a "strange but fitting sanctuary for a meeting of the fearless prophet and the disciple from distant Nazareth." Whatever John the Baptist may have known, that moment marked the inception of the greater prophet's mission.

> To Jesus, it meant the consecration of himself not only to that for which John stood, but also to that vastly larger, broader task that had been revealed to him in the quiet years at Nazareth.[28]

Jesus taught new truths of God to rural folk living in the villages and hills of Galilee, places congenial to Kent's religious sensibilities. Here, simplicity of religious life was best achieved, and shown, in Jesus, who was far removed from the "narrow fanaticism and ceremonialism" of Jerusalem.[29]

FIG. 27. Virgin's Fountain, Nazareth. Postcard, c. 1900.

Kent did not simply invent these nostalgic notions. The New Testament Gospels located much of Jesus' activity in Galilee, a life apart from the grim tragedy unfolding in Jerusalem. Romanticism and conventional Protestant piety supplied the rest. Ernest Renan's *Life of Jesus* was one of the most enduring of many Galilean idylls that gave literary form to such orientalizing sentimentalism.[30] Translations, multiple printings, and imitations such as Henry Van Dyke's Jesus, who "spread His table on the green grass," extended the agrarian Jesus well into the twentieth century.[31]

Selah Merrill, who fashioned a turn-of-the-century career as clergyman, Bible professor, archaeologist, and diplomat, eulogized Galilee, too. A forceful and sometimes not so diplomatic U.S. consul intermittently posted to Jerusalem between 1882 and 1907, Merrill deemed the northern region of Palestine "providentially fitted for the first reception of Christ." Its rolling flora-covered hills were far from "cheerless and dismal" Jerusalem, the "bleak home of priests and Levites" who were hardened and narrowed by dogmatic systems and disposed to reject the innovative teachings of Jesus. The Master found a receptive audience among the "earnest, busy, and industrious" people of Galilee, whose honest labor made "the valleys and hills of Galilee blossom like a rose."[32]

This picture appealed to Victorian Americans, who were partial to hanging gushy poetry and sentimental mottoes on sitting room walls. Protestant anti-ceremonialists among them avidly pursued private religious nostalgia in travelogues, postcards, Holy Land parlor music, and collections of wild flowers affixed to small cards or delicately interleaved inside souvenir books.

When Charles Foster Kent gazed upon the placid Sea of Galilee, he drew deeply from this stream of popular imagination. As Edwin Booth would articulate much later for an audience at Chautauqua, this captivating space of quiet, sacred intrusion cradled the "real incarnation in a real humanity." For Kent, Jesus was a meditative master, an out-of-doors Jesus whom the land of Galilee still evoked in the hearts of Christian pilgrims and students of sacred geography. In "quiet spots, apart from the city," Jesus found his most profound insights and exercised his most lasting influence. Jesus' "great work was that of a teacher," and these places in the Galilean countryside

> afforded the needed opportunity for quiet conversation, for question and answer, and for that intimate personal touch which was the secret of the Master's power.[33]

A few years after writing those words, Kent collaborated with Jesse Lyman Hurlbut on the parlor tour *Palestine through the Stereoscope*. By that time, Hurlbut had been associated with Chautauqua for nearly forty years.

Born in 1843 and educated at Wesleyan University, Hurlbut taught school for a year, and in 1865 took up pastoral duties in the Newark Conference of the Methodist Episcopal Church. Ten years later he came to Chautauqua, met John Heyl Vincent, and began a life-long association with the Assembly. (See figure 8.) Under Vincent, he served as assistant secretary of the Methodist Sunday School Union and Tract Society and as assistant editor of the Society's publications. When Vincent was elected a bishop in 1888, Hurlbut succeeded him as secretary and editor of the Society.[34]

At Chautauqua, Hurlbut directed the Sunday school normal department that had been established to train teachers. From 1882 he was principal of the Literary and Scientific Circle and took a leading role in this program of general education for adults. A sought-after speaker at regional Chautauquas all around the country, Hurlbut authored a popular handbook of biblical geography and edited numerous teachers' manuals which set the standard in the Sunday school movement for a generation.[35] In 1900, after a trip to Palestine, he wrote his first guide for an Underwood & Underwood stereographic tour of the Holy Land.[36] Hurlbut died in 1930 following a debilitating illness. The famous preacher Harry Emerson Fosdick, who had published his own account of travels to Palestine,[37] eulogized Hurlbut while standing in Palestine Park. A more fitting memorial would be hard to imagine, for "on the little hills of Palestine," as poet Rachel Dithridge recalled, Hurlbut had lectured for more than thirty years.

Like John Heyl Vincent and Charles Foster Kent, Hurlbut was passionate about the facts of biblical geography. Like them, he believed that exacting study of the Holy Land would bolster flagging confidence that biblical narratives, once set into their landscape environs, could be relied upon to yield true heavenly treasures. In his *Manual of Biblical Geography*, Hurlbut plotted on colored maps pathways leading to Christian revelation, from the great flood and the patriarchs to the journeys of Jesus and Paul. Sacred truth was accessible in human migrations and settlings, in diagrams and pie charts, in long-buried cities resurrected into the life forms of architectural plan. A panoramic photograph of Jerusalem, complete with vertical and horizontal coordinates, identified with surveyor-like precision every site deemed important to Christian devotion. Engravings of contemporary Palestine, produced in the typical nineteenth-century style of romantic landscapes, suggested that divine presence indeed inhabited those faraway spaces portrayed with such dramatic intensity and exacting gaze.

Hurlbut gladly followed Vincent's dictates to provide teachers such richly imagined spaces of Christian revelation (Vincent, it will be recalled, wrote an introduction to the *Manual of Biblical Geography*). Hurlbut also took naturally to Palestine Park, making it his own by tirelessly giving talks on sacred history while wandering the model's hills and valleys. "We would all sit on the grass at Mount Hermon or wherever he wanted us to be," his daughter Bertha Hurlbut Doughtery later recalled, "and he would again tell a story from the little models [of villages on the hills] of Palestine." Afterward, she added, her father encouraged the forty or fifty children to sail their little boats in the Sea of Galilee.[38]

In such settings, Hurlbut perfected his vivid homiletic style of commentary that would eventually find an even larger following in *Palestine through the Stereoscope*. With Charles Foster Kent's collaboration, the best known of the parlor tours of Palestine became a flagship of Christian commerce delivering its holy lands to Americans ready to buy.

The Tour

The publishing company Underwood & Underwood provided trouble-free world travel to its customers at a time when affluent Americans, more than ever before, were journeying to distant places. The company targeted those with aspirations to stylish tourism but few resources. "Travel of the truest kind" is what one got, a 1910 brochure proclaimed in its promotion of some eighty-five vicarious tours to world destinations. Yet, remarkably, one could travel "without utilizing either ship or railroad, or any of the ordinary bodily conveyances," and gain all the cultural benefits that accrue to the truly wealthy. Equipped with dual-image photos printed on cards, a stereoscope that enabled the two images to blend into a single three-dimensional view, a guidebook, and a patented system of maps to locate the position from which one viewed each scene—with this relatively inexpensive equipment, an Underwood traveler of "wealthy . . . or humble means alike" could partake of "all the possibilities of culture" that world travel promised.[39]

Finding promises of such social privilege irresistible and pressed by advertising testimonials, thousands of armchair travelers bought the products. Even without owning the guidebooks, teachers and students could consult brief commentaries printed on the reverse side of the photographs (an Underwood & Underwood innovation) and embark on fantasy journeys of cultural improvement. By 1901, the manufacturer was producing about twenty-five thousand images per day.[40]

To judge from the six variously priced Underwood & Underwood sets, not to mention the series sold by other firms and individual photographers since 1865, trips to the Holy Land were among the most popular voyages. From Underwood alone one could purchase two short tours of Palestine, one with commentary by Hurlbut. There were "travel lesson" sets, each with commentary—one from the Old Testament and one each on the life of Jesus and the lives of "apostolic heroes." A special "Jerusalem tour" and a journey "covering the wanderings of the children of Israel" through Egypt rounded out the offerings. The publisher reached an even wider market by correlating views of Palestine with the *Uniform Sunday School Lessons*, a long-running series to which both Hurlbut and Vincent made numerous contributions.

Hurlbut and Kent's *Palestine through the Stereoscope* was actually a two-hundred-view compilation and expansion of these previously assembled Underwood & Underwood tours. Under the authors' tutelage, travelers became pilgrims who, by viewing the photos and following the accompanying explanations, entered Palestine at the seacoast port of Jaffa, journeyed to and fro in the land, recalled biblical people and events associated with various sites, and left by way of Damascus. With an assurance born of Protestant iconoclasm, the authors erased or modified much of the contemporary reality of Ottoman Palestine and encouraged their charges to imagine a biblical landscape peopled with familiar figures drawn from the Bible text. Hurlbut and Kent regularly evoked epic events, intimate incidents, and a pastoral Jesus from relatively empty expanses of landscape, disheveled villages, and scruffy Bedouin. The result was, as Lester Vogel put it, an "inspirational diorama," scenes right out of the Bible enlivened by the memory of biblical narratives.[41]

They were enlivened as well by thrilling personal associations, one may add. Hurlbut recalled a moment from his own journey through Palestine when, saddle-weary from a day's ride in the rain, he and his travel companions were greeted with the "inspiring announcement" that they were to dine on "fish from the Sea of Galilee." Perhaps they tasted much the same as those the "fishing firm of Zebedee, Sons & Co. supplied to the high priest's palace!" he added, citing New Testament references.[42]

As Kent's *Biblical Geography and History* had earlier implied, this idyllic place of Bible-centered memory was the true Holy Land, a place sanctified by memories and the reputed simplicity of Christ's ministry. Surely it was not this land populated with Muslims, often viewed with paternalism if not disdain, or the hills and cities dotted with what many a Protestant believed to be misguided and gaudy shrines of indigenous Christians. Always urging respect for such heterodoxy, Hurlbut and Kent nevertheless agreed in substance with the well-known biblical scholar and devout Quaker George Barton. During his travels in 1902–1903, Barton wrote to members of his family that he much preferred reveries among the simple folk of rural Galilee to Jerusalem, which was "much overlaid with unreal traditions," Muslim "fanaticism," showy ritual, and jewel-bedecked clergy. "One could not but feel how different from the real, simple, holy life of the Man of Sorrows was all this gorgeous display," he reflected one Palm Sunday. Especially, Barton added, in view of the Turkish soldiers on guard "to keep these fanatical professed Christians from shedding one another's blood at the very tomb of Christ."[43]

Rather than pretentious ceremonies or shrines encumbered with elaborate legends of the pious, a much better memorial to Jesus would be quiet devotions in the actual places where he taught. Even Christmas carols sung in English and Arabic at a Protestant school in Jerusalem, as Hurlbut and Kent wrote, are more suitable than showy ritual.[44] Understandably off the emotional register of a tour so aflame with Protestant fervor was a more charitable sense of how those holy lands lived in the hearts of different faithful. Muslims were attached to Ishmaelite history and Mohammed's visit to Jerusalem. Jews imagined holy lands—and debated their political consequences—as a Jewish homeland or as a center of cultural and religious renewal for world-dispersed Jewry. In fact, the Holy Land was contested space, materially by Europeans bent on expanding economic and political influence, and mentally by the faithful in search of the primal spiritual wellspring.

Despite occasional acknowledgement that Jews, Muslims, and non-Protestant Christians enjoyed some legitimacy in Palestine, Hurlbut and Kent envisioned a land of strictly biblical, not contemporary, dimensions. And not simply because they wrote for Christians. The land, the real Holy Land, was a place of exclusively Christian revelation, its antecedents in prophecy, and its evangelistic imperatives. At the end of the journey, having roamed through nearly three hundred pages of commentary, Hurlbut and Kent recalled this landscape of Protestant piety one last time. As though thinking of Jesus' command to "make disciples of all the nations" (Matthew 28:19), they invoked St. Paul as paradigmatic hero and disciple-maker:

> Here, fellow pilgrims, we end our journey. . . . We have stood amid the hills of Judah, without the sepulchre of the patriarchs, and around the walls of Jerusalem. . . . We have stood under the trees in the garden where our Lord suffered, have looked up the mountain where he was transfigured, and on the green hill where he died. . . . And here at Damascus, where Paul began the work of converting the world, we end our pilgrimage.[45]

The pilgrimage and its travel spaces were not simply made of piety, biblical story, and encompassing Christian ideology. Hurlbut and Kent offered their reader-pilgrims a place on the team of explorers whose members combined scientific observation of the land with confidence in the historical and religious reliability of the Bible. This representation amounted to a political gesture of some importance. In opposition to strident voices being raised in the churches against scholars who looked to explain the historical origins of the Bible, the title page of *Palestine through the Stereoscope* prominently announced a happy

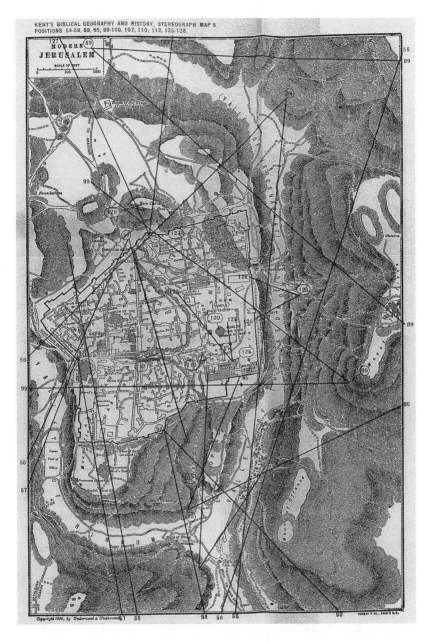

FIG. 28. Map of Jerusalem, from Kent, *Biblical Geography and History*.

concordat between traditionalism and modernism. Hurlbut, a Methodist clergyman, Bible believer, and trusted leader in Sunday school education (his links with the Sunday School Union and Chautauqua were acknowledged), had joined hands with Kent, a New England Congregationalist identified by his Yale professorship and books on biblical history and geography. The parlor tour presented itself as blessed by Bible-centered Protestant orthodoxy, church service, and academic science, precisely the blend of allegiances favored by many university-based biblical scholars at the time.

Moreover, pilgrim-viewers were repeatedly urged, like navigators, to plot their journeys on maps of Ottoman Palestine. Each stereoptic card was numbered and correlated with numbered dots on these maps, from which two bold lines extended outward in a V-shape, indicating a field of vision. This patented system, which had been used nearly fifteen years earlier in Kent's *Biblical Geography and History*, showed exactly how much of the land was recorded in each photo or "viewing position." A pilgrim thus entered an infinitely expanding ideational space that was accessible while standing at each location. Hurlbut and Kent's chatty commentary aided that process by moving pilgrim-viewers from where they stood, beyond foregrounded objects, encompassing more and more territory, until they arrived at a limitless realm of remembered biblical event.

On the maps these imaginative geographies were cumulatively represented by overlapping, superimposed lines, which triangulated, contained, and subdued sacred territory. As John Davis noted, the system subjected Palestine to "commanding perspectives much like an anatomical specimen X-rayed from several different angles."[46] Map, stereographic photos, and commentary thus effectively encoded a geography of devotion and fantasies of a Christianized and Bible-centered Holy Land. At the same time, such virtual journeys emulated the spirit of scientific exploration very much bidding to become a dominant feature of Europe and America at the time.

Hurlbut and Kent, however, saw the tour as a means of combating indifference to the Bible. In an elaborate discussion of pedagogy—to them the technology seemed much more than a mere visual aid to learning—they asserted that stereographs enabled intimate familiarity with places and times often felt to be far removed from modern experience. These tours, then, can make "the Bible *real* to us."

We are not to look on *small, flat* photographic prints, but *through* them, and our eyes are to roam over life-size representations of two

> hundred definite sections of Palestine. . . . We shall make a dead Past
> live again. . . . We must get out of the Present into the Past, and we
> must bring the Past into the living Present, if we are to obtain the
> largest reward for our journey in this land. (emphasis in the original)[47]

Such actualities readily experienced vicariously, yet in realistic fantasy,
bring one into the presence of God, or the Holy Land profoundly spir-
itualized.

> We first need to know intimately—to see, if possible—the very stone
> and earth of which those places [where God spoke through events] are
> composed. Such experiences help us as nothing else can; they are
> magical in their power to give us a vivid realization of actuality in the
> Bible narrative. . . . Now, if in connection with the specially devised
> maps in this book, we give ourselves up to the study of these parts of
> the land, through the stereoscope, then, in a true sense, we may have
> experiences of standing in the very presence of Palestine.[48]

Here is the ideological core of Hurlbut and Kent's visual mapping of
the Holy Land. Like the primal scriptural word, or the Word itself (God
in Christ), the Bible land itself offered a self-authenticating personal
experience of God, which since Martin Luther had justified the privileged authority Protestants gave to individual conscience in matters of
religion.

The parlor tour could evoke such powerful effects because, as so
many assumed at the time, Palestine had remained largely unchanged,
outside that upward march to Christian, Euro-American civilization.
Edward Said, above all, argued that the aura of settled objectivity given
to this idea of the East masked its historical origins in the political
practices and commercial interests of European colonialist nations.[49]
Change in Ottoman Palestine was obvious to Hurlbut and Kent, even
if its inconsistency with the idea of changelessness and their complicity
in the colonialist enterprise were not. There were ruins about, for one
thing, and for another, Hurlbut and Kent found certain aspects of
contemporary Palestine ill suited to their conjuration of a heroic biblical past. Perhaps to alleviate the dissonance, they often alluded to the
land's former prosperity, now dimly echoed in present degradation,
backwardness, or moral turpitude. The distant epoch when the fullness
of God was apparent was a time of economic prosperity, moral fortitude,
and receptivity to faith—all of which has been lost or is dimly reflected
in present circumstances. But Eden may be recovered. "Our constant
endeavor," Hurlbut and Kent told their pilgrim charges,

must be to go back in imagination from the ignoble present of this land into its mighty past; to associate with each place that we shall see its men and its events . . . [and thus] make the noble Past alive and real.[50]

Yet contemporary Palestine kept thrusting its resilient presence onto the focal plane of the camera and across the path of would-be pilgrims. Photographic image and commentary thus regularly framed problematic space between idealized biblical past and contemporary present. In filling this space, Hurlbut and Kent continually created and recreated holy lands while mitigating contradictory ideas and uncomfortable aspects of the place that might challenge the significance they gave to it. The authors took their pilgrim charges not just through a land of Christian recollection. They brought them Holy Lands constructed of romantic expectations, idealized projections, scientific rationality, and theology. And as we shall see, the real-imagined holy fields were seeded with cultural values and political gestures produced in Protestant America.

The True Woman of Amwas

Standing at any given location, Hurlbut and Kent typically pause to orient their pilgrims and indulge tourist ethnography by noting something about the local situation or "native" in view. They then quickly eclipse the contemporary with memories of biblical events. The authors repeatedly urge this double consciousness.

Viewing position 6, "Looking southeast from Mizpah to Jerusalem," is a rather straightforward example.[51] The camera takes a pilgrim-viewer's eye across a broad valley and upward toward distant Jerusalem. An Arab figure, replicating the tourist's gaze, looks into the same distant space from a position a little way down the foregrounded hillside. "Mizpah is fourteen miles from Beth-horon on the road to Jerusalem," Hurlbut and Kent write. The pilgrims are then directed to their maps. "Turn to Map 2 and find figure 6. The branching lines will indicate the range of our outlook from the top of Mizpah towards Jerusalem." Once oriented to the spot at which they stand, the pilgrim-viewers next orient themselves to the Bible, or rather, to the recollection of biblical events. The exact biblical reference appears in a footnote, lest memory stray too far from the authoritative biblical text. "We are standing upon the summit of Mizpah where Samuel judged, and Saul was made king,"

Hurlbut and Kent explain. Directing their charges into the foregrounded visual space, they continue, "Below us, on the slope of the hill, is a native of Palestine, clad in his *abba*, a heavy outer-garment, worn when the air is chilly." Immediately, they expand into that widening cone of sacrality. The hills, then Jerusalem, then historical events appear, like figures deftly brushed onto a landscape canvas:

> Look closely at the left and you can dimly perceive a tall tower. That stands on the Mount of Olives, beyond the city to the east. . . . Notice those roads that climb the mountains and lead to the city. What countless generations of people—the soldiers of Rameses, of Adoni-bezek the Amorite king, of David, of the Chaldeans, in Bible times, and of Arab conquerors in the middle ages, besides pilgrims of many lands in modern days, have walked up those hills toward the sacred city![52]

Evoking a heroic biblical past is more complicated at viewing position 5a, "The Village of Amwas (Emmaus)."[53] Three Arab women, posed rather ornamentally, suggest peaceful, almost leisurely work. Though facing the camera, they look somewhat toward the right, out of frame, as if hesitant to pass. Hardly noticeable in the indistinct background, lying low on the hillside but given prominence in the authors' caption, is the little village of Amwas.

Despite the label, the women in fact constitute the main visual subject. And they impede Hurlbut and Kent's desire to visualize biblical Emmaus amidst contemporary Palestine. To meet the challenge, the authors draw boundaries between themselves (and their pilgrim charges) and this silent image of non-biblical otherness. At the same time, they suggest that these women do not quite measure up to the ideals of true womanhood—motherly virtues of passivity, domesticity, piety, moral purity, cleanliness. Writers and artists widely propagated such ideas in post–Civil War America and often used them to distinguish middle-class Protestant "America" from crude, working-class, immigrant, even morally deficient "America."[54] The "native" women of Amwas are absorbed into Hurlbut and Kent's ambivalent compassion for their differences. In the end, remembered associations with Jesus sweep them away altogether.

The opening in the ground just to the right of the nearest woman, the authors write, is a spring "from which the village people get supplies for drinking, cooking, and such little cleaning as they are disposed to do." Viewer-pilgrims, Hurlbut and Kent imply, are to forgive the "unbearably dirty" village houses (hardly visible on the distant hillside) and pardon

FIG. 29. "The village of Amwas," from
Hurlbut and Kent, *Palestine through the Stereoscope.*
Courtesy of Pitts Theological Library, Emory University.

the inadequacy of the women (very visible in photograph and commentary) because it is such a "toilsome undertaking" to carry water into that distant village for "thorough-going housecleaning." Besides, they add, "fuel is pitifully scanty, and can ill be spared for heating water."[55]

Hurlbut and Kent instruct their pilgrims to notice how the women "carefully shield their faces from a stranger's gaze" and "how erect and graceful" is their poise "even though they belong to the poorer class." Perhaps surprised that such graces of true women could be associated with poor Arabs, the commentators explain that the "habit of carrying

FIG. 30. "Ancient Fountain of the Virgin, where Mary came for water," from
Hurlbut and Kent, *Palestine through the Stereoscope*.

such burdens on the head gives to the working women of oriental lands
a much finer figure and carriage than belong to the women of the
wealthy class." Do heavy work and graceful posture, after all, become
the female poor and expose the corpulent and ill-postured body language of idle wealth?

Or do Hurlbut and Kent admire the gracefully athletic strength of
these women? Viewing a similar scene of water bearers at the ancient
"Fountain of the Virgin," they first note the woman and child in the
foreground, recalling Mary and her son Jesus. Then they add,

How much do you suppose that jar of water will weigh? If one tries to lift a filled jar, as it stands on that corner of the well, he may find it more than he cares to lift. A woman of Nazareth smiles at the awkwardness, picks up the jar in an easy swing, lifts it on her shoulder, and walks away with it in apparent ease.[56]

Is the admiration without qualification? Cathy Gutierrez thinks not, and argues that in Hurlbut's eyes the athletic, even muscular, grace of the indigenous women of Palestine transgresses a Victorian standard and marks them as culturally inferior. These actual women turn True Woman into a strong, laboring "man" (is there a certain attractiveness about them, nevertheless?) and thus violate a gentleman's fantasy of delicate, chaste, and refined domesticity.[57]

A 1901 training manual perhaps put it best. While acknowledging the newly public successes of women, one "must not lose sight of her most divine and sublime mission in life—womanhood and motherhood." Look to Mary, "the perfect mother," the book exhorts. And to Penelope, "the model wife . . . [who exhibits] motherly influence, unswerving faith, ardent love, unchilled hopefulness, and untiring industry."[58] True woman, wife and mother, belongs in the home, protected from the indignities and temptations of worldly and common affairs. Coarse, unrefined women labor openly in Palestine's fields and presumably in America's factories.

The water carriers who emerge out of Hurlbut and Kent's commentary are complexly layered obstacles to realizing biblical fantasy. Economically, they belong to the lower classes, a marker of otherness for those Americans who could afford or at least aspire to travel abroad. Yet they are poised, perhaps ennobled by lower-class work, and evidently morally superior to the idle rich. However, they still fall short of the ideals of domesticity—delicate refinement, cleanliness, good carriage, motherliness, and orderly housekeeping—so cherished in Protestant America.

Eventually, Hurlbut and Kent avert their eyes from the water bearers at Amwas, who have become entangled in this orientalizing thicket of attitude, desire, assumption, and proffered expertise. Pilgrims should look away, too. "Do you know," Hurlbut and Kent write, "that this very path around the little hill, where those women are walking with their water jars freshly filled from the spring, may have been trodden by the torn feet of our Saviour, on that glorious day when He rose from the dead?" (Here the authors cite Luke 24:13–32.)

Thus diverted, pilgrim-viewers are encouraged to embrace familiar accounts of the risen Jesus' appearance on the road to Emmaus. Hurlbut and Kent paraphrase Luke's narrative, urging their charges to "sweep away from the landscape yonder the Amwas of today, with its squalid clay huts and its poverty-stricken inhabitants." Imagine a time of innocent receptivity to Christ, they suggest, plainly in contrast to the "squalid huts" and the "poverty-stricken" yet appealing women in the photograph. "Call up the Emmaus of twenty centuries ago, when these slopes were terraced with vineyards, when a contented, prosperous people were dwelling in stone houses, with domed roofs, when the white front of a synagogue was rising before us." Inside that Edenic garden, the authors imagine Jesus and two disciples breaking bread (are two of the photographed women now transformed, converted into followers of Jesus?).

> Light flashes upon their eyes! They see their Master for a moment, and a moment only, as He vanishes from their sight. That is the one event which gives to yonder village a thrilling universal interest—for it is typical of the deeper spiritual revelation which comes to every disciple who yearns to behold the face of his Master.

They had no need to add that the desolate and uninviting Ottoman landscape, the village of Amwas, evoked these deep passions of Christian devotion, surely not those water bearers.[59]

The Tired and the Wretched

In viewing Amwas, the main strategic problem was how to evoke biblical presence from a photograph that might pull a viewer in some contrary direction. When guiding their charges at viewing position 54, "Women grinding at the mill," Hurlbut and Kent imagine the Bible more directly, as a biblical land that had remained unchanged over the millennia.[60]

Two women pose before an entry door. They appear busy at a small grinding stone. One looks down (shyly avoiding the tourist?), perhaps waiting for the moment to add more grain to the stone; the other gazes away from her work, humorlessly catching the camera's eye. Both grasp the handle of the large grinding wheel. A young child stares intently from the doorstep behind. "How completely the life of to-day in these Oriental lands copies that of two thousand years ago!" Hurlbut and Kent exclaim. "Here in the court of a house are two women grinding at

FIG. 31. "Women grinding at the mill," from
Hurlbut and Kent, *Palestine through the Stereoscope.*
Courtesy of Pitts Theological Library, Emory University.

the mill." (The authors refer to Matthew 24:41.) As Hurlbut and Kent
describe the scene, they construct a holy land of value-laden conceptual
juxtapositions—prosperity, technology, and cultural superiority implicitly laid opposite the poverty, primitiveness, and inferiority that characterize the people caught in their tourist-pilgrim's gaze.

It is "women's work" glimpsed here, they write, a scene of natural,
approved-of domesticity. "One never sees a man turning a mill stone,"
they add. Yet the process is quaint, primitive, and emblematic of how far
technology and rising wealth have carried American society. "But what

a slow and laborious process of making flour!" Although almost every town has a grist mill turned by water power, they add, pilgrim-viewers are looking upon "poorer people [who] save expense by having their own little mills."

The scene is appealing, despite its evident backwardness. Perhaps the women are a little seductive in their unveiled immodesty, even as Hurlbut and Kent define them by laborious poverty and a desire to visualize the Bible directly. Notice the bracelets, they urge. The "bangles, like coins" are fastened around the child's forehead and the "veils left open more than is usual" when men, presumably the photographer and entourage, are near. The large hole for "an oriental key . . . always a clumsy affair" and the rough pavement make a "fair sample" of what must be endured in any town "advanced enough to have its streets paved at all." The women use a mat, not chairs. "How forlorn and hopeless they look!" Hurlbut and Kent declare with sympathy, perhaps dismay, and evident conflict.

Do the women not measure up to the authors' expectations of virtue and beauty even as their unchanged state represents the highly revered Bible? Perhaps their land is *not* the Bible land, which was, as Hurlbut and Kent repeatedly assert, formerly very prosperous. Perhaps their debasement confirms Hurlbut and Kent in their sense of superiority as members of a nation with a much higher regard for women, for "True Woman."

> The lot of woman in a land where almost every family is desperately poor, and where women are regarded as little better than beasts of burden, is such as to give to all women of the working class a tired, wretched, almost despairing look.

Hurlbut and Kent clearly cannot sweep the photographic contemporary entirely out of sight. Their orientalizing gaze imparts to the scene a desperate, unredeemed, "wretched and despairing" quality. What would one have imagined, if not abject pagan need, when the choice of Christianity was first offered? To men of evangelical convictions, the women may even suggest a needy Palestine where Muslim rule, widely regarded as hostile and fanatical, restrained Christian missionaries' works of redemption.

It may be, as Cathy Gutierrez suggests, that for most travelers to Ottoman Palestine indigenous women had their insufficient piety inscribed on their bodies in the language of wretched mendicancy and lack of beauty and modesty. Even Christian women of Palestine often fell shy of Western travelers' expectations. "We can all believe that the Virgin Mary was beautiful," Mark Twain had written of Christian women in Nazareth. "It is not natural to think otherwise; but does it follow that it is our duty to find beauty in these present women of Nazareth?"[61] How much less the non-Christian women of Palestine, writes Gutierrez, whose repugnant looks proclaimed the absence of true religion.[62] As for the women grinding their grain, their immodest parting of their veils was evidence enough for Hurlbut and Kent.

Hurlbut and Kent project this layered ambivalence toward beauty and wretchedness onto natural topography as well. At viewing position 33, "Bethany, where our Lord was anointed by Mary, south from the eastern slope of Olivet," they refer to a New Testament incident while overriding artistic conventions of landscape beauty.[63] The caption directs pilgrims to recall an incident in Jesus' ministry. However, the photograph evokes landscape, not history, as a vehicle of Divinity Sublime.[64] A bit of tree frames the scene and invites one's eye downslope past two Arab figures, then upward to a tiny village set on the first of several rounded hills that roll into the distant horizon. The result proclaims Palestine the picturesque, a dramatically captured but illusive landscape that whispers antiquity, grandeur, and God.

Late-nineteenth-century artists, following a romantic tradition of nature realism, favored this genre of representing Palestine. Dramatic light and shadow, turbulent skies and seas, mountains and valleys of monumental proportion, ruins evocative of antiquity were the main visual elements. Human beings appeared tiny and powerless, mere decorative markers on that natural canvas of the sacred. Where photographs, paintings, and engravings of Palestine might rely on this particular aesthetic, Hurlbut and Kent often comment on filth and disease, disagreeable religious practices, backwardness, poverty, and annoying "natives," all the more to confirm the beauty of biblical Palestine and the superiority of American (and Christian) civilization.

At the beginning of their tour, the authors note small and overcrowded houses. "We shall not find magnificent architecture . . . [or] natural scenery of great beauty and splendor" in the Holy Land, they aver. What is more, there is no "real port at Jaffa," and passengers must make their way ashore through a treacherous reef. What an "immense advantage to business interests" it would be if the situation were made more convenient for passengers and freight. Alas, "the idea does not appeal to the government."[65] At viewing position 2, Hurlbut and Kent are plainly annoyed with the local inhabitants, who obstruct views of

FIG. 32. "Bethany, where our Lord was anointed by Mary," from
Hurlbut and Kent, *Palestine through the Stereoscope.*
Courtesy of Pitts Theological Library, Emory University.

the real Holy Land. "If the few people in a semi-European dress—
combining Paris with Baghdad fashion—were out of the way, we could
easily imagine . . . a Joppa throng as the Apostle Peter saw it."[66] Lepers
outside Jerusalem are repulsive. "Can you endure to look at those
miserable people?" they ask. Yet misery can teach. "What a picture all
this is of that other, deeper, deadlier disease of sin . . . healed alone by the
transforming touch of the Son of God!"[67]

At viewing position 45, "The plain of the Jordan," two Arabs, robed
and armed, gaze out over a vast plain. Rifle-bearing desert roamers set

Fig. 33. "Jerusalem from Scopus," from Wilson, ed., *Picturesque Palestine*.

within an expansive landscape suggest romantic and exotic heroism. But Hurlbut and Kent see devastation, "a once fruitful plain of the Jordan with only stunted trees and bushes growing upon it." Passing through the distasteful, they recall magnificent Jericho, whose stones have "been so completely removed [for modern construction] that only traces of the foundations . . . can be found." And they dismiss the Arabs, wondering what trivia they can be discussing. "We may be sure it is not what we are recalling—the mighty scenes that were enacted on that broad terrace at the foot of the mountain."[68]

Given that Hurlbut and Kent repeatedly flee the contemporary for the biblical past, it is understandable that the photographic image of Bethany suggests degradation to them, not grandeur, despite its aesthetic style. "Few towns of Palestine today are more filthy and poverty-stricken," Hurlbut and Kent write, but in the days of Jesus, Bethany "was apparently a prosperous suburb of Jerusalem." Its present debasement just barely intimates some lost openness to God, or to Jesus' attunement to Nature Sublime. Or, as Kent wrote of the same view, "the quiet atmosphere and the noble vistas remain, and help explain what attracted the Master to this secluded village."[69]

FIG. 34. "The plain of the Jordan, southeast from the ruins of ancient Jericho," from Hurlbut and Kent, *Palestine through the Stereoscope*.

Are pilgrim-viewers supposed to see the wretched village barely visible in the photograph? Or are they to imagine themselves encountering God, like Jesus, in a space of unspoiled "noble vistas"? Or should they recall some inspiring biblical event? In any case, this desperate little village can hardly be home to such a "True Woman" as Martha, beloved disciple of Jesus and homemaker in Bethany (John 11:5).

> What a squalid, miserable place it is! Can you imagine Martha, that careful housekeeper, having her home in such a cluster of hovels? Most of the people living here today are wretchedly poor; that young

woman's string of silver coins glittering over her forehead represents the larger part of the savings of her family.[70]

What is one to do with such a bundle of conflicting requirements imposed on this image of Bethany? "We must sweep away the present," the tour guides advise,

> and build in our thoughts another Bethany on that hillside; for the Palestine of to-day is only a shadow and the ruin of the Palestine two thousand years ago.

Although no dwelling stands from Jesus' time, and "it would tax our credulity" to accept what local tour guides claim to be the ruins of Simon Peter's house or Lazarus's tomb, the earth itself is nonetheless a permanent and reliable witness to God's presence. Geoscripture, not Nature Sublime, is what Hurlbut and Kent read.

> We know that our Lord walked over these paths, and counted yonder village as one of his homes. . . . Try to call up that scene—the sorrowing sisters, the sympathizing friends, the sepulchre with stone before its door. . . . that most marvelous of miracles of Jesus [the raising of Lazarus].[71]

One wonders if the posed Arabs, ornaments of picturesque Palestine displaced by the geography of devotion, nevertheless resist the commentary that ignores them. In looking to the right, out of frame, do they counteract the pilgrims who see a landscape of Edenic Bethany? They look away from the village, as though refusing the palimpsest of biblical story that the tour guides decode. Or perhaps they glimpse something altogether different.

Christianity, the Truly Picturesque

Viewing position 11a depicts "Jerusalem, beautiful for situation, from the southeast, showing the Temple site."[72] Looking toward walled Jerusalem from a hillside to the southeast, one's eye travels downslope, across the Kidron Valley, and fixes on the city's most prominent landmark, the Dome of the Rock. A favorite vantage point for depicting Palestine, especially Jerusalem, as the object of Christian affection, the scene also foregrounds El Kuds, "the holy," one of the most prominent landmarks in Muslim configurations of the Holy Land.[73] Like many other Christians of the day, Hurlbut and Kent summon up specifically

Fig. 35. "Jerusalem, beautiful for situation," from
Hurlbut and Kent, *Palestine through the Stereoscope*.
Courtesy of Pitts Theological Library, Emory University.

Christian memories, while recognizing and quickly marginalizing contemporary Muslim presence in the photographic space.

"That open square . . . is the Haram-es-Sherif [*sic*], or 'Noble Sanctuary,'" Hurlbut and Kent inform their pilgrim-viewers. It covers "in part
the area occupied in ancient times by the Temple and its courts." It is
wrongly called the Mosque of Omar, since Caliph Omar did not build it.
Besides, they add, "strictly speaking, it is not a mosque." Nevertheless,
the building "is of surpassing interest, for directly under that dome is the
great slanting rock on which stood the altar in the Temple of old" (the

authors refer to 2 Chron. 3:1). In the manner of panoramic paintings and photographs, Hurlbut and Kent lead their pilgrims from point to point on that distant background hill, mentioning a few Muslim sites, but mostly creating a landscape of Christian piety, if not possession. The Turkish governor's castle stands on the site where Jesus was condemned to death, and where St. Paul was taken for refuge. The modern tower barely visible beyond a clump of trees marks the headquarters of crusaders organized to "defend the city from the Saracens." Nearby is the Church of the Holy Sepulchre, the site of Jesus' burial. Next to that is a hospice for "pilgrims of the Latin church."

Moving toward the foreground, Hurlbut and Kent focus attention on the walled-in road before which the viewer-pilgrims stand. It "would lead, if we could follow it, past the Garden of Gethsemane and then up the Mount of Olives." The Arab woman looking back at the camera is invisible, or at least bereft of comment, along that pathway of Christian topography.[74]

On closer inspection, that "Noble Sanctuary" at viewing position 19, "The Sacred Rock, where the Temple Altar stood, Mount Moriah," similarly effaces Muslim presence.[75] The enclosed rock "remains almost as it was when David stood upon it and Solomon knelt before his altar there." Hurlbut and Kent linger over architectural details of the richly decorated surrounding space and allude to a cave ("probably a cesspool") underneath the rock, whose "original purpose has been crowded out of thought by fantastic legends that Muslims have told about it." Hurlbut and Kent insist on facts, and they will have only Christianized space.

> We forego the fancies and recall facts enough to make this one of the most impressive places on the earth. On this very spot was David's altar . . . and here stood Solomon's altar. . . . Then for many years the sacrifices ceased, and the rock was heaped with ashes until the Jews built upon it a new altar for the second Temple. . . . Then, after centuries of struggle came the heroes of the New Testament, the Master and the twelve disciples, looking at the sacrifices on this rock and seeing in them new meanings.[76]

Jews hold a similarly ambiguous place in Hurlbut and Kent's configured spaces of the Holy Land. Gazing down on the tumbled ruins at "Traditional Capernaum, Christ's home by the Sea of Galilee" (viewing position 89),[77] the authors fold moral lesson and prophecy fulfilled into their frequently invoked myth of paradise lost. Palestine's former prosperity has become ruin and degradation, just as the prophets and, in the

Fig. 36. "The Sacred Rock, Mount Moriah," from
Hurlbut and Kent, *Palestine through the Stereoscope*.

case of Capernaum, Jesus had foretold. "Can this be Capernaum (biblical Chorazin), once exalted to heaven?" they ask, referring to Matthew
11:21–24, where Jesus prophesied that the unrepentant Jewish town
would be cast down into Hades. "How it has been brought down to the
depths! All that is left of it is a dozen or more miserable huts, outside the
range of our vision." Enumerating Capernaum's diminished grandeur,
however, leaves Hurlbut and Kent dissatisfied. At least the sea remains,
they add, offering a way that contemporary devastation can yet witness
to Jesus' presence. The sea looks "just as it looked of old, except that we
see it deserted, and he saw it alive with ships and fishermen."[78]

FIG. 37. "Shattered remnants of old Chorazin," from
Hurlbut and Kent, *Palestine through the Stereoscope.*
Courtesy of Pitts Theological Library, Emory University.

Moving closer to Capernaum, at viewing position 89a, "Shattered remnants of old Chorazin," the pilgrims view broken columns and building stones sprawled akimbo in tall grasses. An Arab youth—he seems a sculpted part of the pillar on which he sits—carries the viewer-pilgrim's eye through a gentle S-curve, traversing the ruins, moving through the distant valley pass, and then out of frame at the top left. There, Hurlbut and Kent instruct, "We catch a glimpse of the Sea of Galilee."[79]

Hurlbut and Kent convert ruins into an aesthetic object, shaping them into a metaphor of Christian supersession. The remnants of picturesque Jewishness require the Sea of Galilee and memories of Jesus for their fullest significance. "This mass of broken columns and ruined walls is all that remains of the once prosperous city of Chorazin," the tour guides observe, alluding again to the New Testament prophecy. Since the ruins belong to a synagogue, "they interest us deeply." Why? As a memorial to Jesus' activity, the debris of abandoned Judaism marks the spot where Jesus rebuked Chorazin and other cities "because they did not repent." It was a place "where mighty works were wrought."

Conforming to an established iconographic tradition in Christian art, this image of Jewish ruination evokes the supplanting symbols of Christian redemption. The authors are not entirely unsympathetic toward Jews. They are God's children, after all, and not counted among the idolaters of the world. And Hurlbut and Kent find the annual *Tishah B'av* lamentations for the destroyed temple deeply moving.[80] Yet slanderous folk wisdom about Jewish custom occasionally finds its way into their commentary. And they expect that the faith which changed the Apostle Peter "from a narrow Jew to a Christian statesman" will eventually convert Jews to Christianity.[81]

Given such missionary horizons, it is not surprising that the Sea of Galilee and recollections of Jesus' mighty works in the synagogue trump the foregrounded remnants of that mythic (Jewish) world before its fall into unredeemed, but redeemable, darkness. Even the artfully composed Arab—pure ornamentation here and in many other photographs—is anchored to this vanquishing ideology. "The native at the right," Hurlbut and Kent add, "is sitting upon the pedestal of a pillar which once stood before the synagogue."[82] Stripped of any Muslim, Jewish, or indigenous Christian significance, the youth's gaze encourages the eye to move through the scene and, with the help of the tour guides, to glimpse and recall the Sea of Galilee. Hurlbut and Kent urge their charges to hear, once again, the voice of God and the voice of Christian truth.

Holy Land, American Style

Viewing position 37 shows "A barley harvest near Bethlehem." "If we go there," Hurlbut and Kent tell their travelers, "we may look upon a scene which takes us back to the times of the Old Testament."[83] The camera eye gathers together ten figures, evidently Arab, pleasingly posed as

Fig. 38. "A barley harvest near Bethlehem," from
Hurlbut and Kent, *Palestine through the Stereoscope.*
Courtesy of Pitts Theological Library, Emory University.

though caught in a moment at harvest time. Some walk toward the
camera, carrying sheaves of grain. Others bend into the cutting work.
Two figures, apparently women at rest, pass a jug between them. Only a
bearded man, a distant figure, and a woman in the lower right foreground engage the pilgrims' gaze. The harvest scene directly illustrates
the Book of Ruth. Hurlbut and Kent also load the image with affir-
mations of values they evidently cherish: individualism, industry, piety,
frugality, and self-directed political independence.

The tour guides express suspicion, perhaps disdain, for the boss and his wealth. "That gray-bearded, turbaned farmer stands there at ease, while everybody else is hard at work!" they declare. They suppose him to be the "master of the reapers," or perhaps the "owner of the field." "His name might be Boaz, for aught we know" (here the authors refer to Ruth 2–4). Describing primitive harvesting methods, and noting a baby in the sheltered cradle ("perhaps the woman with an armful of sheaves is his mother"), Hurlbut and Kent presume a contemporary Palestine stratified between wealthy and poor, land owner and peasant. They also evaluate it as degraded and oppressed. It is not at all like the United States, where freedom has fashioned a nation that is a suitable heir to the Holy Land of Christian promise, they intimate.

Women and men work "from sunrise to sunset, for a few cents," and take little time for lunch right in the fields, presumably in contrast to the man standing at ease beside the harvest-laden donkey. "Ruth may have looked like one of these women," the authors aver, with her head wrapped in a "coarse veil" and dressed in "common" garments. Yet pilgrim-viewers are urged to imagine harvesters in the days of Ruth and Boaz as "somewhat less ragged and common." For these days in Palestine (understood to be under widely mistrusted and maligned Turkish rule) are "days . . . of oppression and robbery, when the poor are kept wretchedly poor." The times of Ruth and Boaz, by contrast, were "days of quiet, and in the main, of prosperity," not at all anarchic. Weaving a fantasy of pre-industrial, pre-state, agrarian self-sufficiency, presumably the paradise lost to Turkish rule, Hurlbut and Kent continue,

> Except at rare intervals of invasion and subjection the Israelites lived on their mountain summits in peace, tilling their fields, obtaining at home all the necessities of food and clothing, having absolutely no foreign relations, and with little use for a government. They were contented, frugal, and industrious; and when at times foreign foes held sway over them, there was always a Gideon or an Ehud, or an Othniel to appear as the champion of Israel and break the chain of oppression. The whole period of the Judges from Joshua to Samuel sweeps before us as we look upon this harvest field. . . . Each man did what was right in his own eyes, and, while there was a neglect of the rites and ceremonies of the law, there were, upon the whole, prosperity and progress.

The Holy Land evokes a biblical archetype of a political and economic Eden, a place and time of bustling "prosperity and progress" such as, the authors imply, may be found in America. Indeed, at viewing position 8, looking over modern Jerusalem's "wilderness of bulging roofs," Hurlbut and Kent exclaim, "Not much like our bustling American cities, with their tall buildings and wide streets, and varied architecture, is it?" They point out an "almost melancholy monotony in these little one-story and two-story houses, with their bulging domes," but find solace in their sense of cultural superiority and the idealized "city 'beautiful for situation'" where Jesus bore his cross "not far from where we are now standing." The Jerusalem a tourist pilgrim encounters is a "'lorn Syrian town,' but the Jerusalem seen by the inward eye is the Holy City, the center of the world's interest, an image of the heavenly city that hath foundations, whose builder and maker is God." Here the authors cite Hebrews 11:10.[84]

Tour Retrospective

This parlor tour of Palestine is a complexly layered rendering of holy lands. The authors construct Christian space and set its geographical coordinates with evangelical conviction and affirmation—against skeptics—of the Bible's historical trustworthiness. Like modern-day crusaders, Hurlbut and Kent try to subdue an unruly Ottoman Palestine, making its geography conform to images of biblical realities generated from a mix of textual recollections, theological interpretation, and values rooted in Protestant America. Palestine, and especially its women, are somewhat repugnant to them, but tolerable as evidence of biblical (Jesus') prophecy fulfilled and America's cultural superiority. The contemporary land is explainable within an etiological myth that plots an Edenic (and biblical) past ending in contemporary (Turkish-inspired) degradation. They eclipse Muslim and Jewish presence within supersessionist Christianity, which also involves assumptions of United States exceptionalism—notions of political independence, economic progressivism, agrarian virtues, cultural advancement, and economic prosperity. The holy lands Hurlbut and Kent construct through commentary reinforce presumed historical and cultural connections between a United States they know, or long for, and the biblical society they are still able to see, thanks to God's providential ways.

Positioned at the intersection of technical scholarship and popular culture, *Palestine through the Stereoscope* was a mix of nascent archaeology, ethnography, geography, cartography, and biblical literalism, all entangled in ideologically charged renderings of the Holy Land. Much the same amalgam lay at the heart of another Holy Land enterprise, an American research institute that served, more than parlor tours or Chautauqua programs, the technical needs of Bible scholars. However, neither the scholars nor the institute were any less invested in geopiety.

Founded in 1900, the American School of Oriental Research in Jerusalem rapidly became an important center for biblical study. In the decades after World War I, the school played a key role among other nationally based institutions in fostering international cooperation in increasingly specialized study of the Bible. Over the years hundreds of American scholars, graduate students, clergy, even casual travelers availed themselves of the school's hospitality and growing resources.[85]

In the lives of its many members and visitors, the American School surely promoted professional study of the Bible, especially in its ancient Near Eastern setting. But it also provided a unique network of people, activities, chartering documents, and publications which nurtured lively Holy Land consciousness in those who came through its doors. In the 1920s and 1930s, however, the United States experienced new forms of social unrest. Newly urgent political debates at home impinged on that faraway place of desire and fantasy that had become so well established in national life. What newly crafted geographies of the Holy Land would these Jerusalem scholars invent in such new circumstances?

Four

Landscapes of Democracy

The American School of Oriental Research in Jerusalem began modestly in 1900 with little financial backing. However, a dedicated few garnered much in the way of institutional goodwill, for they hoped that such a research venture would stir national pride, stimulate scholarly study, and strengthen religious faith. Some thought it might even compensate for the embarrassing failure in 1884 of a research organization modeled after the very successful, and British, Palestine Exploration Fund.[1]

For more than a half century, most scholars associated with the new initiative would follow the general approach to Holy Land exploration that Edward Robinson had established in the 1840s. They would help develop a community of seminary and university scholars who, deploying specific skills and theoretical perspectives, would define the "ancient Near East" as a new field of professional study.[2] Despite the increasing secularization of knowledge during these years, many would continue imagining Near Eastern Palestine as ancient, but vestigially present, biblical space, a mostly Christianized heritage awaiting reclamation.

However, the years spanning two world wars brought stressful changes to the United States—and newly intense configurations of Holy Land infatuations. Holy lands constructed of the familiar elements of geopiety would be encoded in scholarly activities, and now supported by increasingly technical bodies of knowledge and given voice in the strident political debates of the 1920s–40s.

One of the prime movers of the American School in Jerusalem was J. Henry Thayer, professor of the New Testament at Harvard University and president of the Society of Biblical Literature and Exegesis. In an 1895 meeting of the Society, Thayer put the case for American exploration of Palestine. Consider, he said, that the French had already started a school with its own scholarly journal, all to advance "Biblical learning and missionary work." Could the Americans do any less? Warming to his task, Thayer summoned up a genealogy of ancestral pioneers—rough-and-ready explorers, meticulous scientists, and soldiers of the faith—to arouse slumbering colleagues to their patriotic duty.

> Shall the countrymen of Robinson and Thomson, Lynch and Merrill, Eli Smith and Van Dyck, look on unconcerned? Shall a Society, organized for the express purpose of stimulating and diffusing a scholarly knowledge of the Sacred Word, remain seated with folded hands, taking no part or lot in the matter?[3]

Thayer's call to activism drew some of its political urgency from an explosive growth in Holy Land tourism, the public's infatuation with discovering holy lands that confirmed the Bible, and governments which, in growing nationalistic competition, saw strategic value in Holy Land exploration.[4] While perhaps implicitly acknowledging the power of these factors, Thayer chose his own heroes from a roster of popular Christian explorers who combined more or less technical learning with lives as churchmen and public intellectuals. Like Chautauqua's leaders and other promoters of surrogate study tours to the Holy Land, these pioneers accepted the Bible as inerrant Scripture, unfurled American flags in the Promised Land, and searched out geographical facts to defend biblical truth against its detractors.[5]

For many of Thayer's colleagues in 1895, the pedigree he cited was both cultural heritage and fresh memory. They had witnessed the founding of the American Palestine Exploration Society in 1870 and its early demise fourteen years later. Most had sanctioned its chartering documents, which encouraged on-the-ground research to illustrate the Bible and refute new literary and historical theories that challenged traditional notions of biblical authorship and divine inspiration. The Society's second president, Roswell D. Hitchcock, was friend, colleague, and biographer of the greatly revered Edward Robinson, the most gifted explorer-hero Thayer summoned up in his call to action.[6]

Robinson was well known to academics for his distinguished philological studies, but he achieved public stardom, nineteenth-century

FIG. 39. Edward Robinson.
Courtesy of Hamilton College, Clinton, New York.

style, with his accounts of travels to Syria and Palestine in 1838 and 1852.[7] Robinson produced the first truly rigorous study of Palestine's surface features for the English-speaking world. Notably, he evaluated modern Arabic place-names to establish linguistic and geographic connections with ancient biblical peoples. Joining this evidence with careful evaluations of other sources and fresh geographical observations, Robinson identified genuine, as opposed to legendary, biblical sites and strengthened belief in the Bible's historical reliability.[8] In the process, he advanced quasi-political claims to the land itself. Refined maps of biblical geography imposed emotional affinity, a sense of personal kinship to biblical presence, on what to many Americans were uninspiring provinces of the foreign Ottoman Empire.

Robinson's reports took form as a travel diary that, along with numerous excerpts published in newspapers and journals, achieved surprising popularity.[9] On the advice of friends, Robinson abandoned his original plan for a technical work and wrote more in the vernacular style of Holy Land discovery narratives filled with personal comments and religious devotion. He relieved long stretches of scientific tedium with vignettes of local people and customs, scriptural illustration, and digressions to recall narratives of Old and New Testament events.

Robinson was as dedicated to Christ as he was submissive to scientific method and Mistress Holy Land herself. The Holy Land, like science, demanded meticulous devotion, and she revealed herself to reverent seeker and scientist alike who, like the ancient Israelites, stood poised to know thoroughly what God had provided. Robinson interwove personal narrative with scientific research, he told his readers, so as to "exhibit the manner in which the Promised Land unfolded itself before our eyes, and the processes by which we were led to the conclusions and opinions advanced in this work."[10]

Moreover, particular aspects of American experience offered special access to Holy Land truth. From his earliest New England childhood, Robinson wrote, scenes from the Bible had made a deep impression on him. As an adult with sensibilities formed by uniquely American experience, his youthful impression became a strong desire to visit the places where formative events had occurred.

> Indeed in no country of the world, perhaps, is such a feeling more widely diffused than in New England; in no country are the Scriptures better known, or more highly prized. From his earliest years the child is there accustomed not only to read the Bible for himself; but he also reads or listens to it in the morning and evening devotions of the family, in the daily village-school, in the Sunday-school and Bible-class, and in the weekly ministrations of the sanctuary.[11]

Quickly setting an international standard for critical work in biblical geography, Robinson's harmonious blend of American exceptionalism, piety, and rigorous scholarship would characterize the short-lived American Palestine Exploration Society as well as much subsequent Holy Land research. He also began a process by which American politicians and diplomats would soon compete with their more experienced

European counterparts in sending scholarly explorers to lay claim to Ottoman Palestine in the name of science, fatherland, and the Bible.[12] A colleague's eulogy for Robinson eloquently caught that nationalist sentiment:

> Resolved, that his departure takes from our country the patriarch of sacred scholarship, an untiring student, a careful, learned and sagacious author whose works have enriched our own libraries, done honor to the American name abroad and written his own name with that of our Nation upon the land and language of the Bible.[13]

To claim the Holy Land for one's own nation—the naturalness of that colonialist metaphor reflected deep connections between nineteenth-century Protestant religion and the United States's emerging imperial policies.[14] It could easily have been applied to another of Thayer's explorer-heroes, William M. Thomson. A missionary in Palestine for more than forty years, Thomson had provided local assistance on Robinson's journey of 1852. Shortly thereafter, it will be recalled, he achieved unusual literary fame with the lavishly illustrated *The Land and the Book*, a report of his travels that popularized the notion that the Holy Land's physical characteristics spoke directly of Christ.[15]

For Thomson, Protestants held a particular right to this land, just as their version of Christianity, by divine promise, supplanted non-Christian religions. Because Abraham, traveler through Canaan, had been justified by his belief in God, so latter-day Christians, heirs to Abraham through faith, should explore the Promised Land unhindered, whether equipped with scholarly training, an adventurer's pious courage, or both, which was Robinson's mien. "To walk through the land is the exact purport of my visit," Thomson told his readers. "And I mean to make it mine from Dan to Beersheba before I leave it."[16]

Thomson's readers probably needed no convincing. Many likely felt dispossessed, given the widely accepted opinion that the medieval Crusaders' aim to restore the Holy Land to Christian influence was finally being realized in Anglo-European explorations and, after World War I, in political control by Great Britain.[17] Others undoubtedly had encountered reports of righteous invaders recapitulating the biblical conquest of Canaan with cameras, paint brushes, notebooks, sextants, and evangelical zeal. American travelers, like their counterparts from European nations, ardently displayed their national flag at sacred spots, over their tents, on their backs, or streaming from parasols; one diarist

FIG. 40. "Encampment on the River Belus,"
from Lynch, *Expedition to the River Jordan and the Dead Sea.*

complained huffily about a prim Victorian lady who took "possession of each place she passed thru."[18]

William Francis Lynch, included among Professor Thayer's heroic explorers, fit this mold of imperious crusade, if a little incongruously. Described as an "earnest Christian and lover of adventure,"[19] Lynch embodied the very ideas of science-authorized Christian piety and staking-a-claim adventures. In 1848, bearing the requisite permission from Turkish authorities, he led, in his words, "young, muscular, native born Americans of sober habits" on a somewhat preposterous flag-planting expedition down the Jordan River into the Dead Sea. Afterward, Lynch quickly popularized his exploits with a report illustrated with wood engravings claimed to be "true to nature" but drawn with conventional romantic drama.[20] His circumnavigation of the Dead Sea and geographical survey of the Jordan Rift were firsts among American explorers, and his brazen conquest in the name of science, the American Navy, and "native born" Americans earned him a place in the litany of Professor Thayer's heroes.

Another was Selah Merrill, Congregational clergyman, theological seminary professor, and American consul in Jerusalem during the years

1882–85, 1891–93, and 1898–1907. In 1875–77, he had been staff archaeologist, then leader, of a rather unsuccessful expedition east of the Jordan River on behalf of the short-lived American Palestine Exploration Society. The final reports were incomplete, but the under-trained Merrill trumpeted his work anyway in a highly romanticized account of his travels.[21]

Merrill avidly fed the public's appetite for pious heroics. Saying he had sought appointment as consul to enable him to explore the Holy Land, Merrill amassed a huge collection of antiquities and natural history specimens that eventually found its way to the Harvard Semitic Museum. He wrote discovery books on Jerusalem, a sentimental idyll on Jesus' Galilee, and numerous popular essays dealing with local curiosities and archaeological findings. He also promoted the Holy Land infatuations of others and collaborated in producing *Picturesque Palestine*, a consummate example of armchair journeys into the manufactured spaces of the Holy Land.[22]

Not one to discourage private enterprise either, Merrill once enthusiastically endorsed a scheme to boil, cool, and ship some thirty-four tons of purified Jordan River water to the United States. Merrill was considerably less generous toward Jews and the Protestant residents of the American Colony in Jerusalem, whom he publicly disparaged, even vilified.[23] As a highly visible government representative, Bible student, and Holy Land explorer, Selah Merrill embodied, perhaps more than any other American figure at the time, the entangled strains of adventure expeditions, *Realpolitik*, Christian triumphalism, and scholarly possession of a biblically signposted Holy Land. One alarmed critic, the consul general of Beirut, complained that Merrill "considered the whole of Palestine and its works to be his special bailiwick."[24]

J. Henry Thayer's rhetorical praise of famous men had quick effect. Within five years a formal proposal gained financial pledges from twenty institutions and thirteen individuals. With governing resolutions voted, the school's doors could open and American biblical scholars could set about (re)claiming the Holy Land for science, America, and God. As much as they could, that is, with limited funds and a rented room in the New Grand Hotel, just inside the walled city of Jerusalem. About a kilometer away were the American consulate and the good offices of Selah Merrill. The effort at concerted scholarly exploration looked something like an American protectorate. At the least, it had claims on official and personal assistance, which Merrill gladly supplied.[25]

AMERICAN CONSULATE AND TOWER OF DAVID, JERUSALEM.

FIG. 41. American consulate, from DeHass, *Buried Cities*.
Next door is the New Grand Hotel, where the American School
would be located in 1900. By that time the consulate had moved
to new quarters not far away, beyond the walls of the old city.

By this time, around 1900, Thayer's stirring address had been reduced to the necessary tedium of resolution and constitution that would
govern the school. Religiously non-sectarian and forward-looking in
admitting both men and women, the school's stated purpose was to
"enable properly qualified persons to prosecute Biblical, linguistic, archaeological, historical, and other kindred studies and researches under
more favorable conditions than can be secured at a distance from the
Holy Land."[26]

Invisible in this formulation of non-sectarian academic purpose,
however, were two important factors. First, study of the Bible and the
Holy Land as envisioned by the school's founders was largely a Protestant affair. It would be two to three decades before significant numbers
of Jewish and Roman Catholic scholars would participate.[27] Second,
the animating piety and spirit of Edward Robinson would in effect
define a culture of the "properly qualified" and their main activities at
the school. Indeed, from the beginning well into mid-century, Robinson's
harmonious blend of scientific rationalism, geopiety, patriotism, and
Protestant devotion to the Bible was strongly in evidence. George
Barton, for example, the distinguished Quaker scholar of Assyriology,

the Bible, and archaeology, and the school's third annual director, retraced some of Robinson's explorations and tried to pinpoint as-yet-unlocated biblical events. Barton's published account of those journeys conformed to the popular type: a scholar-pilgrim's diary of discovery in a Christianized Holy Land. Like Hurlbut and Kent in their parlor tours, Barton sought refuge in biblical memory, listening for "echoes of the footsteps of the religious heroes of both Testaments." Decrying modernization, he found unmediated encounters with biblical reality hard to come by, but no less desirable or attainable on that account. Muslim residents, whom he often dismissed as "fanatics," got in the way, as did those non-Quakerish "ecclesiastical trappings [that] would overlay so thoroughly the reality of the past as to rob it of all significance."[28]

William Foxwell Albright, the American School's director from 1920 to 1929 and the major influence on the school's development, was more circumspect, but no less at home in this Protestant ethos. Despite his success at encouraging scholarly cooperation across sectarian and national divisions, Albright's first field studies as well as typical programs for resident students and scholars followed Robinson's lead. Geography and archaeology went hand in hand to build confidence in the Bible and establish the background and precise locations of biblical events. Like Robinson, Albright fed the public's hunger for Bible-centered romance, partly because the school's financial solvency depended on it. "These unassuming mounds among the hills of Ephraim and Benjamin are of the greatest interest to us," Albright once wrote for readers of the school's non-technical *Bulletin;*

> They represent authentic monuments of the Israelite past. Every stone and potsherd they conceal is hallowed by us by association with the great names of the Bible. Who can think of the tells which mark ancient Mizpah and Gibeah without a thrill as memory calls up the shade of Samuel, and the heroic figure of Saul?[29]

James Montgomery, chair of the American School's executive committee and editor of the *Bulletin* for thirty years, drew on such sentiments more explicitly to help secure financial support of the fledgling school. "If America is to maintain an honorable place in the international plan for archaeological work in Palestine," he said after World War I, "increased income must be obtained at once . . . and all lovers of the Bible are earnestly urged to come to our aid."[30] It was, after all, a matter of civic honor and duty, especially for Americans, to respond to this new opportunity. The "preeminently Bible-studying land" (Montgomery echoed Robinson here) should play its part, "now that Palestine has fallen into Christian and civilized hands."[31]

Montgomery had some success and the Jerusalem school grew. But radical changes were in the air at home. Finding cultural benchmarks in classical antiquity, such as were embodied in the St. Louis World's Fair, was losing its popular appeal. At the same time, increasingly vigorous study of the ancient Near East was pushing the limits of antiquity far beyond Greece and Rome. Moreover, social turmoil was intensifying in the United States. Waves of European immigrants, socialist philosophies, excesses of capitalist enterprise, racial conflict, and two world wars—all posed challenges to the easy optimism of turn-of-the-century America and the unquestioned presumption that Protestant America was heir to the promises of the Holy Land.

These were also the years, it will be recalled, of inventive entrepreneurial responses to fever-pitch interest in the Holy Land. Models, World's Fair spectacles, exhibits of landscape paintings, photographs and postcards, diaries and travelogues, parlor music, cabinets of Bible-land artifacts—these were some of the items of Holy Land consciousness that were becoming mass-marketed commodities. Many were apt to show up in homes, churches, and local libraries, along with sensationalized reports of archaeological discoveries, Bible dictionaries, and atlases purposefully coordinated with the expanding curricula of the American Sunday school movement.

In the early days of the American School, William Foxwell Albright, Chester Charlton McCown, and Max Leopold Margolis developed their professional careers in relation to this flowing stream of cultural imagination. They also responded to changing political circumstances. Deeply committed to harmonized ideologies of science and Protestant Christianity, Albright and McCown imagined the Holy Land primarily as biblical space fraught with declarations of God's purposes and events to be recovered, revered, and relived in historical knowledge. Margolis, an ardent Zionist, joined the same canons of scientific and historical inquiry to a quite different ideational space, an ancient Holy Land of national independence reenacted as a cultural and religious renaissance for Jews and Judaism.

All three men deployed technical scholarship to imagine divinely sanctioned truths rooted in the Holy Land that helped them negotiate the political crosswinds blowing across the America of their day. While reinscribing many vernacular representations of the Holy Land onto the body of biblical scholarship, each invented a holy land nuanced for his own time. And all three men advanced programs at the American School of Oriental Research, that mighty propagator of scholarly knowledge and spaces of Holy Land consciousness.

Albright's Holy Land: A Fountainhead

Seeing himself as distinctly removed from those untrained adventurer-pilgrim travelers of an earlier century, Albright made his way through Egypt to British Mandate Palestine in December 1919.[32] He was twenty-eight years old and about to begin postgraduate research as the Thayer Fellow of the American School in Jerusalem. The following year he would begin his distinguished service as director of the School, a position he held from 1920 to 1929 and again from 1933 to 1936, while pursuing an extraordinarily productive career at Johns Hopkins University, 1929–58. Epitomizing what was then called "Oriental studies," Albright would preside over major efforts, especially by his many students, to deploy linguistic, archaeological, literary, and material studies to advance scientific knowledge of the Bible and promote a theological view of Western intellectual history.[33]

In mid-summer of 1921, flush with early successes, Albright told his mother about the pleasures of living and working in Jerusalem. "It is the first place I have yet been in," he wrote, "where I really wanted to stay. There is not a spot in the whole world which suits me like Jerusalem, not only for its associations, but also because of the opportunities for research at the fountain head, and because of the cultivated cosmopolitan atmosphere which I love." Carried along by this rush of feeling, Albright extolled the wondrous variety of people who made their way to Jerusalem. "It is all interesting," he said, his prose swelling with post-war optimism. Marching under the banner of "our beautiful international science," he added, "little bands of scholars in the various countries are again exchanging discoveries and methods, while our knowledge of the lands where human material and spiritual civilization originated increases by leaps and bounds."[34]

When he confessed such delight in Jerusalem, Albright was already preparing an essay that would evince similar enthusiasm for the ideologies of evolutionary advancement, lionized science, and privileged origins. He wanted to help his Christian readers realize that accelerating post-war archaeological research was uncovering "the mighty sweep and momentum of the spirit of progress in man, ever striving forward

Fig. 42. William Foxwell Albright, c. 1950.
Courtesy of the Ferdinand Hamburger, Jr. Archives,
Johns Hopkins University.

and upward" toward its culmination in Christian civilization. No one could detect divine providence in history so clearly as "the reverent archaeologist" whose one great aim was "to know the past as it really was, and to deduce the laws which govern the development of man toward that ultimate goal which the Creator has set for him."

In the service of such ambitions, Albright continued, archaeology in Palestine held a "peculiar interest that no other branch of the science has." Being carried on at the fountainhead, excavations could confirm and reinforce in Albright's reader and, just as importantly, in Albright himself deep emotional attachment to an idealized Holy Land. It was a land of religious imagination and historical facticity, a place of beginnings etched in desert tracings and sandstone ruins, yet pregnant with ultimate value and significance. In its most revered, almost sainted application, Albright suggested, archaeology laid bare the birthplace of the Bible, the

> land where the sacredest of human possessions came into being, and [where] hardly a mile of its surface is not hallowed by Biblical associations. In the illustration, elucidation, and, if need be, confirmation of this masterpiece of world literature archaeology justifies itself finely.[35]

The following year, Albright referred to the land exposed by archaeology and imagined by piety as the "cradle" of Christianity. Sure that the 1920s turmoil in Palestine meant "little in comparison to the eternal verities of religion," Albright made his own claim to ownership. He dismissed the current troubles as a "contest between Jew and Arab" for control of the Holy Land. It was the ancient, universally influential place, not the modern protectorate of the British Empire, that was to be recovered and revered. "To the Christian," Albright continued, recasting the fervor of his nineteenth-century predecessors, "Palestine has a personal attraction as the cradle of his faith and the enduring witness to the genuineness of the documents upon which that faith is primarily based." By using all available information to illuminate the Bible, every teacher and student would be able to see "revelation as a logical, consistent whole, and to combine his data into a solid foundation for confidence in the purposes of God and the destiny of man."[36]

About a decade later, Albright observed that the results of such grand endeavors made him and his readers "spectators at the unfolding of the greatest drama of history, the origin and early development of our own civilization and our own religion."[37] In 1940, Albright presented a compelling and comprehensive rendering of that drama by tracing, as he told the readers of *From the Stone Age to Christianity*, "our Christian civilization of the West to its earliest sources."[38] Two years later, he described his purpose in writing *Archaeology and the Religion of Israel* as "nothing less than the ultimate reconstruction, as far as possible, of the route, which our cultural ancestors traversed in order to reach Judeo-Christian heights of spiritual insight and ethical monotheism."[39]

Imagining the Holy Land in a narrative of evolutionary perfection did not simply appeal to Bible-centered sensibilities and traditional geopiety. It had a political bite as well. From this ancient "fountain-head" flowed democratic values and a social organization that Albright, without specifying matters too closely, accepted as consistent with American forms of Christianity and Judaism. Thanks to the results of increasingly scientific archaeology, Albright wrote in 1922, enlightened people could now see that these institutions, which had evolved over thousands of years, had "an inherent stability and a permanent value." Measured against such granite-hard and empirically tried foundations, "hasty generalizations of modern speculative sociology" (by which he apparently meant Marxist/Leninist philosophy) looked quite insubstantial. In a gesture of containment, Albright declared checkmate:

> Our radical Socialist friends would do well to immerse themselves in the study of archaeology before attempting to repeat an experiment which failed a thousand times before the abortive communism of Mazdak, so like that of Lenine [*sic*], fifteen centuries later.[40]

When Albright wrote these words, the United States was coming to terms with increased immigration from Eastern Europe. The Russian revolution of 1917 was a fresh memory and growing numbers of Socialists and Leninists clamored for a newly ordered society in Europe and North America. Turmoil swirled about big business, labor unions, and voting rights. A war had been fought and sloganeered to "save democracy." It was a time in the United States, as James Weinstein put it, in which "few active intellectuals avoided the challenge of socialism."[41] Journals of opinion and Christian theology were filled with debate about the virtues and vices of socialism, especially its Marxist forms.[42]

Evidently, Albright believed that Near Eastern and especially biblical antiquity spoke to the anxieties of 1920s America. For him, correctly recovered history explained and justified the superior value of non-socialist (presumably democratic) institutions that had survived the winnowing tests of evolution. By asserting continuities with a land and civilization rooted in the Bible's permanent values and, moreover, by presenting those connections as natural and unassailable, Albright tried to counter early-twentieth-century rumblings of revolutionary change. Palestine, the ancient biblical land constructed out of archaeology and religious memory, was the mythic place that nurtured his sense of identity as American, democrat, and Christian.

Nearly twenty years later, Albright would suggest that the waters streaming from the sacred land of the Bible had even nourished modern empirical rationalism, against which new totalitarian regimes were destined to fail. Since empirical reasoning, an evolutionary stage beyond pre-logical rationality, had developed out of the experience of biblical peoples, Albright declared, the "Judeo-Christian tradition," which embodied true religion and the seeds of clearheaded, empirical, and scientific rationality, offered the only defense against modern-day regression to raw primitivism. The political pressures of totalitarian empires, by whatever name, threatened to plunge the world into pre-logical, irrational chaos. Yet Judaism and Christianity, joined in evolutionary advance to the discovery of scientific rationality, offered a common resistance in a world under threat from totalitarian ambition.[43] Thus joined together in their development, scientists, Jews, and Christians should now unite in defending the Bible and opposing those forces of darkness.

> In these days when the tyranny of European dictators employs every means to eradicate Judaism and Christianity from their empires, it is incredibly [sic] folly to attack the Bible because it was written in a day when the sun was still believed to revolve around the earth. . . . The religious insights of the Bible remain unsurpassed and have sustained our western civilization for nearly two thousand years since the collapse of pagan culture.[44]

For all their sophisticated scholarly authority, Albright's declarations shared the tone and reductionism of wartime propaganda. Authors, artists, and government agencies routinely invoked heroic images of the cross, the Holy Land, or the "Judeo-Christian tradition" as self-evident surrogates for allied European and North American resistance to fascism and, later, communist Russia.[45]

Louis Finkelstein, chancellor of the Jewish Theological Seminary in New York, did his part as well. He organized a conference to "rally intellectual and spiritual forces" to meet the threat of totalitarianism and build "more secure foundations for democracy."[46] Each partici-pant, Albright among them, addressed the Nazi and Marxist threats by showing how the disciplines of science, philosophy, and religion were entirely supportive of democratic, not totalitarian, values.

It seems hardly accidental that *From the Stone Age to Christianity*, published at the beginning of World War II, concluded by offering a similarly urgent defense of a beleaguered West. "Yet today we see Occi-dental civilization tottering," Albright wrote, referring to a broad recru-descence of tendencies that were sending the world back to primitive states of disorder. "We see scientific methods and discoveries judged by Marxist and racist gauges instead of by independent scientific stan-dards." In such a world, Albright pleaded, we need a return to biblical faith.[47] And, one may add, a return to secure historical knowledge. On that bedrock, Albright believed, he could recover and enter the spaces of the "real" Holy Land, the salutary Holy Land, cradle of Judaism and Christianity, source of empirical rationalism and true religion, the foun-tainhead of waters most sweet.

McCown's Holy Land: A Democracy of God

Chester Charlton McCown never escaped the thrall of a Holy Land of Christian devotion, especially the Galilean countryside, which evoked appealing images of biblical peoples and an out-of-doors Jesus. Like Albright, he also imagined the Holy Land in the rhetoric of opposi-tional politics. Ancient Palestine gave birth to Jesus and, in resistance to tyrannical empires, to Jesus' ethic of egalitarian social justice. That, McCown felt, was a message still relevant to the United States as she faced urgent calls in the 1920s–50s for social change and reform.

A Methodist minister and professor of the New Testament at the Pacific School of Religion, McCown made his first trip to Palestine in the fall of 1920. Acting Director Albright welcomed the new Thayer Research Fellow. Always cautious, he was pleased to discover an unex-pected affinity with McCown, who was older and rather austere, yet deferential toward Albright's authority. "So far at least we have got on very well," Albright told his mother early that October.

> He is here to work and not to enjoy a vacation. He is a very good
> Greek scholar, trained in Germany, and tho about fifteen years older
> than I am is not disposed to resent our relative place on the faculty of
> the School. Dr. McCown and I, being both evangelicals, of Methodist

antecedents and liberal theology, seem, at least so far, to agree thruout in our religious and critical views.[48]

During that year, McCown followed his own research interests, but also took field trips with Albright to study geography and archaeology. With the director's encouragement and the help of a native speaker of Arabic, he also undertook systematic studies of local Arab Christian and Muslim religious practices.[49]

During Albright's absence in 1929–31, McCown returned to direct the American School, including its expedition to biblical Jerash jointly undertaken with Yale University. He was Annual Professor and acting director in 1935–36. As director of the Pacific School of Religion's Palestine Institute (1936–47), and though not a field archaeologist, McCown built a considerable reputation for expertise in biblical geography and archaeology as well as New Testament history and theology. He served the Pacific School of Religion as professor, and twice as dean.

On McCown's retirement in 1947, Albright celebrated their nearly three decades of association. Albright admired McCown's "nobility of character" and dutiful "capacity for painstaking labor and intelligent grasp of [academic research] problems . . . and his rare combination of talents for family life, personal relationships, professional life and scholarly activities."[50] The intellectual kinship that Albright had felt with McCown as a young man had remained strongly in evidence, too. Both men believed that under God's direction human beings were making moral and cultural progress. Both looked for a theological payoff from the broad range of ancient Near Eastern studies. And both shared a fearless penchant for ambitious narratives of intellectual history.[51]

In British Mandate Palestine, McCown was drawn to open spaces away from the clutter and shouts of urban life, and to the night, when the clear waters of poetry ran their strongest. Like George Adam Smith, whose lyrical Historical Geography of the Holy Land captivated the reading public through some twenty-five editions between 1894 and 1931,[52] McCown sought to sense the poetic "atmosphere of antiquity." And like Edward Robinson, he sifted pious legend, disappointing for the truly religious, from historical fact. From the gleanings, McCown described ancient Palestine of Jesus' day, the better to inform authentic Christian practice of his own day.

To understand the New Testament, McCown wrote in 1920, "one should spend the day under the bright sunlight examining the ancient ruins of a city, and then, as the sun sets, climb to some point of vantage and sit and think it all over."[53] McCown did just that, perhaps to help offset the privations he felt while living in Jerusalem, which was "very far from being in the van of civilization."[54] Like generations of pilgrims before him, McCown sought a glorious biblical city whose soul was at rest, beyond the daytime hubbub of grime and poverty. "Such a panorama of white buildings!" he wrote one evening after a walk about Jerusalem's medieval walls. "White tombstones dotting the hillsides, with occasional splotches of green trees and the long line of gray walls." The world seemed asleep, save for

> the ravens we disturbed as we went along the city walls and which flew out, dark silhouettes against the moonlit sky. Was it on such a night almost as bright as the day, but with a mocking ghostly uncertainty in its light, that Jesus and his disciples took their way across the brook Kidron to the Mount of Olives, where in the uncertain shadows the officers from the high priest sought him with torches and swords and staves?[55]

McCown traveled everywhere that first year with camera and tripod. He took hundreds of snapshots, carefully filed the negatives, and gathered selected prints for later use. Some found their way into popular lectures, seminary classes, and museum exhibits. McCown pasted others into souvenir-like albums. He affixed a few to the typed pages of an unfinished travel guide entitled "On Foot in the Mountains of Judea." Decrying modern conveniences and tours that encouraged superficial visits, McCown offered a "tramping trip" for intrepid travelers who refused too much comfort—a note, it will be recalled, that Charles Foster Kent had struck some years earlier. Like many of his fellow travelers to Palestine, McCown desired to recover the primitive originality of things biblical, and longed to quicken faith through fresh discovery, vivid descriptions of people, and recollections of biblical history.[56]

McCown disdained the cheap sentimentalism of many popular Bible guides. But he lived and photographed a version of them, too. His snapshots that are most suggestive of Christian pilgrimage, for example, recall stereographic tours, which encouraged a viewer to imagine the Holy Land as it really was, but which to us seem a fantasy enabled by the illusory realism of photographs. Other McCown photographs embody the idea of Palestine as the "fifth gospel," a place where even barren topography is fraught with testimony.[57]

Indigenous peoples of Palestine appear in this world of Christian witness, but as convention dictated, they mostly illustrate some feature

FIG. 43. Chester Charlton McCown dressed for explorations, c. 1920.
Courtesy of the Pacific School of Religion and
Badè Institute for Biblical Archaeology.

FIG. 44. Road to Bethany. Photo by C. C. McCown.
Courtesy of the Pacific School of Religion and
Badè Institute for Biblical Archaeology.

of the Bible. In McCown's "Tomb of Lazarus," they ornamentally frame a Christian subject. Another snapshot blends the ornamental with McCown's ethnographical interest—in this case, a scientist's look at rural Arab shrines. The result follows the familiar aesthetic of Palestine the picturesque.[58]

McCown adopted the social position and perspectival conventions common to most mass-produced Holy Land memorabilia of the time. His was the gaze of an outsider who reinforced an unequal social relationship between photographer and posed subject. Artists and McCown—as well as commentators on and viewers of photos—created an alterity of things familiar and foreign, revered and ignored. These were biblical people, yet they were valued mostly as ornamental frames for Christian dioramas. The land was forbidding, yet contemplating its appearance and constructing its geography opened transcendent universal realities of true religion.

In 1952, near the end of his life, McCown was preparing an essay that was to be his consummate portrait of early Christianity. He painted with an Orientalist's eye, a geographer's palette, and a theologian's passion. Picking up the metaphor that had become vernacular commonplace, McCown wrote that the Holy Land itself constituted a "fifth

FIG. 45. Tomb of Lazarus. Photo by C. C. McCown.
Courtesy of the Pacific School of Religion and
Badè Institute for Biblical Archaeology.

Fig. 46. Weli Ibrahim. Photo by C. C. McCown.
Courtesy of the Pacific School of Religion and
Badè Institute for Biblical Archaeology.

gospel." Sandstone ruins, the "changeless mountain, river and sea," the hills and lakes of Galilee all spoke of glorious events. Annually awakening flora recalled a rural teacher who responded to the land's "smiling invitation to the out-of-doors. There we can follow him," McCown wrote,

> the "Master of the rugged hills, the desert, and the storm swept sea," Master also of the open road, the flower-strewn plain, the sunny olive-clad valleys, and the shining blue lake.[59]

Henry van Dyke had made this out-of-doors Jesus famous in a series of popular magazine essays nearly fifty years earlier.[60] Then, a younger McCown was not entirely happy with its soft focus. In the year America's great depression began, McCown depicted Jesus as a fairly astringent successor to sharp-tongued biblical prophets. Impatient with governmental restraints and formed by a desert ethos of individualism, these prophets bitterly opposed organized "civilization," which brought "growth of luxury, extravagance, and social injustice." They followed a nomadic ethic, McCown wrote, and demanded "economic justice, economic democracy . . . in the distribution of the good things with which God has blessed the earth." They wanted to "make the most of life in industrious and independent simplicity."[61]

God-empowered Jesus opposed the social institutions of his age in the name of those same nomadic ideals, McCown wrote.

> The very geography of Palestine had providentially conspired to prevent the blood of the Hebrews from ever becoming completely poisoned by the virus of a greedy agricultural-commercial conception of life.... From the ancient nomadic ideal he [Jesus] inherited his hatred of wealth and luxury, his love for simplicity in living and for democratic brotherliness in economic and social relationships.[62]

A prophet in his own time, this child of the Holy Land's particular geography still offered to McCown a bracing political philosophy nearly two millennia later. In the aftermath of the First World War, when issues of Bolshevist revolution, democratic survival, and nationalist and internationalist politics were hotly debated in the United States, McCown reclaimed both Jesus and the Holy Land as participants in contemporary political debates.[63] Jesus was, McCown wrote in *The Genesis of the Social Gospel*, "neither communist, Bolshevist, nor socialist." He was instead a prophet of the heart.

Protestant ethicists and theologians had long emphasized that meaningful social change flows from an inward conversion of the will, not from imposed regulation and duty. For McCown, Jesus embodied that conviction, in effect imagined as the model for Protestant formulations of social ethics.

> The issues of life are out of the heart. Laws cannot affect the will, but only the outward conduct, and outward conduct is of importance only as expressing the will. Jesus had all the sympathy for the wrongs of the poor that any communist could ask. His purpose to do away with these wrongs was steadfast, but his method poles apart from those of the socialist, the communist, and the modern reformer-by-legislation.

In enunciating these principles, Jesus went "far beyond the best of his immediate predecessors" (by which McCown, like many a triumphalist Christian theologian, meant beyond the best that Judaism had to offer).

> Jesus demanded a peaceable and teachable temper, a modesty and kindliness that made aggression and injustice toward anyone impossible; he demanded also the willingness to suffer for righteousness' sake, the readiness to sacrifice all that was dearest in the interest of the kingdom.... Jesus insisted, not on passive endurance, but on sacrificial

activity for the sake of the kingdom. . . . If he was to save the world, he must include the oppressed poor in his salvation, and the social organization which was responsible for their oppression must be transformed.[64]

How to cure social ills, then? Jesus answered in a way that surmounted the temptations posed by both secular activism and spiritual quietism, wrote McCown. Jesus said "No!" to spiritually empty materialism (just feed the hungry); "No!" to nationalist revolutions (just transform the world through political revolution); and "No!" to religious apathy (just wait patiently for God to overcome the world's suffering). There was another way. Jesus lived and proclaimed an "oriental realism" which required acts of sacrifice in order that God's Kingdom, the "Democracy of God," might come on earth.[65]

The history that produced this Jesus was partly a function of geography, the lay of the land that, as McCown asserted, "had providentially conspired" to keep the nomadic ideal coursing through generations of Hebraic peoples. McCown construed Jesus' homeland as a biblical landscape—the only Holy Land that mattered to him—a place whose deserts favored the ways of austere individualism within communality, but not anarchy. Its hills had received nomadic peoples, cradled the biblical prophets, and nurtured the prophets' God-directed assaults on economic injustice. Finally, this Holy Land had given birth to Jesus, an incipient economic democrat who proclaimed a self-sacrificing ethic leading to a "Democracy of God." And this, for McCown, was a perduring antidote to the despairing politics of disengagement and the repressive activism of revolutionaries.[66]

One sunny Friday in mid-April 1949, Chester McCown brought something like this democratic Holy Land before an audience in Berkeley, California. Civic leaders had gathered at the Berkeley City Commons Club, about a block from the main campus of the university. The building's elegant stone-and-ironwork façade still bespeaks the comfortable demeanor of the urban elite who regularly met in those days to promote, as the club's *Bulletin* declared, "good fellowship and community solidarity, civic pride and intelligence, national and international understanding."[67]

A past president of the club, McCown brought a collection of photographs that day to illustrate a talk entitled "Arab Justice, a Spring-Time Parley." Taken during McCown's first year in Palestine, the photographs depicted a gathering of Bedouin elders who, in long night discussions over strong, sweet coffee and a feast of lamb, had settled communal obligations incurred by a private killing. The reporter for the *Bulletin* noted the "picturesque simplicity and good common sense of the Arab farmer in Palestine" whose social rituals repaired the torn fabric of wilderness society. "No policeman or other representative of government was present to supervise," he wrote, "and none would enforce the verdict. The settlement had been reached under public participation and no culprit dared defy unanimous public opinion."[68]

McCown had long been attracted to these nomadic folk. They suggested biblical types and universal aspects of religion. Perhaps the "springtime parley" that had captured McCown's imagination in 1920 offered something more. Did the Bedouin live that ancient nomadic ideal, however vestigially, which McCown would later claim to have driven the biblical prophets and Jesus? Did these people born of Holy Land space, like Jesus the social gospel prophet, remain relevant as contemporary political commentary?

The "nomadic ideal" that McCown (and many others) found so appealing has long since lost its prestige among biblical scholars. It was a powerful construct that associated the ancestral and prophetic literary traditions in the Bible with European romanticism and idealized reports of Arab life.[69] Yet for McCown, "nomadism" was a settled and uncomplicated fact of early Israel's emergence in Canaan. The "nomadic ideal" was an objective value trait of those immigrants from the desert who were ancestors to the prophets who preceded Jesus. For his Berkeley audience, McCown seems to have enlivened those dwellers on Palestine's steppes with similar romance. They were austere, independent people who were admirably suspicious of centralized governments, zealous for individual liberty, and careful to ensure community consensus. Their justice would require no policeman "to supervise [. . . or] enforce the verdict."

As McCown had written two decades earlier, the rugged mountains of ancient Judea "constantly invited the Bedouin from his still more barren desert" into a geographic zone of religious significance, where the "rough hills bred a hearty, prolific, and adventurous race, given to plain living and high thinking." These migrants might have been monetarily poor among the nations. But they "became the world's teachers in those matters in which their gifts and their austere mountain home had made them preeminent, morals and religion."[70] These morals and religion, I suggest, were born of a Holy Land configured for McCown in terms of Jesus and his particular vision of an inner-directed, socially powerful "Democracy of God."

FIG. 47. Max Leopold Margolis, c. 1920.
Courtesy of the Center for Judaic Studies,
Philadelphia, Pennsylvania.

Margolis: Holy Land Homeland

When Albright and McCown first went to Jerusalem, Max Leopold Margolis, at fifty-three, was already a highly respected scholar. Since 1908 he had been a professor of philology at Dropsie College in Philadelphia. He was editor of the *Journal of Biblical Literature*, a position he held from 1914 to 1922, and then of the *Journal of the American Oriental Society* (1922–32). Author of many learned works on the Bible and Rabbinics, Margolis was committed to historically oriented modes of inquiry, which were now increasingly linked to archaeological data.

Nonetheless, Margolis recognized that Christians dominated this scholarly approach to the Bible, and that they generally ascribed religious importance to the Hebrew Bible, or Old Testament, only insofar as the "old" witness to God's covenant had been perfected in the "new" covenant of Christ, or the New Testament. Sometimes this scholarship, particularly in nineteenth-century Germany, was downright hostile to Jews and Judaism.

Given this situation, Margolis urged in 1910 and again in 1915 that the people for whom the "language of Scriptures is in large measure a living tongue" must claim their rightful place among modern students of the Bible, many of whom were associated with the American School in Jerusalem. Resisting a theologically prescribed guild while speaking from its margins, Margolis urged Jewish scholars to defend the Hebrew Bible as fundamentally a Jewish book, even while accepting that it had been incorporated into the Christian Scriptures and read in ways that were often antithetical to Jewish understandings. Moreover, Jews must rescue the Bible from neglect by a community that, under the conditions of European and North American modernity, had largely abandoned its own Book. Jews must join the guild dominated by Christians and embrace the historical and philological training required to set forth the Bible's correct relevance for Jewish, rather than Christian, practice.[71]

When he wrote those words, Margolis had already shown what was possible by writing a scholarly commentary on the Book of Micah.[72] He also carried his message to wider audiences. Margolis lectured on the Bible at the Jewish Chautauqua Society (modeled on John Heyl Vincent's Chautauqua Institution) and frequently commented on Bible study and contemporary Jewish affairs in popular magazines.[73] It is not surprising that he embraced Zionism, too, for it similarly claimed space from the margins of a European world in which Jews were persecuted, or at the very least accorded little political and cultural relevance.

Following an ambivalent awakening in 1907, Margolis resigned from what was then a decidedly anti-Zionist faculty at the Hebrew Union College in Cincinnati and vigorously embraced the cause. Margolis recognized the socialist, secular, and colonizing aspects of the Zionist movement, but he believed even more fervently in its promise to revitalize Jewish culture and religion among Jews who might choose not to settle a new homeland. In this regard, Margolis imagined the Holy Land not so much as a place of biblical origin (as McCown and Albright did) but above all as a nationalistic destination. Writing in 1907, Margolis explained that physical return, repentance, and revitalized religious life came together in the Zionist cause.

> In going back (*teshuvah*) to Jewish life and Jewish ideals and Jewish hopes lies our salvation. Its work must necessarily consist, on the one hand, in strengthening the hands of those who volunteer to build up the waste places on the hills of Palestine and, on the other, in building up the Jewish consciousness in the Diaspora Jew.[74]

The Holy Land, then, was a physical and ideational space of reclaimed national and spiritual identity. Its "waste places" (note that the land is rhetorically emptied of its current residents) were to be populated in settlement and possessed in cultural renaissance. As Margolis would suggest after a year of travel and study in Palestine, the Holy Land could also become a place of proud, but not prideful, Jewish independence exercised through American-style democratic sensibilities.

Margolis first traveled to British Mandate Palestine in 1924. It was an anxious and heady time for Americans at home. Post–World War I prosperity was under way for some, but for the poor, threatening Klansmen roamed country roads and city streets. Fears of Bolshevist revolution and labor strife—the same fears that brought forth Albright's and McCown's defenses of democracy—fed the demons of isolationism, anti-Semitism, and xenophobia. Recalling his month-long journey to Palestine, Margolis reflected on the conditions of shipboard confinement that temporarily kept these troubles at bay. Thrown together, "traveling humanity seeks and finds its own level," he wrote. Few travelers of "Nordic prejudice" espouse "the doctrine that America is for Americans and Christians only," and even "caste distinctions are for the moment discarded."[75]

Margolis accepted an appointment as Annual Professor at the American School in Jerusalem. Albright, then in his fifth year as director, noted for readers of the school's *Bulletin* that Margolis's training and research fit his own topographical studies of the ancient biblical land-scape "extraordinarily well."[76] The gesture of welcoming inclusion, for all its truth and goodwill, sidestepped political fault lines. In those days, Albright was less friendly to the Zionist cause than he would later become. And Margolis deeply believed in the Zionist dream. One out-come was that they harnessed their scholarship to different construc-tions of holy land.

Margolis's affection for Palestine was stirred less in retrospect, by evoking biblical associations, than in prospect, by witnessing and cel-ebrating, as he wrote, the "dawn of the national resurrection."[77] Of course, he trekked through a reassembled landscape of biblical desire—such walks were, after all, a dominant feature of the American School's activities at the time. Margolis reported on land traversed, places ob-served and named, hills dug into and identified as this or that biblical location. He paid homage to Albright, Edward Robinson, and a host of earlier scholar-pilgrim travelers by imposing an affective geography of biblical events on the hills of Palestine, always alive with biblical mem-ory. "We passed through Kesla, the biblical Chesalon," he wrote for readers back home,

> and in getting to it the hoofs of our horses must have trodden the mountain which in the book of Joshua is called Seir. . . . Gradually we descended, on towards the Low Lands, crossing and recrossing the scenes of mighty battles between the Israelites and the Philistines, the ground where Samson performed his feats before he was robbed of his strength by the treacherous Delilah.[78]

A Holy Land reconstituted in biblical memory and sought after by count-less earlier pilgrims now lay open to scientific conquest and religious awakening.

> We are after the pulsating life that ceased to be, but once was there; the spirit with which in bygone days it was animate; the workings of the divine breath in men and movements long past. Exploration of sites and excavations must needs be carried on upon the very spot, though the explorers and excavators come from afar.[79]

Despite occasional flights of such romantic fancy, Margolis gave surprisingly little attention to biblical sites in his reports. He was far more stirred by contemporary conditions in Palestine and their power to inspire a Jewish future. In contrast to Albright, who prioritized archaeo-logical work that probed biblical origins, Margolis looked for inspiration in the Jewishness of life in Tel Aviv, and in the excavation of places that could evoke an idealized memory of Jewish nationhood in Greco-Roman times. The Holy Land was not just biblical land, not the cradle of Western civilization, not the lightening sky of democracy's dawning. The Holy Land was an ancient homeland, and now, under the watchful gaze of British authorities, it might even be a homeland regained, its settlers inspired by ancient images of heroic aspirations toward national independence.

Ancient sites of home rule called for excavation, too. In addressing students at the Jewish Institute of Religion in 1925, Margolis pleaded for archaeological explorations at Beth-ther, the second-century site of Jewish nationalist Bar Cochba's fortifications. Then, turning to Stephen Wise, an ardent Zionist and president of the school, he urged fundraising for such excavations: "I put it up to him as a sacred duty, in the name of historical science of antiquity and by all that stirs Jewish sentiment for a most glorious period in Jewish history."[80]

Margolis believed that a Holy Land uncovered and known would inspire a much broader cultural and religious revival.

> We Zionists clamor for the one land where the Jews may constitute the majority and where alone a full national Jewish life becomes possible. Palestine is just now within the grasp of the Jewish people. For any Jew to obstruct the path to the land of the fathers is treason, treason to the cause of the Jewish people, treason to the cause of Judaism.[81]

On the matter of actual political sovereignty for a Jewish state, however, Margolis was circumspect, at least in his publications. The question drew to itself an unstable mix of issues and dilemmas that still, even today, inflame Zionist politics in America. What of the rights of non-Jews who had lived for generations in the region then called British Mandate Palestine? How could one counter charges of divided national allegiance leveled at Jews who supported Zionism while remaining citizens and residents of the United States? And what of the personal discomfort felt by Jews who chose to live in the United States while others built up a Jewish homeland elsewhere? As for life in America, how could support for Zionism be disentangled from "Nordic prejudice," the host of exclusions that contributed to the conflicting demands of assimilation, ethnic identification, and the desire to create a safe haven for Jews?[82]

Margolis and other cultural Zionists (Mordecai Kaplan, Judah Magnes, Israel Friedlander, and Louis Finkelstein, for example) believed that a properly executed revival of Jewry in Palestine would counteract such deleterious political pressures. The solution was thought to be apolitical. "Education, rather than politics, was the decisive Zionist act."[83] One heart, beating in the breast of an ardent Zionist and loyal American, could safely support cultural renaissance for all Jews and argue the necessity of a politically sanctioned safe haven for the persecuted. The new Zion should be created, Margolis wrote in 1917,

> not only for the oppressed Jewish people, but in particular for the suppressed Jewish soul, to the end that, released from her prison, she may, like the dove sent out by Noah, find a rest for the sole of her foot.[84]

As early as 1907, Margolis wrote an essay that brought the weight of his authority and technical scholarship to bear on this particular conception of the Zionist imperative. The patriarch Joseph, he claimed, was both a historical figure and a timeless exemplar of something repeatedly experienced in Jewish history. Joseph was an admired Egyptian Jew of "dual allegiance" (Margolis's phrase ennobled a demeaning accusation frequently leveled at Jews). He was also a "type of the Diaspora Jew who, through rigid discipline and self-control, rises to the position of a court-favorite." Other Jews, other "types," lived in ancient Palestine, fully at home and devoted to "the God of promises, not yet the God of fulfillment; the God of a nation in the making, not yet the God of a nation consummated."

Moses, the great teacher and giver of Torah, is a timeless exhortation to all the Josephs who continue to live outside of the Promised Land. On the one hand, Moses was of the Diaspora, and knew that for "Israel to realize itself to the full of its capacity, it must have a soil under its feet, a home wherein it may dwell securely, free to develop its powers." On the other hand, Moses looked to "a home for the suppressed Jewish soul."[85]

Both Moses and Joseph, Margolis implied, are instructive for American Jews. Like Joseph, Jews could be successful (and loyal) in any Diaspora homeland. And like Moses, they could look to what the "God of promises" demands—attention to spiritual vitality and settlement of a land where Israel, the people of God, might freely develop to its fullest capacity. With safe haven in Jewish Palestine, the Zionist movement could be fully sacralized, overcoming the limits of its secular origins. With the Holy Land fully materialized, Zion could become more than a centuries-old pious hope. Cultural, spiritual, and secular energies could be concentrated in a renewed world center, that ultimate point of sacredness from which human beings derive their highest moral and religious principles.

This Holy Land of Jewish renewal would not rise up, alive, merely in mental constructs of biblical origins. It would be both spirit and material, a vital contemporary reality and dawning future rooted in ethnicity and soil, but without compromising the demands of fatherland patriotism. "From redeemed Zion," Margolis wrote in 1918,

> there will be shed luster upon scattered Jewry, who in their various abodes will continue loyal citizens, and while loving their many fatherlands will cherish the mother country, the seat of Jewish culture in the land of the fathers.[86]

After his year in Jerusalem, Margolis linked the newly founded Hebrew University to this vision of material, cultural, and spiritual revitalization. "In the dawn of national resurrection," he wrote, the truths of Judaism would be distilled in the "laboratories and institutes on Mount Scopus, the place from which in ancient days men could see the Temple." The university would serve as a "lesser Sanctuary, that out of Zion once more may go forth the Torah, and the word of the Lord from Jerusalem."[87]

With similar enthusiasm, Margolis noted reassuring scenes of revitalized Jewish life as he traveled through Palestine. He marveled at economic miracles and vernacular Hebrew; the normalcy of self-determined Jewish life; the shuttered public face of Shabbat in "wholly Jewish" Tel Aviv.[88] He was greatly moved in observing *Tisha B'av*, where

> not an eye remains dry. It is gripping, overwhelming. It is an event hallowed by centuries, from the time when Roman soldiers guarded the approaches and the Jews had to buy the privilege of weeping for the departed glories. Today a Jewish policeman keeps order.[89]

The note of pride in that reversal of governance (even while recognizing the fact of British rule) suggests the delicate positioning of a desired Jewish majority in this Holy Land of Zion. The Palestinian Jew is "free politically," Margolis wrote, suggesting an Americanized vision of Zionist social order. "Free to speak his own language, free to bring up his children in Jewish schools," and moreover, free "to walk with head erect," Margolis wrote. Yet a Jew in Palestine "need not become provocative" and the rights of others could be guarded. Therein lay political wisdom and future well-being.[90] And, one might add, the installation of values prized in America, now imagined as a better rule for the hearts of settlers creating a Holy Land of Zionist imagination.

Retrospective

In looking forward to a Holy Land of Jewish renewal, Max Margolis was no less scholarly and no less romantic than Albright and McCown. Albright imagined Bible times and the "cradle" of Western civilization as scholarly defense of democracy under threat. In similar circumstances, McCown constructed a place whose uniqueness nurtured Jesus' enduring hope for the "Democracy of God." Margolis negotiated the perils of minority politics at home by plotting an affective geography of a Jewish homeland shaped by American ideals of democratic rights.

Three American scholars, three "holy lands." Images of the Holy Land were entangled with shared ideologies of scientific discovery and privileged American values, and embedded in the exegesis of text and artifact. Each man gave voice to learned discourse about the Holy Land and constructed spaces of moral and political imperative. Each lived his own version of a Holy Land myth, American style, inspired in part by the American School in Jerusalem, the great nurturer of Holy Land travels and enabler of fantasy realism.

Travelers required real maps, however, something more than those metaphorical charts of romanticized Holy Land prose and scholarly discourse. Even surrogate travelers, whether joining parlor tours or wandering through Chautauqua's Palestine, demanded the assurance of cartography that their holy lands were anchored in real territory, on the ground, so to speak. Yet what if Holy Land maps were special cases of conjuration, too? In a basic Euclidean sense, of course, maps could be true or false. But suppose that even the most scientifically and historically accurate maps of the Holy Land were themselves vehicles of Holy Land myth and articulators of holy lands at home?

Five

Mapmakers and Their Holy Lands

Jack Nowse had been traveling for a few weeks in British Mandate Palestine. It was 1936. Mounting tensions were erupting into what one historian would later call "the great Palestine revolt" as tectonic forces of European colonialist encroachment, Zionism, and emergent Arab nationalism collided.[1] The *New York Times* regularly reported on the troubles. "Nazareth Police Stoned, Strike throughout the Nation," proclaimed one headline in late April. "Two Arabs Killed, Fifteen Wounded," reported another, referring to anti-British demonstrations in Haifa, Acre, Nablus, and Jaffa. Other reports spoke of terrorist attacks and boycotts—Jew against Arab, Arab against Jew.[2]

About May 5th of that year, Jack Nowse visited "Jacob's Well," an ancient site of pilgrimage about thirty miles north of Jerusalem. A postcard he purchased and sent to a friend at the *National Petroleum News* pictured, not the famous well, but its custodian, a Greek Orthodox convent planted inside a walled garden of slender Mediterranean cedars. One of the buildings wore a deeply sculpted cross on its façade, as though it were offering benediction to the surrounding fields. It was an image of tranquility, a throwback to less troubled times, or perhaps a suggestion of the old conviction that spiritual renewal takes root in cloistered retreat.

Jack Nowse would have none of that. He was a sampler of things, a man keenly aware of surface, depths, and aquifers. He was prospecting the layered deposits of biblical memory, and he all but ignored the

FIG. 48. "Convent of Jacob's Well and Mt. Gerizim." Postcard, c. 1935.

photographed memento that he had used to record the effort. "Jacob's Well is within this building," he wrote.

> Still actively in use, 175 ft. deep thru solid limestone rock. We drew water from it and drank it. We are going pretty slowly now account of the Riots everywhere. It is wonderful to relive the old Bible scenes.[3]

Jack Nowse needed no cartographer. His scrawled words were themselves a map, drawn with the codes of geological description (the well and its water), news journalism (the riots everywhere), and the rhetoric of biblical reenactment. Had Nowse drawn a map of the site, it might have had something in common with Jack Finegan's projection of "Jacob's Well and Environs" more than thirty years later. Finegan included his map in Holy Land mementos of a different sort, a compendium of scholarly reports on "things which can be found, chiefly in Palestine, which are connected with or cast light upon the life of Jesus and the existence of the early Church."[4]

Although a sketch, Finegan's map seems similar in purpose to modern road maps, which in recent memory were mostly published and distributed by major oil companies. Typically, one would find minimal indication of topography and maximal information for travelers. Roads, towns, and villages—how to get somewhere and what to see of interest

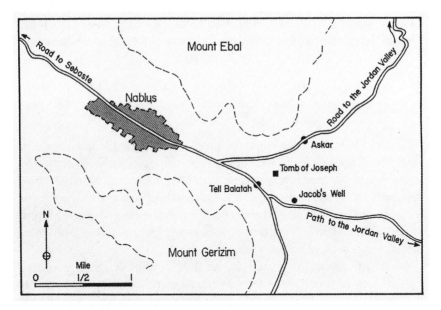

FIG. 49. "Jacob's Well and Environs," from Finegan, *Archeology of the New Testament*. Used by permission of the estate of Jack Finegan.

along the way—these are the main points. Masked by the self-presentation of factuality and utilitarian space are numerous contingent, historical scenarios. For example, what issues came into play in selecting what was to be shown or not shown on the map? How were decisions made and on what basis? How were the production, sale, and use of road maps in America related to the history of Automobile Triumphant, whose life story encodes values, folk mythology, longings, obsessions, government highway programs, and the destruction of city centers?

The map of "Jacob's Well and Environs" invites similar interrogation. It indicates directionality of travel: for example, toward Sebaste in the northwest, and the Jordan Valley in the east. But why is the road that turns to the south unmarked? Why would no one need, or want, to know what lies beyond the map's frame in that direction? And why is the scope of "environs" limited to plotting two named mountains, the village of Askar, the town of Nablus, a place of ancient ruins (Tell Balatah, but ambiguously marked, as if the road goes through it), and a couple of tourist attractions?

The answers lie partly in uncertainties of place and partly in a suppressed narrative of Jesus' travel from the Jordan Valley westward to

Galilee, passing through Samaria, as recorded in the Gospel of John. "Immediately prior to his journey from Judea to Galilee through Samaria," Finegan writes,

> Jesus had been engaged in baptizing (Jn 4:1) and had had certain relationships with John the Baptist (Jn 3:25f), therefore it is probable that he came up at this time from the Jordan valley.

The map, then, locates a biblical narrative in geographically represented space. As sketch artist and cartographer, Finegan gathered up a series of historical witnesses and plausible suppositions to illustrate something far more stable, the point, he wrote, "where these routes converge in the vicinity of Jacob's Well and proceed through the pass between Mounts Gerizim and Ebal."[5] It is the point of convergence where Jesus-story, Jesus-event, took place.

Yet this patina of objectivity masks the map's character as controlled fiction. It purports to represent the world—in this case, ancient Palestine—as it really was at a certain time, but without disclosing the value-laden choices by which that world came to be and the particular interests it served, both in production and reception. "Maps are never value-free images," J. B. Harley has written, and "except in the narrowest Euclidean sense they are not in themselves true or false." Whether obviously propagandistic, such as a map of "Greater Syria" that ignores modern Israel, or "disinterested" and scientific, such as the nineteenth-century survey of Palestine by the Palestine Exploration Fund, maps are purposeful articulations of reality. Each is a way of "structuring the human world which is biased toward, promoted by, and exerts influence upon particular sets of social relations."[6]

In Finegan's map of Jacob's Well, cartographic convention and the presumption of disinterested mapmaking proclaim none of this. The map speaks of the factuality of plotted locations, while Finegan's commentary discloses ambiguity and uncertainty, but always tends to reinforce confidence that New Testament accounts of Jesus' life are trustworthy and capable of illustration on the ground.[7]

For example, archaeologist G. Ernest Wright identified ancient Shechem with ruins located at Tell Balatah. On the one hand, the Hebrew *shechem* might be preserved, though corrupted, in the "Sychar" of the Jesus narrative (some ancient Greek manuscripts read "Suchem"), or perhaps in the name of the modern village of Askar, located more than half a mile from ancient Shechem. On the other hand, if New Testament Sychar is modern Askar, its location seems implausibly far away for what the Jesus story suggested was a villager's routine trek out for water. Besides, Askar has its own well. So where was it that Jesus met a Samaritan woman beside a well, at Shechem (= Sychar = Tell Balatah) or Askar? Moreover, ancient Shechem ceased to exist about a century before Jesus' day.[8] So could the woman who met Jesus have been a Samaritan resident of ancient Shechem (= Sychar), as the New Testament reports? Perhaps a village (modern Balatah) survived the larger town's destruction, as suggested by Wright, and so could have been home to the woman who came out to meet Jesus.

Finegan approved of that idea without dismissing all the difficulties. Thus his commentary preserved the integrity of the New Testament account while justifying an odd feature of his sketch map. A road bisects Tell Balatah, just as it does modern Askar and Nablus, as though the ancient ruins were still an inhabited village, presumably modern Balatah. Thus the supposed descendent of ancient Shechem is an unnamed absence, or rather is present only in cartographic symbol, as an unmarked village bisected by a roadway. In effect, Finegan's map represented disambiguated territory and New Testament narrative: the Samaritan woman came out to Jesus from ancient Shechem (corrupted into "Sychar" but labeled Tell Balatah), where the road runs through.

Then there is "Jacob's Well," which Jewish, Christian, and Muslim traditions have long identified with a specific water source in the area. Yet, outside the New Testament, the Bible does not mention it, although Jacob is said to have dwelt in the vicinity of Shechem and to have given his son Joseph a field there (hence the traditional location of Joseph's tomb). Nonetheless, André Parrot, one of many in a line of distinguished scholars and Holy Land travelers, declared that no holy place in Palestine "had more reason to be considered authentic than Jacob's Well."[9] Joining that company, Finegan showcased the Medeba map, a mosaic installation in the floor of a Byzantine church. As part of his rendering of the Holy Land as a pilgrimage destination and a Christian story of salvation, the sixth-century artisan captioned a red-roofed chapel with the words "Here [is] the Well of Jacob." The ancient reference, perhaps the sheer vividness of its antiquity, moved Finegan to speak with untroubled finality, as though scribbling a postcard witness: "This corresponds with the deep well that is still today on the southeastern outskirts of the village of Balatah."

However, no references to Jacob's Well are older than the fourth century. They occur in an account of Christian pilgrimage and in Eusebius's *Onamasticon*, a work that undertook to fix the location of all biblical sites.[10] Moreover, the artisans of the Medeba map probably used Eusebius's work as one of their sources.[11] Although the map depicted contemporary places, such as churches, and offers valuable historical information for that reason, it also channeled into decorative map-making the impulses that drove early Christian pilgrims to illustrate the topography and toponymy of their faith.

Clearly, Finegan's sketch map converted much indeterminacy into a particular, seemingly unambiguous place. But "Jacob's Well and Environs" was not simply inert space "out there" with the ontological status of a river or hillside. The map represented the journey space of a New Testament narrative realized in cartography. It projected constructed space onto a disambiguated two-dimensional plane, space that had been imagined and animated in relation to the values and interests of the mapmaker and commentator.

Moreover, Finegan's map of Jacob's Well is part of a cumulative history of such constructions. That is, Finegan belonged to historically contingent social space. He participated in those networks of Christians, traditions, and religious practices that had over time assured the continuing vitality of Jacob's Well as a real-imagined place of great religious significance. Over some sixteen centuries of making pilgrimages, reciting legends, studying the Bible, writing theological treatises and popular travelogues, depicting geography and mapping holy territory, Christians had constructed cultural affinity with one another and a resonant place called Jacob's Well. They assigned empowering privilege to the social realities of that physical-ideational place and repeatedly rendered this common heritage into maps and geographical commentary.

In the early nineteenth century, for example, Edward Robinson finely calibrated Jacob's Well for an Anglo-European culture awakening to the power of scientific rationalism and its challenges to traditional doctrinal use of the Bible. His general approach to biblical geography was so persuasive that it quickly became paradigmatic for subsequent travelers and scholars.

First, Jacob's Well had to be located definitively by deploying rigorous historical investigation. Reports of pilgrims, local legend, and centuries-old shrines were not sufficient. Pious tradition required independent corroboration. If the location were precisely identified, then the associated Jesus narrative could be accepted more confidently as historically reliable and, in a shift of logical ground, religiously trustworthy as well. Traveling to the reputed location, Robinson carefully considered local topography, ancient sources, and biblical text. Offering a mix of deduction and supposition, he assured himself that the traditional site of Jacob's Well, though unattested before the fourth century, was "actually the spot where our Lord held his conversation with the Samaritan woman" some three hundred years earlier. That condition satisfied, Robinson immediately configured the physical place as devotional space, as a spot of earth (the "real" place) that could satisfy the desire to encounter Jesus and encourage the reaffirmation of certain Christian beliefs.

> Here the Saviour, wearied with his journey, sat upon the well, and taught the poor Samaritan woman those great truths which have broken down the separating wall between Jews and Gentiles: "God is a spirit; and they that worship him, must worship him in spirit and truth." (John 4:24)

Later, Robinson returned to his tent and, though fatigued, remarked that he was "refreshed in spirit as we read anew, and in the midst of the very scenes, the account of our Saviour's visit and sublime teaching."[12]

Following a similar procedure for hundreds of other sites, Robinson summoned the authority of scientific analysis to survey the land and defend Bible-centered Christianity. He laid the foundation for a newly modern but emotionally charged geography of biblical Palestine. Detailed maps drawn by Heinrich Kiepert, chiefly based on Robinson's maps and published to accompany Robinson and Smith's *Biblical Researches in Palestine and Adjacent Regions*, imposed this newly animated social space on what was to most Anglo-Europeans an uninteresting part of the Ottoman Empire.[13] In Robinson and Kiepert, canons of modern cartography joined with apologetics to strengthen an ancient, mostly Christian practice of locating the places where biblical events occurred. Or, better, Robinson and Kiepert encoded socially constructed spaces of Christianity and Christian geopiety in the language of cartography. Part of their success was likely due to the growing authority accorded to scientific rationalism at the time.

Frederick Bliss, an American archaeologist in the employ of the British, put the matter more succinctly some years later. Bliss imagined the earthen surface, not the church built upon it, as holy, as a catalyst of biblical memory and devotion. Jacob's Well is "one of the most interesting places in Palestine," he wrote in 1894. Why? Because it is among the least disputed as to location, and moreover because it is "a link between the histories of the Old and New Testaments." Thus the ancient

Christian belief that human history had moved from an old to a new dispensation found a confirming corollary in the indisputability of physical place. Moreover, the defining essence of Christianity, presumably its triumphal separation from its tribal origins in Judaism, was tied to this same place. "It is a spot where the universality of the Christian religion was proclaimed in definite terms." Such a location merits respect and custodial care, Bliss added. "The site has been greatly neglected, and I am glad to announce . . . that at last proper care is being taken of the place."[14]

Reflecting a commonly held antipathy toward non-Protestant Christianity, Harry Emerson Fosdick, a famous preacher and author of many studies of the Bible, had harsher words for those custodians of Jacob's Well. However, he was no less enthusiastic than Bliss about definitively locating the sites of biblical events. Nor did he doubt the power of place to yield authentic, timeless Christian experience, even if nowadays his vision of Christianity seems tied to the nostalgic longings of an increasingly urbanized 1920s–30s America. In Palestine, "only the out-of-doors matters very much," Fosdick told his readers, since "almost everything that men have put under a roof they have spoiled for the intelligent visitor." Alas, even Jacob's Well, "one of the most arresting sites in Palestine," has not escaped this plague of Catholic devotion.

> That deeply impressive spot, one of the most certain identifications of site in Palestine . . . is enclosed in an ugly half-finished church . . . a painful example of ecclesiastical maltreatment of a sacred place; but even so, one may sit in the open air outside the church and make the events of John's vivid chapter seem visually real.[15]

If Fosdick configured and fantasized Jacob's Well as arresting "out-of-doors" space, most other travelers of the time did so as well. George Adam Smith, the great biblical scholar, geographer, and lyricist of Holy Land travels, took his readers to the summit of Mount Ebal and figuratively surveyed the entire land. He felt its geographic smallness and marveled that such a tiny land could have so influenced "the history of the whole world." The explanation, however, was nearby.

> Down below us, at the mouth of the glen, lies a little heap of brown stones. The road comes up to it by which the patriarchs first entered the land, and the shadow of a telegraph pole falls upon it. It is Jacob's Well.

"Neither in this mountain nor in Jerusalem shall ye worship the Father; but the time cometh and now is, when true worshippers shall worship the Father in spirit and truth."[16]

Hurlbut and Kent led their pilgrim-viewers to Jacob's Well, too. With stereographic photographs and elaborate commentary they created a visual counterpart to that biblical and Christian space that Smith and Fosdick had so lyrically imagined.

> How wonderfully real that meeting between Christ and the Samaritan woman becomes as we stand here by the very same well, with the very same Mount Gerizim, the seat of the Samaritan worship, before us.

Recall that meeting, Hurlbut and Kent urged their reader-viewer pilgrims. "Read once more the entire conversation held on this very spot, and see if it was not one of the most wonderful revelations ever given to a soul."

And look, the tour guides added, pointing to another scene. "Here is a woman of Samaria, just drawing water." She is allowed a role in this imaginative Christian drama, but as a contemporary non-Christian in the conjured space, she is an outsider, too. So Hurlbut and Kent diminish her presence, in effect reinforcing their own construction of a Christianized Jacob's well.

> Indeed she is a real Samaritan woman, who has come from the very village of Iskar (Sychar of the Bible), that the woman came from whom Christ met. . . . We wonder whether the woman who came from Sychar to this well eighteen hundred years ago was dressed in a striped gown, and wore earrings and beads. Certainly those women did not find this copper bucket at hand for drawing water.

Even the contemporary well cannot measure up to what Christian space demands, the abundant and eternally flowing waters of Jesus.

> Every traveler now receives a cup of water from the depths of the patriarch's well, but whoever drinks it runs much risk, for its cleanliness is open to serious question. . . . if it were fully cleared out it would undoubtedly be a perennial spring.[17]

I have cited these typical examples to suggest that despite reflecting vastly more rigorous training and sophisticated scholarship, Jack Finegan's sketch map of Jacob's Well belongs in the history of socially constructed and inhabited spaces of Christian geopiety. Moreover, Finegan evoked

FIG. 50. "A Samaritan woman at Jacob's well,"
from Hurlbut and Kent, *Palestine through the Stereoscope*.

that history not just with commentary and map, but also with one of its
favored icons, a Samaritan woman drawing water at Jacob's Well. Similar to the photograph used by Hurlbut and Kent, the image required
and received no comment, because its importance was culturally self-
evident. A triumphant gesture, it determined what was indeterminate
and compressed Jesus' valorized journey into a single image. It invited
contemplation of what Christians have made of that narrative, that
place, that Jesus, over the centuries.[18]

In this regard, photograph and map perform similar ideological
work. As Denis Wood put the matter, maps "make present—they repre-

sent—the accumulated thought and labor of the past." They bespeak "the milieu we simultaneously live in and collaborate on bringing into being." Maps have only one fundamental use, the

> connecting up what-we-have-done (money we have exchanged, sur-
> veys we have carried out, walks we have taken) *through the map*—
> property or mental, thematic, or general reference—with what we
> want to do or have to do, with what we find pressing. But if only one
> use . . . *many livings*.[19]

From this perspective, Finegan's sketch map of Jacob's Well connected past and present, understood socially and spatially as involving networks of people and ideas inhabiting a social and historical continuum of many generations. His drawing encoded many lives lived—religious commitments made, paganism vanquished, trips taken, unscientific piety made rational, Scripture defended against skeptics. And lives to be lived? They were embedded as well: acting on renewed confidence in the Bible's reliability and strengthened religious faith; reaching for a Holy Land desired, claimed, and celebrated in ideational travel; modeling archaeology as a privileged pathway to definitive historical truth.

Save perhaps that Finegan's technical biblical scholarship drew so deeply on the vernacular vocabulary of Holy Land geopiety, not much here is very surprising, least of all to Jack Finegan. He was aware, at the least, of his investment in theological work, in articulating and supporting religious faith. "Archeology must be as rigorously scientific as possible," he told his readers. But admittedly, his archaeological compendium was a pilgrimage of sorts, too. For, without any sense of incongruity, he said that his book might have been dedicated "to the remembrance of Melito of Sardis," a Christian bishop in Asia Minor who in the mid-second century "went to the East and came to the place where these things were preached and done."[20]

The point is that, as geographer and cartographer, Finegan assembled facts into a constructed space that embodied social and cultural dynamics, the numerous ambiguities of narrative and place, complex expectations, and particular histories of attachment to a real-imagined Holy Land. His map gathered these past livings and connected them to future livings, the many purposes and receptions the map would find.

The map was ostensibly utilitarian, intended to show Jacob's Well and its environs. The names of places and routes; the map's title; the relative sizes of type; the use of boldface characters, solid lines, and

hatched lines; the interplay of blank and filled spaces—all these cartographic conventions seemed straightforward, their conveyance of meaning self-evident. Yet these conventions involved the less evident, what
Harley called subliminal geometry and representational hierarchies.

Finegan (and any other mapmaker, according to Harley) would
assemble information and designate places relative to some particular
interest (e.g., population, climate, administrative borders, or relevance
to archaeology and Christian theology). Representations of geographical reality, e.g., roads, towns, and historic sites, might reflect other kinds
of social power or stratification which a mapmaker brings to the territory (e.g., a bibliocentric Protestant religious community, or Finegan's
purposeful Christianizing gaze that relegates non-Christian interests to
blank spaces or invisibility).[21] In short, maps embody specific purposes
and choices, as well as the "prejudices, biases, and partialities (not to
mention the less frequently observed art, curiosity, elegance, focus, care,
imagination, attention, intelligence and scholarship) their makers bring
to their labors."[22] Yet maps are not simply individually authored cre-
ations. They also inscribe social realities and social formations, the network of people, communities, and nations that have vivified and will
continue to animate cartographic space with specific cultural interests,
traditions, values, and ideological commitments.

Moreover, for a variety of complex reasons map users seem prone to
accept maps as simple statements of factuality. Maps "appear to represent facts pertaining to mother earth herself," S. W. Boggs wrote. "Ve-
racity and authority are often attributed to them far beyond their just
desserts." They are ubiquitous in modern life, and even when not obviously propagandistic, they speak with the voices of careful draftsman-
ship and scientific surveys. Users, being highly suggestible, take maps as
neutral, truthful, unbiased, and complete. A map's layout, its conventional symbols and codes of meaning, its explanatory "keys"—the rules
or rhetoric of presentation—keep invisible the necessarily selective
processes of production, hide ambiguity, and efface vested interests.
Such "cartohypnosis" masks constructed spatial relationships, scenarios
of history, and lines of social, political, and economic power that a map
may authorize or promote as natural.[23]

Given these considerations, Finegan's map of Jacob's Well and its
environs, indeed any map, is a very complicated thing. Its authority and
power of persuasion depend partly on unexamined attitudes toward
modern maps, but also on participating in the very history and condition, the social reality, that the map helps construct. By enabling fantasy

travel to a specifically imagined biblical and Christian Holy Land, Finegan's map maintains a set of social formations—for example, a church community, a group of scholars within an academic discipline, a culturally specific sense of attachment to place. These constitute the various livings, the histories and social realities that convert protean geospace into specific place, a territory of particular, often suppressed, interests. In a word, a Holy Land at home in Finegan's America.

Two influential Bible atlases may serve to make such gently postmodern perspectives more concrete. One, published by cleric and educator Lyman Coleman, appeared just before the Civil War. Ernest Wright and Floyd Filson, an archaeologist and a theologian, offered theirs as World War II came to an end. The works reflected, of course, vastly different social worlds and academic concerns, and each could be understood within several historical trajectories. For my purposes, it is most important to investigate something of the social space, the many livings, that these maps imply, and to reimagine the holy lands, each specific to its ideologically charged social and historical contexts, that these maps embody.

Geo(carto)graphy for the Winning of Souls

Lyman Coleman was an intense man, as flinty and resolute as the granite hills of Hampshire County, Massachusetts, where he was born in 1796. Wanting to become a teacher and clergyman, Coleman put himself through Yale College without the blessing of his father. William Coleman was so aggrieved by his son's refusal to take up medicine—the profession of both father and grandfather—that he offered no financial assistance whatsoever. As Lyman later recalled, his father never once inquired as to his academic progress.

Lyman Coleman would not be deterred, however. He taught a little and borrowed from friends, and finally graduated from Yale in 1817. He studied theology during the years 1820–24 and then served a Congregational parish, his only one, from 1825 to 1832. Like most American clergymen-scholars at the time, he also studied in Germany, and like many he visited Palestine and Egypt, making his last visit in 1856. From early middle age, Coleman seemed to have set his course, sailing through some fifty years as school administrator and teacher of classics and German in various private schools and colleges in the eastern United States. From 1861 until his death in 1882, he was a professor of Greek and Latin at Lafayette College in Easton, Pennsylvania.[24]

After a second trip to Palestine to study and contemplate, as he later wrote, the hills and winding shores of Galilee, whose "varied beauties . . . held and charmed the eye of Jesus of Nazareth," Coleman fixed his passion for the winning of souls ever more intently on promoting the study of the geography of Palestine. He wanted to bring to all institutions of learning the natural landscapes and human habitations that sheltered and made possible the events of revelation. Only so, he said in the preface to his *Historical Textbook and Atlas of Biblical Geography*, could students be carried back "to live in the bygone days of history, and to become living actors in its stirring scenes," and acquire the "knowledge which it is most important for them to know—the knowledge that may make them wise unto eternal life." Only so could educators "allure the young and assist them in an interested and intelligent perusal of the Book of God," and overcome the "profound ignorance" of the cities and towns of Scripture, indeed ignorance of Scripture itself, among members of the general public. "Sacred History and Geography," Coleman opined with regret, "has no place in our public systems of education."

> What school or academy, even when proposing a course of study peculiarly select and religious—what system of Public Education—what College or Theological Seminary even, includes in its plan of study the Geography and History of the Bible?

His humble and laborious efforts, Coleman concluded, at least had religious neutrality as their special claim to public favor. His textbook offered "to our Institutions of Learning of whatever grade or name, an opportunity for introducing the study of the Bible into their course of education, without disturbing the denominational or sectarian prejudice of any religious creed." He meant, of course, sectarianism among the Christian churches. Coleman hoped that, in the end, such careful study of geography, including plotting of journeys and events on finely engraved maps, would be an effective tool of Christian evangelism. Coleman wrote that the study of biblical geography would win the young to a "more interested and profitable perusal of the word of God." Expressing an idea that Chautauqua's John Heyl Vincent would later transform into a mighty enterprise, Coleman added that such study of the Bible would teach students

> what power divine it has to enrich the mind, refine the taste, to rejoice the heart, and to convert the soul.[25]

Coleman's *Atlas* became something of an enduring classic in mid- and late-nineteenth-century America. First published in 1854 and revised in 1859, it was reprinted virtually every year until 1899. An accompanying *Wall Map of Palestine*, published in the late 1850s, was a standard pedagogical tool for many years. New maps and George Adam Smith's more lyrical, yet scholarly, treatment of Holy Land geography swept Coleman's *Atlas* aside toward the end of the century.[26]

Coleman spoke to readers largely untroubled by the skeptical literary and historical studies that would emerge later to challenge traditional understandings of the Bible. Moses authored the first five books—a point presumed and not discussed. The Bible is literally true as written. The chronology of world history is to follow the Bible's reckoning and narrative structures (the chronology of Jesus' ministry was even calculated to the exact day). Coleman resolved inconsistencies, whether arising within the Bible or posed by extra-biblical considerations, by settling on what was most in agreement with the "sacred narrative" itself.

The *Atlas* stood in the company of countless Holy Land travel diaries, including those whose accounts had by the mid-nineteenth century taken up residence in the vernacular discourse of Holy Land consciousness. Coleman summarized biblical accounts (his retelling of history), noted geographical features (his own and others' field observations), and drew copious quotations from fellow Christian travelers. He presented, at each spot visited, "the most reliable conclusions of modern research." With landscape charted additionally in sentimental prose, Coleman reaffirmed that the Bible was a trustworthy guide to the very spots where revelation had occurred. "In following the footsteps of Jesus from Bethany," he wrote in an entirely typical passage,

> in following in his triumphant entry into Jerusalem, as we turn the summit of the southeastern declivity of this part of the Mount of Olives, we observe distinct traces of a village over against us. . . . The road to Bethpage turns boldly off to the left, and at the entrance into the village meets that which leads from it to Jerusalem. Just here the disciples "found the colt tied by the door without" in the place where these two ways meet. (Mark xi.4)[27]

Like the Byzantine Medeba map and later travel accounts, Coleman's *Atlas* and geographical commentary amounted to an updated retelling of the Christian story of salvation in its geographical aspect and an enforced Christianization of the Holy Land. After the invention of photography, it was but a short step to lavishly illustrated travelogues and stereographic parlor tours.

Cartography carried a full share of this burden. Modeling his atlas on Edward Robinson's maps, later reduced by Heinrich Kiepert,[28] Coleman mainly illustrated Scriptural narratives, as indeed Holy Land maps had done from the very earliest attempts by Christians and Jews to fix the locations of biblical events.[29] One could visualize ancient and modern Jerusalem (the frontispiece), the "World as Known to the Hebrews" (map 2), "Palestine under the Judges and Kings" (map 4), and "Palestine in the Time of Jesus" (map 5, which was on the largest scale). Or a reader might follow the "Routes of the Israelites through the Desert" (map 3), the "Travels of Our Saviour" (map 6), and the "Missionary Tours of the Apostle Paul" (map 7). Of course, the rhetorical conventions of each map hid its history of production, its entanglements with ideologically charged social space, its appeals to authority, and the hypotheses it accepted or discarded. Map space more simply matched a biblical event with a specific location and expressed (or masked, depending on one's perspective) the evangelical hopes that were invested in mastering the geography of the Bible. And each map did so with an air of settled neutrality.

Yet what of the social realities embedded in such utilitarian functionality? Take, for example, the title of map 3 and its printer's typography, which I reproduce here as closely as possible.

THE ROUTES of the **ISRAELITES** from Egypt through the
DESERT. CANAAN at the time of the Conquest

Bold typeface and capital letters both encapsulated the underlying biblical narrative and embraced the theme of a single people moving toward a singular goal, "the Conquest." The expression reflected customary use, going far back into the history of biblical mapmaking and commentary. It surely described the overall tone of the underlying narrative, which typically speaks of "entering" the land that God had assigned to the offspring of Abraham and "dispossessing," even destroying, its inhabitants. Hoary usage and status as map title reaffirmed the Hebrews' entitlement, and of course they, as victors, preserved the story. Yet, in pre–Civil War America, such biblical claims of a political and moral right to territory might have been heard in a new key. Could there be a happy congruence, perhaps just an enabling echo, of popular notions of America's beginnings in righteous victory over savage pagans?

Fig. 51. "Our Predecessors Viewing the 'Promised Land'."
Aultman Miller & Co., Akron, Ohio, 1888.

Countless celebrations and treatises propagated images of a "new" exodus people, a Christian people of high moral purpose who were following their manifest destiny to expand Christian civilization in the pagan wilderness of North America.[30] Along the way, of course, the newcomers subdued or killed the local "Canaanites" (when they could not befriend them). Or they relegated them to the mournful sideline, as one 1880s advertising card more benignly suggested. Pictured was a pioneering family looking westward toward industrial prowess and unlimited possibility, while an American Indian faced eastward, resigned to his defeat and excluded from the limitless promise of the western horizon. The title neatly caught the sense of exclusionary entitlement and biblically inspired narrative of American beginnings: "Our Predecessors Viewing the 'Promised Land'."

It is doubtful that the title to Coleman's map directly reinforced such vernacular images of America's national history. Readers of the Bible, taking up the perspective of the Bible itself, had long used invasion or conquest to describe the movement of Hebrews into the Promised Land. But Coleman's usage did nothing to weaken the reservoir of active metaphor that had made such Bible-based analogies a powerful force in American culture. With an emphasis that implied that he had met and overcome at least some moral reservation, Coleman depicted an ancient biblical people taking from the undeserving what was theirs by divine gift. The vanquished Canaanites, Coleman wrote,

> had wearied the long-suffering of God by their sins. Their iniquity was now full. . . . Their extermination was necessary for the accomplishment of the Divine purpose in making the descendants of Abraham the depositories of His word, and preserving among them a pure religion.[31]

On Coleman's map, a continuous double line (hand-tinted in red) marked the route taken by those Abrahamic trustees of pure religion. Broken double lines depicted alternative routes that had been proposed by other scholars. The uncertainty derived from the Bible itself, but the compulsion to override it lay with the commentators. "The route is quite conjectural," Coleman admitted in his explanation of map 3. Yet, in deference to Robinson's authority and the route he thought likely, the solid red line simply negated Coleman's admission and proclaimed certainty. Alternative proposals, the broken lines of lesser rank in the representational hierarchy, commanded less attention, even skepticism.

Similarly, the question of exactly where Moses would have received the law of God seemed to demand of commentators a definitive answer. An inset map, "Mountains of Sinai," reflected the importance given to the issue, as well as the theological weight this narrative carried in both Christian and Jewish communities. In topographical relief, the cartographer showed the "wider range of ground" amidst sharp and craggy peaks that would, as Coleman explained, alone of all the narrow valleys in the mountainous region, have offered space for the "hosts of Israel . . . when they received the law from Sinai." In his commentary, Coleman quoted extensively from Robinson's vivid account of coming upon the place, the only place that suited both the Bible's indications of topography and Robinson's romanticized notion of wildness out of which had erupted the civilizing law of God.

> As we advanced, the valley still opened wider and wider, with a gentle ascent, and became full of shrubs and tufts of herbs, shut in on one side by lofty granite ridges, with rugged, shattered peaks, a thousand feet high, while the face of Horeb [where the Bible says the Torah was received] rose directly before us. Both my companion and myself involuntarily exclaimed, "Here is room enough for a large encampment!"[32]

Lurking in this interplay of map and commentary was an unwavering belief that religious truth can be credible only if it is implanted, that is, attached to an actual event in an actual place available for discovery and plotting with geographical coordinates. One must know with certainty where events occurred, so as to get closer—in imagination and reconstruction, of course—to the original moment of divine disclosure. Therein lay purchase on the history of God's revealed truth. Thus indeterminacy, even admitted ignorance, must be vanquished. It may be laid to rest by gaining increasingly exact and true knowledge (the underlying premise of detailed scholarly commentary and maps). Or it may be overcome with cartographic symbols such as clear lines tracing the desert wanderings (map 3), color-coding the travels of Jesus (map 6), or setting forth the missionary journeys of Paul (map 7). Uncertainty may even be mitigated by diversion. "The travels of our Lord," Coleman wrote, even though ill-defined by the Gospel narratives (and so presenting a problem for piety sustained by geography), should nonetheless be plotted and pondered in the interest of creating a sense of evangelical purpose among the young. Such a map

serves to impress the mind with the extent of his [Jesus'] travels and
the wearisome life which he lived, in his labor of love, going about
everywhere doing good.[33]

In the Gospels, Jesus was laboring in love while eventually turning
toward Jerusalem, the city of shame and triumph that Coleman showcased in the frontispiece to his *Atlas*. Two maps, one of ancient and the
other of modern Jerusalem, plotted layers of historical features and selec-
tively identified modern structures and sites. As though to justify the
privileged position he had given to Jerusalem in the lineup of maps,
Coleman noted that "Jerusalem is the great central point to which the
bearings and distance of cities and countries may be referred."[34] The deci-
sion may not have been simply a matter of cartographic convenience.

Christians, like Jews, had always seen Jerusalem as the centering
manifestation of God's redemption. Christians, moreover, tended to see
the establishment of the eschatological, heavenly New Jerusalem as the
consummating event of that divine initiative begun in Jesus. Many
ancient maps, such as the one uncovered in the church at Medeba,
embodied those convictions by depicting the city in larger scale than
her immediate surroundings, or sometimes, as in the Renaissance, high-
lighting her as cartographic art. Even more grandly, Jerusalem appeared
in some medieval maps at the center of the known world, reflecting not
only theological conviction but political claims which later, as European trade and exploration expanded in the early modern period, mir-
rored mercantile ambitions as well.[35]

Coleman was a part of this mythic and iconographic tradition, even
if he refused the visual sentimentalism of many nineteenth-century
Holy Land travel books, which prominently displayed Jerusalem, el-
egantly sketched, painted, or photographed from the east, isolated,
often washed in supernal light. Coleman projected privilege by locating
it in the frontispiece, and in the maps sketched successive defensive
walls that evoked the Holy City's royal past. Commentary brought mythi-
cally charged social space to the territory, those generations of Christian
travelers and pilgrims who, fixing on the Holy City as precious object,
were moved to lamentation over its lost magnificence. At the very least,
such ruination echoed the fall from Eden and implied divine judgment
on transgression. Christians often attributed that malfeasance to the
Jews because, in the cosmic struggle of good against evil, Jews had chosen
the wrong side and rejected Jesus as Messiah. "Jerusalem retains few
traces of her ancient grandeur," Coleman wrote. And yet

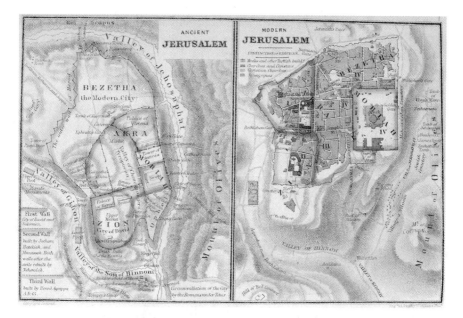

FIG. 52. Maps of ancient and modern Jerusalem,
from Coleman, *Historical Textbook and Atlas of Biblical Geography.*

> You are standing where stood the compassionate Saviour as he beheld
> the devoted city and wept over it . . . the sacred city—Zion, city of our
> God. There sits the sacred city, like a bereaved and desolate widow,
> mourning over her absent and rejected Lord, beautiful still, though
> desolate and in ruins.

This is mythic Jerusalem, a powerful, age-old conjuration of biblical
narrative, memory, symbolic characters, and religious devotion oriented toward transcendent meaning beyond the mundane world. Here
is the real-imagined place of eternal struggle and possession, the place
where Christian truth was proffered and rejected once upon a time, but
as myth, an event of transformative power that happens all the time.

> This holy city, so renowned in the history of the Jewish nation and the
> world, so celebrated in sacred song as beautiful for situation, an eternal
> excellency, the joy of many nations. . . . here on her rocky heights, she
> sits dreary, silent, and solitary, amid surrounding desolation.[36]

There was yet little relief for travelers and pilgrims, Coleman suggested. In an "Explanation of the Frontispiece," amidst lists of structures

and sites, mostly of Christian interest, Coleman added three annotations. The Armenian Convent is "the only building in Jerusalem which presents any appearance of comfort." The Jews' Quarter is "the most wretched in the city." And in Zion's Gate near the "Wailing Place of the Jews," a pilgrim will find "the wretched abode of lepers." In offering these notes, and only these, Coleman seemed to tap the depths of mythic imagination, as though a traveler's discomfort, even paternal disgust at the city's degraded condition, confirmed a distorted shadow of her former glory.

Jerusalem's three defensive walls, built over about a thousand years, were earthly measures of that departed glory. Cartography emphasized a hierarchical understanding of the city-space, a place of royal power exercised and maintained, of prosperous expansion, of defense and challenge to royal control, and finally of devastation under Roman suppression. Of course, this embedded version of history illustrated the selective rendering of events found in the Bible itself. Conventional symbols added confirming certainty to the retelling. Solid lines and an overlay of color gave the impression that the limits of the city, the borders of its material splendor, were assuredly known. Seeing the walls, even if only as abstract representations, also supported the idea of mythic grandeur and introduced another complication. Was Jerusalem's past mythic and worldly glory imagined in part with a template of modern European and American experience with nation-states?[37]

In any case, Coleman visualized a retelling of Jerusalem's history in its observed and measured geographical aspect, just as his seventeenth-century progenitor Edward Wells, one of the inventors of modern historical geography, had done.[38] This and other maps supported social formations of Christian evangelism and may even have reinforced popular American narratives of national origin. Map and commentary encoded commitment to a notion of religious truth as anchored in the real—the material, not fanciful, space. Christian revelation was inherent in certain historical events, which could be vitalized by treks through the land and the making of maps. And yet Coleman evoked mythic, eternal Jerusalem, too. He called up the long march of Christian pilgrims and explorers, poets, artists, and theologians who had celebrated her former grandeur and lamented her contemporary misery. All these "livings," and surely others that I have not seen, Coleman brought to the territory, the mapped Holy Land, the space for winning young souls.

Mapmakers and Crusaders for Biblical Archaeology

George Ernest Wright and Floyd Vivian Filson were midwesterners, Presbyterians, and teachers of theology students. Filson was in his mid-thirties and a professor of the New Testament at Presbyterian (later McCormick) Theological Seminary in Chicago when Wright, then just twenty-two, began his studies there in 1931. An alumnus of the seminary, Filson had joined the faculty in 1923. Over some forty years, he built a notable, though self-effacing, career as a theologian, biblical interpreter, and historian of early Christianity. Filson served as dean of the seminary, then as its acting president during 1954–56, and after retirement in 1967 remained a vigorous researcher, publisher, and contributor to ecumenical activities until his death.[39]

Filson and Wright became faculty colleagues in 1939, and soon thereafter they collaboratively edited *The Westminster Historical Atlas to the Bible*. This book was destined to become the premier Bible atlas for mid-twentieth-century America. It would also become a forceful weapon, one of many that Wright would inspire, in what David Noel Freedman later described as the "biblical archaeological crusade."[40]

Wright and a number of other brilliant students of William Foxwell Albright constituted the campaign's elite corps during the 1950s and 1960s. Propagating their teacher's linguistically rigorous and archaeologically informed approach to understanding the Bible, they raised up students of like mind and training, reprinted Albright's more accessible writings, and published new scholarship of their own. Principally led by Wright, the group planned and published reference works which not only became authoritative in the field, but helped Albright's sons and grandsons, as they spoke of themselves, establish a commanding presence on the landscape of American university-based biblical studies. In these ambitious enterprises, members of the Albright school deployed philology and archaeology in a battle to defeat what they (and Albright) saw as sterile, subjective studies of the Bible. Only positive facts—objectively arrived-at truths about history, language, and material remains—could rightly illuminate the Bible and its religious teachings.[41]

Wright found his way into the Albright circle at Presbyterian Seminary. Arriving in 1931, he studied the Old Testament with Ovid Sellers, who had been a student of Albright's a decade earlier in Jerusalem. Sellers had continued the association, and he soon steered his promising pupil toward graduate study with Albright. At the time, Albright had recently begun his long tenure as professor and chair of Semitics at the Johns Hopkins University. He was already quite famous as a linguist, archaeologist, Bible scholar, and the director (from 1920 to 1929) of the American School of Oriental Research in Jerusalem.[42]

In 1934, with a fresh divinity degree from McCormick, Wright signed up for the Kyle Memorial Excavations at Bethel, directed by Albright. He was immediately entranced—with archaeology, surely, but even more with its master practitioner. Albright was a "one-man show," Wright later recalled.

> He was at it day and night, overseeing every little thing, working hours upon hours out there in the field after the dig was over . . . working out every detail of the relationship of walls to walls, and so on, working this out all in his head, then doing pottery with everyone around, teaching everyone the rudiments of pottery chronology while he made notes on the pottery at the same time.[43]

Wright later studied formally with Albright and received his Ph.D. in 1937. Teaching at McCormick Seminary from 1939 to 1958, and then at Harvard University until his death in 1974, Wright earned fame and affection as a bold archaeologist, an inspiring teacher, a visionary leader of the American School of Oriental Research, and a theologian. His most enduring monuments, eulogists seemed to agree, were his numerous contributions to Near Eastern and biblical archaeology.[44] Part of that legacy was *The Westminster Historical Atlas,* co-edited by Wright and Filson and published in 1945 as World War II was coming to an end, nearly a hundred years after Lyman Coleman had first commended his handbook to the public.[45]

While reflecting Wright's and Filson's deep commitment to Christian theology, the work was modernly erudite, congruent with archaeological interests, and redolent of Albright. As well as encouraging the project, Albright contributed an introductory essay, "The Rediscovery of the Biblical World," which set the *Atlas* within a narrative of advances made possible by increasingly scientific archaeology (one of Albright's favorite themes). He also offered a foundational "Chronology of Ancient History."[46]

The new work quickly supplanted George Adam Smith's *Historical Atlas of the Holy Land,* which had gone out of print during the Second World War. Smith's handbook was closely tied to the romantic piety of the previous century, something the Albrighteans wanted no part of, and in any case it had not taken sufficient advantage of what an

Albrightean crusader took to be the revolutionary gains of modern archaeology.[47]

Nevertheless, a fair number of photographs evoked Smith's lyrical geopiety and the more broadly conventional iconography of Holy Land travel. At one point, for example, a reader encountered a half-page photograph of the "Wilderness of Judah." To its left was a large map of "Southern Palestine," and immediately below, the opening paragraphs of a long chapter entitled "Southern Palestine in Biblical Times." The arrangement of textual space was as good as a narrative. Readers had traveled to southern Palestine, perhaps using the map to find their way, and now awaited a guide's explanation for the view that unfolded before their eyes. Looking past an Arab horseman, who gazed across the receding folds of barren hillsides, Wright and Filson evoked Palestine the empty and picturesque, forever irresistible in the eyes of her lover. "The bleakness of the area is forbidding," they wrote in the photo caption, "but the visitor never tires of watching the ever-changing pastel shades of color in views such as this."[48]

Other photographs stood in the tradition of scriptural illustration, such as "The Sea of Galilee," which depicted fishermen launching their boat onto the waters. The caption identified the image as a "view northward along the northwest shore of the lake," and then directed viewers outside the frame: "Just left of the foreground is the 'Plain of Gennesaret.'" Christians who knew their Bible could not fail to realize that their tour guide had just evoked memories of Jesus' healing activities in this area (Matthew 14:34), as well as his call for his disciples to become "fishers of men" (Luke 5:1–11). It is surely no accident that this evocative photograph, so reminiscent of vernacular travel literature, headed a chapter of commentary, "Palestine during the Ministry of Jesus." As though recalling William Thomson from a century earlier, Wright and Filson declared anew—even in an atlas cast in the discourses of archaeology, positivist history, and science—that the land itself yet bore witness to those wondrous events of God's activity on earth.[49]

Virtually without competition for more than twenty-five years, the *Westminster Atlas* went through many printings, including a revision in 1956 and a translation into Spanish in 1992.[50] "Wright and Filson" was on the must-purchase list of countless students (I among them) who entered expanding university and college programs in the study of religion and theology during the 1960s.[51] The book's success surprised even Albright, who told his star pupil that he was "positively astonished at the way the *Atlas* still sells."[52] When printings ceased in the early

1970s, the publisher had sold more than 87,000 copies, an impressive number considering that in 1968 membership in the Society of Biblical Literature, the oldest American association of biblical scholars, stood at about 2,700.[53]

In their *Atlas*, Wright and Filson advanced the biblical archaeological crusade, but they sang the *cantus firmus* of Lyman Coleman. Coleman had seen his handbook as serving Christian evangelism while dispelling ignorance of the Bible and making it less forbidding to students. "Acquaintance with the History, Chronology, and Geography of the Bible," Coleman told schoolteachers in 1867,

> would lend new attractions to this holy book, and by the grace of God might win them to such a perusal of His word as would enlighten the eyes, rejoice the heart, and convert the soul.[54]

Wright and Filson's version of this evangelical purpose, or perhaps its sublimation, was embedded in their reach for a culminating synthesis. They blended geography and archeological discovery with ancient Near Eastern history and religion (in a narrative shaped toward contemporary theological relevance), and focused their commentary mostly through the privileged perspective of the Bible itself. The integrated package brought the social spaces of the Albright school and its biblical archaeological crusade to Holy Land territory, and with theological banners unfurled.

The Bible records in the main actual history, not legendary fantasies, Wright and Filson suggested to their readers. It tells of God's encounters with human beings, and this "theology of recital," as Wright wrote elsewhere, constitutes the heart of biblical theology. Geographical study of the land (as all the old travel books and atlases had asserted or implied) and modern archaeology (as Albright and his students repeatedly proclaimed) are necessary, not only to delineate the background of the Bible, but to discern its message for a new generation. "Geography, history, and religion," Wright and Filson told their readers,

> are so inextricably bound together in it [the Bible] that the religious message cannot be truly understood without attention to the settings and conditions of the revelation.[55]

To understand truly is to proclaim—this had always been the point of Bible study, especially among Protestants. The dictum energized Coleman's *Atlas* as well as Wright and Filson's. The authors conjured up an ancient people whom they viewed, not in their historical complexity, but as "Israel," a quasi-historical theological type, a unique bearer of revelation and exemplar of both faith and apostasy.

This biblical people "lived in the world, yet were not quite united with it," an interpretation reminiscent of New Testament descriptions of a Christ-centered life.[56] "Israel" created a unique book, Wright and Filson wrote, reformulating a claim fundamental to Bible-centered evangelism. It is the only Scripture "for whose comprehension the study of historical geography is a fact," because it is the only book focused on God's actions in actual human history. Ancient Israel lived in a "providentially provided setting," the authors continued, a setting in which her "prophetic minds" preserved the "relatively high moral purity and austerity" of ancestral monotheism. Those same prophetic minds fought to save Israelite religion from "the degrading, polytheistic nature worship of Canaan." In this point, Wright and Filson echoed Albright, but also, perhaps unwittingly, Lyman Coleman, who, it will be recalled, had declared that "Divine Purpose" ordained destruction for the iniquitous Canaanites so as to preserve "pure religion" among the invading Hebrews.[57] For Wright and Filson, the prophets understood that idol-smashing purity. They taught that the "real purpose and blessing of God for his people were not to be found in riches, political power, and cultural distinction." Presumably God's blessing was to be found in an idealized sphere of privatized, apolitical religious practice, a decidedly Protestant—and American—formulation.

Coursing through many centuries, these prophetic insights eventually found expression beyond tribal ethnicity in "world-scope" Christianity. A certain geographical isolation in ancient Palestine, Wright and Filson wrote, combined with persistent elements of spiritual and cultural separateness, eventually led to Judaism and its "unique spiritual heritage." However admirable, even this achievement was surpassed, and with the irresistibility of divine plan.

> Under the stimulus of Hellenistic influence and Roman rule, the setting was created in the first century for a fuller revelation of the world scope of God's purpose. The days when detachment could be creative and fruitful were past; it was time for Israel to give her gifts to the world.[58]

Such foundational claims, which amounted to an incipient, comprehensive theological narrative, gave to the Wright and Filson *Atlas* a particular theological substance, even as the handbook conformed to its genus, historical geography in the service of elucidating the Bible. Finely drawn maps, engraved and printed in stunning color, depicted Palestine's physical topography and neighboring political empires during specified pre-Christian and early Christian centuries (plates 1, 3, 11, and 13). The largest-scale projections were reserved for three sectional maps of ancient Palestine in non-specific "biblical time," on which were located all towns, villages, and places mentioned anywhere in the Bible (plates 8–10). However, at the heart of the collection was something conventional, even generic, to Bible atlases: a series of maps that encouraged readers to track iconic "Israel" and nascent "Church" on their journey through history, according to the temporal sequencing of the canonical narratives. Maps depicting the Exodus from Egypt, tribal claims during the time of the judges, the times of Jesus, the journeys of Paul, and the like helped readers visualize the Bible's version of events. In this way cartography reiterated selected narratives that were, in Wright's readings, especially useful in supporting a theology of salvation history. Map and commentary also advanced the Albrightean crusade by demonstrating how archaeological data enabled a more objective, cartographically projected understanding of the Bible and renewed confidence in the Bible's historical reliability.

For example, consider plate 5, "The Exodus from Egypt." The title of the map immediately invoked biblical narrative, of course. Thematic trajectory, a way of defining the end of the story, appeared on the map among several ancient roadways, but distinguished from these by a dashed line in red. The key to the map explained that the line marked the "Probable Route of the Exodus and Main Phase of the Conquest." One would never have guessed that the factuality of such a journey was beginning to be vigorously disputed at the time.[59]

The map evoked broader images of habitual movements—trade routes, roads through the wilderness, the ancient track toward the land of the Philistines. It also suggested a similar everyday, unmediated "reality" for iconic Israel's purposeful movement toward triumphal conquest. Wright, who took responsibility for this section of the *Atlas*, reinforced in commentary the impression given by the map. This movement from Egypt was not fantasy, but real history, and trustworthily reconstructed by Wright, who occasionally toned down the Bible's exaggerated numbers and explained some of its miraculous events as natural occurrences.

The conquest was a "storming" of Canaan from the east, Wright wrote, aimed at wresting the land from its decadent inhabitants. The

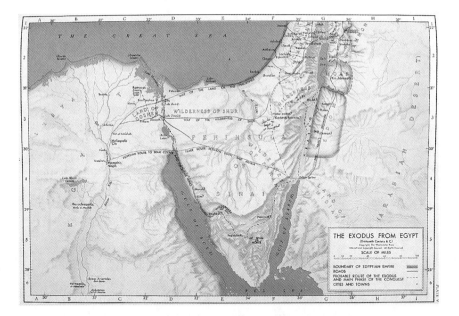

FIG. 53. "The Exodus from Egypt," reproduced from Wright
and Filson, *Westminster Historical Atlas to the Bible.*
Used by permission of Westminster John Knox Press.

Canaanite system of "nation-states" permitted and perhaps encouraged
such "warfare and bickering" as would "drain the energy and vitality of
any people." Likewise, its social organization was "unhealthy," for an
aristocratic "feudal system" exploited a "lower class of serfs and slaves."
Perhaps expressing his impression of post–World War II America,
Wright added without evidence that "an independent and energetic
middle class was non-existent."

Furthermore, abject paganism, which Wright itemized with lurid
pleasure, was a factor in Canaanite weakness. The "extremely low level"
of Canaanite religion may have hindered the "development of civilization," he declared. Even if the influence of religion on community life
was difficult to discern, the record of barbarity "must be pointed out."
Polytheism was abhorrent enough, but the gods "had no moral character whatsoever [and] certainly the brutality of the mythology [was] far
worse than anywhere else in the Near East at that time." Worship
entailed "the most demoralizing practices then in existence." Child
sacrifice, large-scale snake worship, sacred prostitution—"It is difficult,"

he wrote, "to see how a religion of such debasing character could have had any stabilizing or vitalizing effect whatsoever upon the civilization." Then, as though recognizing the moral ambiguity of a "conquest" that is both rapacious destruction and divine gift, and as if to explain the extraordinary amount of energy he had devoted to the matter, Wright concluded,

> It was small loss to the world when in parts of the Palestinian hill country it [Canaanite barbarity] was virtually annihilated. The purity and righteous holiness of the God of Israel were now to be demonstrated against this background of pagan and immoral religion. The intransigence and hostility of the religious leaders of Israel toward the people and religion of Canaan is thus to be seen in its *true perspective*. (Emphasis mine)

Correctly understood, conquest was the providential outcome of a righteous God's relentless demand for undivided devotion. It completed a chain of "stirring events" which constituted the beginning of "Israel's history as a nation."[60] Invasion and conquest were easily justified by feelings of superiority entangled in a bundle of convictions about biblical uniqueness, true religion, and unshakeable moral compass—the *cantus firmus* of Lyman Coleman.

In amplifying the outsiders' claim to Canaan by divine gift and moral right, the *Atlas* implicitly—and perhaps unwittingly—iterated claims to a homeland for ethnically bounded Israelites (Jews), and no one else. The scholarly picture of ancient Israel as unitary and unique, as a morally superior, God-justified taker of land, fell together with the geography of ancient Palestine as a mostly empty homeland conquered in the service of divine purpose. Just this version of nationalist narrative, with all its simplifications and vested interests, had underpinned early Zionist colonies in Palestine, and after World War II it found political realization in the state of Israel. Viewed from the side of Arab opposition, European and North American biblical scholarship seemed complicit in the "myopia of the West," which, in the powerful machinery of colonialism, had tended to devalue any claims to Palestine or its past that might be raised by Arab peoples.[61]

Clearly, the line showing the "Probable Route of the Exodus and Main Phase of the Conquest" was hardly just a matter of neutral geography, or even of archaeologically (and scientifically) oriented reconstruction. It created a real-imagined Holy Land territory, a Promised Land, out of a defining moral vision and a readily accepted sense of triumphal righteousness that was amenable to biblical preaching and Zionist politics alike. This was a spiritual inheritance, part of that Holy Land social space of prophetic witness that Wright embraced and lived, and eagerly brought to America in geography and mapmaking. Perhaps also implied was a notion of political virtue in post-war America, whose middle class, empowered by the New Deal and then by wartime, the authors valued for its independence and energy. Such an America, as Wright's teacher Albright had written in 1940, was a biblically grounded bulwark against civilization-destroying, godless totalitarianism.[62]

The second edition of the *Atlas* appeared in 1956, at the height of America's Cold War with the Soviet Union. By then, America's postwar prosperity was in full swing, and a prosperous middle class was becoming a powerhouse of economic and social change. Could Wright's indirect praise of middle-class values have been heard as a salutary defense, as a link with Judeo-Christian tradition, not pagan Canaanite, in this newly anxious time?[63]

On the whole, the map of Exodus gave an impression of precision. Where there was doubt, the cartographer provided appropriate symbols, such as question marks positioned after place-names (e.g., the stages of encampment along the route from Egypt) and hatched lines indicating uncertain boundaries for kingdoms with which, according to the Bible, Moses had to reckon.

Yet the visual sense of settled history and geography, and behind that, a biblical narrative in the main confirmed, is fragile, even a little illusory. Partly owing to the effects of cartohypnosis, and partly because of an insistent drive to match each narrative event with a confirmed geographical locality, Bible atlases regularly suggest that scholars know much more than they actually do.[64] In Wright and Filson, for example, the location, or even existence, of the "Way of the Wilderness of Shur," while perhaps plausible, is not as certain as its solid-line symbol suggests. Indeed, compared to other ancient roadways similarly marked on the map, it is far less traceable on the landscape. The Bible occasionally uses the word "Shur," but the somewhat murky references still, as they did in Wright and Filson's day, obscure what "Shur" meant or exactly where biblical writers thought it to be located.[65] Moreover, identifying the cities of Succoth, Pithom, and Baal-Zephon, the first landmarks in the biblical account of the departure from Egypt, involves a web of assessed archaeological remains, deduction, and supposition, all acknowledged by Wright and Filson. The map, however, located the "Way of the Wilderness of Shur" and these cities without a trace of indeterminacy, just as Lyman Coleman's map (based on Edward Robinson) exuded confidence, even if his locations for the cities were markedly at odds with those of Wright and Filson. These roadways, towns, and villages, even where commentary seemed hesitant, enjoyed the same ontological status as rivers and mountains, or the shorelines of the modern Gulf of Suez.

Then there is Mount Nebo (or Pisgah), from which Moses is said to have viewed the whole of the Promised Land. Its location near Jericho at the end of the route toward conquest elicited no comment and merited no question mark. Lyman Coleman, following Edward Robinson, had opined that the actual biblical site would never be found. The site traditionally identified with Nebo simply did not fit the biblical description, even though there were ruins of ancient churches in the area and a spring named after Moses. In any case, its attestation was no older than the fourth-century Christian writer Eusebius. Nevertheless, like Coleman, Wright and Filson pinpointed it on their maps anyway.[66] Too much was at stake, too much vital social experience, it seems, to do otherwise.

Centuries earlier, in 1659, Nicolas Visscher the Elder had drawn the "Holy Land as Moses Viewed it from Mt. Pisgah." His projection, which looked west and north from the trans-Jordan plateau, became "the predominant Dutch delineation for the next 150 years."[67] The narrative moment had long been memorialized in topological exegesis, in which Moses was said to have seen far beyond Canaan to the advent of Jesus, the Redeemer. The sight from Pisgah was carried metaphorically into literature and music, and captured with typical Victorian sentimentalism by the French artist James Tissot.[68] Mount Nebo was a favorite stopping point of countless travelers to the Holy Land, who walked over the places cartographers could only draw. Frank DeHass, the American consul in Jerusalem in the 1870s, wrote that a dream of his life had finally been realized when he stood on the spot, quite satisfied that all doubts had been overcome by meticulous observation and induction. Biblical scholar and Assyriologist George Barton climbed up the summit and gushed, "This was a great day. Think of standing where Moses stood and getting his view of Canaan!"[69] And, of course, a space so vital with livings—personal and cultural histories of faith and romantic attachments—had to be included in Hurlbut and Kent's parlor tour. Like Jacob's Well, Mount Nebo was a spot that enabled fantasies of a past to rise up, vital and captivating.

> Can you not with the mind's eye see on that summit a venerable form, standing erect and alone, gazing upon the land of promise, to whose

borders he led the hosts of Israel, though he was not permitted to enter? To look upon the land, and then to lie down upon the mount and die—this was the sublime end of the sublime life of Moses, the Man of God.[70]

On the map, the "probable route of the Exodus and main phase of the conquest" skirted the kingdoms of Edom and Moab, just to the south of Mount Nebo, on the way to traversing the kingdom of Sihon. These kingdoms appear again in plate 4, "The Land of Canaan before the Israelite Conquest," where a note indicates that they were "founded during the 13th century." Both maps give a strong impression of centralized political order, with sovereign territorial powers and defined borders (even if the eastern limits were marked as uncertain). This picture comported with Wright and Filson's commentary, which essentially paraphrased the biblical account of Numbers 20–21 and 33. The authors spoke of military strategy, kings, borders, kingdoms, and capitals, as Moses led "a new generation of Israelites" through the "first phase of conquest" that left them "in possession of the territory of Transjordan between Bashan and the River Arnon."[71]

This account and its accompanying visualization in the map, even though plausible and conventional, imposed clarity on ambiguity, and perhaps wrongly applied modern experience of centralized nation-states to biblical accounts. Wright and Filson knew of a reference to "Bedouin tribes of Edom" from the thirteenth-century reign of the Egyptian ruler Merneptah. That date was enough for them to declare a thirteenth-century origin for Edom. But did the inscription, a report by an Egyptian official about non-Egyptians passing by a fortified outpost, establish a "kingdom" of Edom? And what would "kingdom" mean in a geographic region that, as archaeological research in Wright's day had shown and as has been later confirmed, supported local agricultural villages, and perhaps some mining?[72] Wright may simply have accepted the picture of Numbers 20 more or less at face value. He could then imagine not a region of localized communities, or of Bedouin groups, but a unified political entity, all "Edom" arrayed against all "Israel," with whom Moses tried to negotiate passage through organized and clearly defined "territory" (Numbers 20:14–21). In any case, even if Wright and Filson might, if pressed, have admitted some doubt, the map assuredly created that "kingdom" as a reality for their readers.

Moreover, translating the Hebrew word *gebûl* in Numbers 20:16 as "territory," or sometimes in other texts as (territorial) "border," assumes a political entity exercising sovereignty through bureaucratic and military control. The map codifies the assumption by indicating defined borders, as in the cases of Edom and Moab, or as tribal claims to territory, in plate 6. Acknowledging that the information about borders is incomplete only embeds the assumption more deeply.

However, a translation of "frontier," meaning the contested, fluid edges of actual or claimed political influence, might better suit the traditionally organized, decentralized systems of local communities and kinship organization that the Bible mostly reflects. As John Rogerson cautiously suggested,

> the rendering [of *gebûl* as] "border" is misleading if for modern readers it suggests borders as understood by modern nation-states, that is, clearly marked boundaries which, in some cases, are defended either by continuous physical obstacles or border guards or both and within which the nation-state exercises complete sovereignty.[73]

Rogerson argued that if his reservations had merit, then Bible maps of even the monarchical period in ancient Israel, when one most intuitively imagines a unified nation-state, may mislead. He considered, for example, a 1997 portrayal of King David's monarchy, very similar to plate 7 in Wright and Filson's *Atlas*. The map gave the impression, and probably assumed, wrote Rogerson, that David controlled large areas of land and that these areas of control could be indicated by lines and shading. Is that presupposition of modern nation-states appropriate, Rogerson asked? Possibly not. He called for historians and cartographers to rethink how maps might represent traditional, pre-capitalist sociopolitical formations without imposing modern ideas of the nation-state.

In the end, I suspect that the cluster of problematic nationalist and ethnocentric assumptions—an ethnically defined people, a nation-state, kingdoms, borders, capitals, and territory—were well suited to the cultural experience of Wright and Filson, as indeed of their readers. This way of imagining the people whom Moses encountered, or even the "Israelites," was so deeply embedded in Victorian Anglo-European scholarship that alternatives were not easily conceivable, and in any case might have challenged confidence in the perspectives governing the underlying biblical narrative. Since Numbers 20 may have been composed several centuries after the time Moses was supposed to have lived, alternatives might have challenged the relevance of the narrative for tracing the route and the historical reality of conquest. Alternatives would surely have complicated acceptance of modern nationalist narratives.[74]

In this situation, cartography not only illustrated the biblical story. It also carried certain culturally specific understandings of society and politics, to which the story referred. In a word, the map constructed familiar, rather than alien, social realities, and so reinforced spiritual and cultural identification with a reputedly unitary ancient biblical people.

In their commentary, Wright and Filson naturally admitted many historical uncertainties. And of course, they worked to bring the biblical record and archaeological data into a mutually supportive relationship. Those struggles, those decisions, those commitments and exclusions were mostly invisible on maps driven by a traditional impulse to ground events of biblical history in material geography. Besides rigorous scholarship, what finally seemed to matter (and perhaps what was offered as a palliative to doubt) was a theological version of the past, and a Bible theology subtly confirmed insofar as archaeology and mapmaking purported to track the story. "Historical questions must not obscure the central facts," Wright summed up for his readers, and those facts were

> that at least some Israelites suffered slavery in Egypt, that they were freed in a wonderful deliverance, that they were led victoriously into the Promised Land after years of murmuring and faintheartedness, and that in these remarkable events the Israelites saw the hand of their God, a gracious God who had taken pity on their afflictions and saved them for his providential purpose.[75]

It is this providential purpose that the authors' commentary encouraged readers to see in maps, and it was nowhere more dramatically evident than in the treatment of Jerusalem and New Testament history. Filson, who was responsible for most of the material dealing with Christian origins, devoted four maps and a chapter to Jerusalem, "by far the most important city in the Bible." He was aware that Muslims, Jews, and Christians all lavished great attention and affection on this city. Nonetheless, he gave a certain primacy to a theologically shaped historical narrative that went far beyond the literary limits of the Bible to include the "Church" (a quasi-historical type, which seems similar in that way to "Israel"). In Jerusalem, Filson wrote,

> was the Temple, the focal point of Israelite and Jewish religious life and aspiration. Here David and Solomon, Isaiah and Jeremiah, Ezra and Nehemiah, lived and labored. Here, too, a portion of the ministry of Jesus took place; here he was crucified and raised up, and here the Christian Church was founded.

Filson noted that after a seventh-century conquest, Jerusalem became, next to Mecca and Medina, the "most important holy place of the Moslem world." For all these reasons, then, Jerusalem is a city holy to "Christians, Jews, and Moslems." Yet, in a final summary (does it claim primacy, or merely recognize his primary audience?), Filson referred to Revelation 21:2, 24. The allusion evoked centuries of Christian attachment to a mythic, heavenly "New Jerusalem." It was surely not a vision of space that incorporated the particular on-the-ground social realities of competing ideologies and affections.[76]

In counterpoint, plate 18 depicted the earthly city, singularly imagined and lifted up in elevation—as a large-scale relief map shows. No other site garnered such lavish attention. Jerusalem belongs to a space of grandeur, perhaps to the poetic lore of a city "beautiful for situation," which was so often pictured in vernacular travel accounts and souvenirs. Four maps concentrated on boundaries, defensive walls, and monumental structures. These reflected both the biases and the physical constraints of nearly a century of archaeological investigation. However, like much excavative interest, the maps also defined the city's reassembled reality only in terms of hierarchical spaces of centralized royal and theocratic power. First there was Jerusalem of "Israelite" times (ruled by David, Solomon, and Hezekiah), then the city in the "time of Christ" (governed and made resplendent by King Herod), and finally the city in "Christian Times," when the Roman Empire was on its way to sanctioning Christianity as the official imperial religion. (The tomb of Queen Helena, who was responsible for associating so many sites in Roman Palestine with New Testament narratives, is duly marked.) This wider post-biblical horizon found notable expression in plate 16, which traced the expansion of the "Church" from St. Paul (c. 45 C.E.) to Emperor Constantine and his mother, Queen Helena (c. 325 C.E.).

A fourth map, "Jerusalem Today," projected a very particular sense of the contemporary city. Aside from designating a few Israeli municipal buildings, cartography was silent about the politico-religious situation of the 1950s. Rather, the map was oriented to a spatialized culture of religious memory, one deeply formed by Protestant Bible study and persistent quests for intimations of a biblical past. The Church of the Holy Sepulchre and Gethsemane Church, for example, were landmarks, but also points of spatial continuity with worship and pilgrimage that memorialized New Testament events. Bible research institutions, vehicles by which the past may be discovered, such as the

American School of Oriental Research or Israel's Department of Antiquities, received their due. Other than El-Aksa within the Haram Esh-Sherîf, there were no mosques, and the positioning of the Haram visually preserved not Islamic history but a link with preceding biblical temples.

The map designated no synagogues, either. These communities did not evince biblical origins—their relation to the Bible was indirect, filtered through rabbinical traditions. In any case, they played no essential role in Wright and Filson's theological narrative. It is true that a reader could locate the Wailing Wall. However, Filson's commentary imagined this site as a vestige of the ancient temple of Jesus' day. The wall was clearly a better fit in a geography of Christian memory than it was a vital space constructed of Jewish longing, which at the time had been made perhaps more intense because Jews living in the new state of Israel were denied access. Elsewhere, a photograph of "The Wailing Wall" showed readers the place where Jews "lament the loss of their Temple." The photograph complemented Filson's emphasis on the same page that in the first phase of Christian history, before its triumphant spread to non-Jewish communities, Jesus' ministry was "deliberately limited to Jews."[77]

The historical sweep of these four maps, despite the title given the *Atlas*, extended beyond the limits of the Bible itself. From Jerusalem came "Old Testament" royal history that led to providential outcomes in "New Testament" Jesus (an echo of the Christian metaphor of Christ as King?) and subsequent expansion into "Christian times." This narrowing of narrative content and expansion of its range had been a familiar feature of many earlier Bible atlases. It found notable precedent in George Adam Smith, who explicitly related his geographical study of the Holy Land to an abiding concern with the missionary advancement of Christianity.[78]

In sum, Wright and Filson's *Atlas*, despite its powerful synthesis of new historical and archaeological knowledge, still evoked its kinship with earlier sacred geographies. The toponymy of faith seemed strong. Maps and explanations reaffirmed and reiterated Christian constructions of the Bible, implanted places and events in the land associated with its narratives, and brought the social spaces of Christian devotion, theology, and proclamation to the territory of the Holy Land. The *Atlas* staked a broad intellectual and Christian-oriented, Bible-centered claim to the past of Palestine.[79] And it tacitly aligned its picture of biblical origins with American values and emergent narratives of Zionism. It would be some years before Israeli scholars produced a Bible atlas that in its Jewish and Zionist assumptions would rival the embedded theological and political perspectives of the Wright and Filson project.[80]

Jack Nowse took the measure of Jacob's Well and relived "the old Bible scenes." Jack Finegan mapped the places where these "things were preached and done." Lyman Coleman sought to win souls to God. Wright and Filson advanced a crusade of biblical archaeology, and so charted the course of a Bible truly understood and its events truly mapped, its Christian story truly told. In particular ways, each conjured up holy lands for Americans at home, and their maps implied not only enormously thoughtful erudition, but the many livings brought to the territory called holy.

Epilogue
A *Touch of the Real*

While G. Ernest Wright was preparing the 1956 edition of *The West-minster Historical Atlas to the Bible*, he was at work on an essay that had been commissioned a few years earlier by editors of the *National Geographic Magazine*. "I think the money in this project is wonderful," Wright wrote to his teacher, William Foxwell Albright, while express-ing misgivings. Magazine editors had rejected his first attempt as too technical. They were not expecting an archaeological history of Pales-tine, Wright surmised, but what was for him a distasteful "series of stories of archaeologists at work proving the Bible!"[1]

Nevertheless, Wright revised his work—and took the money, which he dutifully shared with Albright. The result was a sophisticated version of that which had been refused, and, like the *Westminster Atlas*, in accord with the biblical archaeological crusade that Wright was so avidly pursuing. Illustrated with maps and ten stunning full-color paintings by Henry J. Soulen, the essay, or perhaps a *National Geographic* editor, announced that archaeologists had combined science and shrewd deduction to "paint an ever clearer picture of life in Biblical days."[2] Wright himself characterized the piece as telling a story of how excava-tions had

> shed a brilliant new light on the wandering herdsmen who gave the world three of its great faiths—Judaism, Christianity, and Islam—as well as its most influential religious document, the Bible.

The artist enlivened Wright's text with paintings of Bible scenes, some of which depicted narrative events. Soulen imbued his paintings with historical rectitude and utter realism—life carefully imagined from the details of text and ground, from the Bible and excavations. Like Wright, Soulen had been to the places he painted. "By camel, by car, and afoot," an editor noted, Soulen had "visited and sketched most of the places immortalized in Scripture." He had studied countless archaeological reports as well as pottery to come up with his renderings. Together, archaeologist–biblical scholar Wright and painter Soulen offered reassurance as to the Bible's reliability. They guided surrogate travels to Holy Land spaces constructed of archaeological science, biblical memory, theology, and romance. They retold the biblical story that was now illuminated—never challenged—by the archaeologist's spade and materialized in the visual fantasy of oil paintings that were "as accurate as the latest archaeological studies can make them."[3]

Real history, revitalized Bible, real place, fantasy of the real enabled by imaginative art and scientific inquiry—these are motifs that have run through the various holy land spaces I have described in previous chapters. The impulse to invent this particular scrubbed-up Holy Land seems genetically coded by now. It is embedded in the DNA of American society, dispersed in new generations of travelers who seek a touch of the real in their recreated holy lands, and in publishers who feed the insatiable hunger. Even in the twenty-first century.

At a recent gathering of religion scholars, publisher HarperSanFrancisco and authors John Dominic Crossan and Jonathan Reed, backed by the Society of Biblical Literature, publicly celebrated the "birthday" of a new book, *Excavating Jesus*.[4] Taking turns at the podium, Crossan and Reed spoke to their assembled colleagues, maintaining in the artifice of public presentation the claim of their book, that Reed, an archaeologist, and Crossan, a textual scholar, had worked independently before integrating their results. Reed showed slides of the "top ten" archaeological discoveries; Crossan "excavated" the redactional layers of New Testament narrative. Together, as the front cover of their book proclaimed, they offered "key discoveries for understanding Jesus and his world." In the darkness of the slide presentations, an editor from HarperSanFrancisco, a subsidiary of HarperCollins, slipped up to the raised platform and set a single copy of the celebrated book on the speakers' table. As the lights went up, a somewhat embarrassed Crossan acknowledged the gesture as being "from our sponsor."

Writers of ad copy, of course, were less hesitant. Crossan and Reed, they announced, presented "for the first time exact visual recreations of 1st century sites according to modern archeological findings."[5] Readers of the book's dust jacket were invited to join this "fascinating and highly readable journey . . . as you walk with two of the world's foremost experts in the footsteps of Jesus." The Society of Biblical Literature, a partner with HarperSanFrancisco's parent company in publishing major reference works, contributed (or permitted) an effusive program note. The live presentation, convention-goers were told, would provide "a breathtaking visual tour of Jesus' world and a dramatic picture of his life as a divinely mandated, Torah-based opposition to the injustice that was the Kingdom of Rome."[6]

Both book and public celebration seem a familiar blend of American marketing savvy, scholarly inquiry, imaginative synthesis of information, and desire to lay hold of the "real" Jesus. The authors of *Excavating Jesus* walk in the great company of scholarly and popular investigators, mostly assembled since the nineteenth century, who sought to find the original, historical Jesus. They searched for the man unadorned by legend, the godly teacher before fervent faith and temporal power had transformed him into the formidable Savior of the World. For Crossan and Reed, Jesus, an observant Jewish peasant, actively resisted the repressive, urbanizing, and commercializing kingdom of Rome by preaching the "kingdom of God, a call for distributive justice on earth."[7]

If this Jesus seems a little like a contemporary American progressive social critic, the quest for him is also contemporary, a matter of longing today to experience a Holy Land of biblical yesterday. *Excavating Jesus* assembles forensics, non-technical explanations, photographs, and full-color paintings to carry readers through the layers of earth and text and time to the land where Jesus lived and died. The book depicts the geographical setting and social environment of authentic Jesus activity, as reconstructed by Crossan and Reed, of course. They are tour guides who winsomely and lightly bear considerable scholarly authority.

I use the term "tour guide" advisedly. Crossan and Reed present a masterfully crafted narrative, figuratively digging down through the stone and mortar shrines of Eastern Orthodox and Roman Catholic devotion, leading their readers to pre-church sites of Jesus and the movement he inspired. They close in on Jesus as he really was. But they also uncover the focal points of geopiety, those beguiling realities that lie beneath the soil of modern Israel. Readers are encouraged to imagine the village where Jesus was born, the house in Capernaum where he may have tarried, the place he was buried, all carefully distinguished from later ecclesiastical overlay, the *in*authentic "Holy Land" created out of elaborated Christian piety. Did the Emperor Constantine build a royal mausoleum at the actual site of Jesus' burial, the authors ask? Well, he surely transformed dusty Palestine into a Christian Holy Land of shrine and monument. Nonetheless,

> we think that along with St. Peter's House in Capernaum [earlier rendered more ambiguously as a place of early Christian, perhaps Peter's, habitation] the Holy Sepulcher in Jerusalem is one of the few Christian holy sites with any credibility.

Similarly, Crossan and Reed bypass the Roman Catholic shrines of Nazareth and show their readers the "first-century Jewish hamlet . . . Jesus' Nazareth," the tiny village that was home to Jesus and where all families, though poor, were "observantly Jewish." It was a town of no religious discord, where families

> presumably . . . circumcised their sons, celebrated Passover, took a day from work on the Sabbath, and valued the traditions of Moses and the prophets.[8]

Nazareth is a place stripped down to its original first-century dimensions, necessarily—Crossan and Reed are clear about this—a matter of interpreting excavated ground and analyzed text. Yet Nazareth is iconic. It is an idealized and idyllic hamlet, a unitary space, an "entirely Jewish" village in an ethnically and geographically bounded "Jewish homeland," a town in which there was no "religious discord." In effect, Crossan and Reed create affective geography. They map value-laden space constructed out of Jesus' assigned presence-in-absence, Christian attachments to Jesus, and desire for the "real." In short, the authors employ imaginative and sophisticated scholarship to create a new version of that ancient trek to the places where God's turn toward human need actually occurred.

Artwork is integral to the journey. Twelve paintings by Balage Balogh, said to be the "best archaeological artist in Israel today," offer "historically accurate recreations of first-century sites," according to the dust jacket. There is as much desire as history here. Or perhaps it is Holy Land fantasy enabled by a meticulously constructed "real" that is obviously representational.

For example, Balogh depicts the economically deprived, peasant, all-Jewish hamlet of Nazareth without a trace of any discomforting features that would have been associated with actual poverty. For all its professed realism and historical accuracy, which one should not doubt, the painting also draws upon the conventional vocabulary of the picturesque Holy Land. A bucolic cluster of rectangular one-story houses, all in good repair, cling to a verdant hillside. Little plots of green and brown suggest orderly cultivation of the earth; in the foreground, vineyard workers labor near cutaway bedrock used for crushing grapes. The scene suggests appealing industry and evokes a nostalgic kinship with these agrarian people living close to the soil. A fieldstone wall to the right, in perfect repair, holds back the soil of terraced vineyards. Its pleasing S-curve frames the main composition and visually balances gentle hills that roll off into inviting promise. There is no sign of dirt, thirst, ill health, or tattered clothing. Nothing of hardscrabble poverty. The caption reads simply "Reconstruction of First-Century Nazareth." A painting positioned on the opposite page depicts "Twenty-First-Century Nazareth" from the identical vantage point. In the foreground, that same hillside slopes toward the town, arid and uncultivated. On the right, a wall of coarser, slightly neglected fieldstone curves away into the distance. The Basilica of the Annunciation dominates the modern cityscape—the Christianized Holy Land. The wall seems a harbinger of antiquity, a call to uncover that more authentic Holy Land of biblical memory that lies beneath the soil of modernity and abandonment.

A smaller version of the painting of first-century Nazareth converts this romanticized landscape into calculated illustration. Details, such as collection vats and Galilean-made storage jars, are identified by numbers superimposed on the image. It is still an idealized Holy Land scene, but controlled by historical rectitude and the excavators' desire for artifacts of the quotidian "real." Here, the authors tell their readers, is the "hometown of Jesus."[9]

Other paintings sometimes evoke Gospel narratives in the manner of older travelogues, that is, by direct allusion to Scripture. Balogh renders Capernaum, for example, the "site most frequently associated with Jesus' ministry," in two paintings. One depicts a typical courtyard house in the town, neatly arranged and showing no signs of unskilled construction or disrepair. Here one is to imagine "the simple peasant life of a Galilean family," explain Crossan and Reed. The authors point out feature number five, a flat roof, as being made of "thatch and mud as presumed in Mark 2, where friends of the paralytic 'dig through' the roof to lower him to Jesus." A second view of the town is as a fisherman might have seen it from his boat every working day. The low-lying village, fishers at work on the lake, some on shore mending nets, townspeople mingling along the open shoreline, all blend in a Holy Land of untroubled ordinariness. Of course Balogh relied on the excavators of ground and text. But the image also suggests Christian social space, an accumulation of devotion and Bible study that has made this particular place into something evocative and lived, mentally focused on Christian response. Like many a painting and postcard before, the image recalls the Gospel stories of Jesus' life among fishers turned "fishers of men." The perspective, Capernaum viewed from inside a typical "Galilean boat," invites active participation. It is as though one is actually sitting in the boat, perhaps standing and drawing a net, perhaps with Jesus himself. That is not too far from the intertextual reality of explanation and illustration. Crossan and Reed tell us that the painting shows a vessel exactly like that which was recently discovered by archaeologists. The artifact is surely "unlikely" to have been "the actual boat used by Jesus," they assure us. Nevertheless, elsewhere they state that "it could certainly hold thirteen people" and is now "usually called the 'Jesus Boat.'"[10] At the least, authors and painter distance themselves from such unscholarly enthusiasm for holy relics. At the same time, they give it voice as well, and so allow it to thrive amidst their own search for the realistic "Reconstruction of First-Century Capernaum."

It is perhaps sufficient to note the strength and persistence of such vernacular piety in creating idealized holy lands, even if only raised to consciousness by sly allusion. Biblical scholars continue to play a role in the old story. If not a model, then a photograph. If not a photo, then a map. If not a map, then a painting. If not these, then assemblages of Holy Land knowledge shaped for political relevance. All desire to convey a touch of the real, while all enable a fantasy of a real-imagined place of surrogate travel.

Notes

Introduction

1. See <http://www.inisrael.com/holyland/model.html> (accessed March 8, 2002).

2. The term "geopiety" was coined by John Kirkland Wright in his *Human Nature in Geography* (Cambridge, Mass.: Harvard University Press, 1965). Cited in Lester Vogel, *To See a Promised Land: Americans and the Holy Land in the Nineteenth Century* (University Park: Pennsylvania State University Press, 1993), 7–8.

3. Ruth Kark, ed., *The Land That Became Israel: Studies in Historical Geography* (New Haven: Yale University Press, 1990), 21. In the same volume, note Yehoshua ben-Arieh, "Perceptions and Images of the Holy Land," 37–53.

4. See especially Moshe Davis, *America and the Holy Land*, With Eyes toward Zion 4 (Westport, Conn.: Praeger, 1995); Jehuda Reinharz and Anita Shapira, eds., *Essential Papers on Zionism* (New York: New York University Press, 1996); Samuel Halperin, *The Political World of American Zionism* (Detroit: Wayne State University Press, 1961).

5. Vogel, *Promised Land*, 216. Among other resources, see Yehoshua ben-Arieh, *The Rediscovery of the Holy Land in the Nineteenth Century* (Jerusalem: Magnes, 1979); Davis, *America and the Holy Land*; Gershon Greenberg, *The Holy Land in American Religious Thought, 1620–1948: The Symbiosis of American Religious Approaches to Scripture's Sacred Territory* (Lanham, Md.: University Press of America, 1994).

6. Cullen Murphy, "Travel: Hallowed Ground," *Atlantic Monthly* 276, no. 6 (1995): 54–62.

7. There is as yet no comprehensive treatment of these vernacular products and propagators of Holy Land consciousness. John Davis emphasizes visual representations in *The Landscape of Belief: Encountering the Holy Land in Nineteenth-Century American Art and Culture* (Princeton, N.J.: Princeton University Press, 1996).

8. "City of Jerusalem. Site Dedicated with Most Unique and Interesting Ceremonial Rites in the Presence of Thousands," *World's Fair Bulletin* 4, no. 10 (August 1903): 38.

9. Terry Eagleton, *Ideology: An Introduction* (New York: Verso, 1991); John Thompson, *Studies in the Theory of Ideology* (Berkeley and Los Angeles: University of California Press, 1984).

10. Edward Soja, *Thirdspace: Journeys to Los Angeles and Other Real-and-Imagined Places* (Oxford: Blackwell, 1996).

11. Soja, *Thirdspace*, 311.

1. Lakeside at Chautauqua's Holy Land

1. "A Summer at Chautauqua," *The Tribune Monthly* 2, no. 9 (September 1890): 76.

2. "Palestine Park Tour: A Unique Presentation of the Bible Story in Three Dimensions," Department of Religion, Chautauqua Institution, undated.

3. Franklin B. Laundry, *Guide Book for a Walking Tour of Palestine Park* (Chautauqua, N.Y.: Chautauqua Institution, 1985). A 1997 brochure announces lectures by

Presbyterian minister William P. Lytle entitled "Palestine Park: A Journey through Biblical Times." The bookstore sells audio tapes of lecture tours led in 1995 by Dr. Noel Calhoun, a Presbyterian minister and longtime Chautauquan.

4. D. H. Post, "Chautauqua," *Harper's New Monthly Magazine* 59 (June–November 1879): 353–54. See Lester Vogel, "Staying Home for the Sights: Surrogate Destinations in America for Holy Land Travel," in *Pilgrims and Travelers to the Holy Land,* Studies in Jewish Civilization 7, ed. Bryan F. Le Beau and Menachem Mor (Omaha, Neb.: Creighton University Press, 1996), 251–67.

5. John Sears (*Sacred Places: American Tourist Attractions in the Nineteenth Century* [New York: Oxford University Press, 1989]) has investigated places of natural wonder as sites where tourism and quests for sacred space converge.

6. Leon H. Vincent, *John Heyl Vincent: A Biographical Sketch* (New York: Macmillan, 1925), 69–79. Leon Vincent drew on his uncle's travel diaries for this account. Other biographical materials may be found in Sarah Knowles Bolton, "The Rev. John H. Vincent, D.D.," included in Bolton's *How Success Is Won: Twelve Biographies of Successful Men* (Boston: D. Lothrop, 1885); Edward Albert Trimmer, "John Heyl Vincent: An Evangelist for Education" (Ed.D. diss., Columbia University, 1986); Theodore Flood, "Old Chautauqua Days," *Chautauquan* 131, no. 5 (August 1891): 560–93; *John Heyl Vincent, February 23, 1832–May 9, 1920,* Commemorative Exercises, August 1, 1920 (Chautauqua, N.Y.: Chautauqua Institution, 1920); Jesse Lyman Hurlbut, *The Story of Chautauqua* (New York: G. P. Putnam's Sons, 1921), 11–26; *American National Biography,* vol. 22 (New York: Oxford University Press, 1999), 372–73.

7. Hurlbut, *Story of Chautauqua,* 13–14; Kate F. Kimball, "Leaves from the Life of Bishop John H. Vincent. I. The Palestine Class: A Unique Experiment in Pedagogy," *Chautauquan* 72, no. 14 (December 1913): 273–77. See the first of Vincent's many published aids for Sunday school instruction, *Little Footprints in Bible Lands; or, Simple Lessons in Sacred History and Geography for the Use of Palestine Classes and Sabbath Schools* (New York: Carlton and Porter, 1861).

8. L. Vincent, *John Heyl Vincent,* 75–76.

9. Kimball, "Leaves from the Life," 277.

10. See Vincent's introduction to Jesse Lyman Hurlbut, *Manual of Biblical Geography: A Text-Book on Bible History* (Chicago: Rand McNally, 1884), vi–vii.

11. Hurlbut, *Story of Chautauqua,* 16–18. See John Heyl Vincent, *Curiosities of the Bible: Pertaining to Scripture Persons, Places, and Things, Comprising Prize Questions and Answers, Bible Studies and Exercises Founded upon and Answered in the Bible . . . with Many Reference Tables and Maps* (New York: E. B. Treat, 1875). This book was enormously popular and underwent revisions and at least twelve printings through 1908. See also Vincent, *Biblical Exploration; or, How to Study the Bible* (New York: Hunt and Eaton, 1877).

12. Hurlbut, *Story of Chautauqua,* 18–21.

13. Kenneth O. Brown, *Holy Ground: A Study of the American Camp Meeting* (New York: Garland, 1992); Melvin Easterday Dieter, *The Holiness Revival of the Nineteenth Century* (Metuchen, N.J.: Scarecrow, 1980).

14. Lewis Miller, introduction to *The Chautauqua Movement,* by John Heyl Vincent (Boston: Chautauqua, 1886), 5. The book's appendix offers a valuable compendium of information drawn directly from newspapers published for participants

during the first decade of Chautauqua's summer sessions. See also R. M. Warren, *Chautauqua Sketches: Fair Point and the Sunday School Assembly* (Buffalo, N.Y.: H. H. Otis, 1878) and "A Summer at Chautauqua," *Tribune Monthly* 2, no. 9 (September 1890; New York: Tribune Association). See also F. P. Noble, "Chautauqua as a New Factor in American Life," *New England Magazine*, n.s., 2 (1890): 90–101.

15. J. H. Vincent, *Movement*, 260–62, a summary drawn from official sources, perhaps among them G. L. Westgate, *Official Report of the National Sunday-School Teachers' Assembly, Held at Fair Point, Chautauqua County, N.Y., on the Borders of Chautauqua Lake, August 4–18, 1874* (New York: Sunday School Union, 1875).

16. J. H. Vincent, *Movement*, 256–57.

17. Theodore Morrison, *Chautauqua: A Center for Education, Religion, and the Arts in America* (Chicago: University of Chicago Press, 1974); Richard Kenneth Bonnell, "The Chautauqua University: Pioneer University without Walls, 1883–1898" (Ph.D. diss., Kent State University, 1988); John Harrison Thornton, "Chautauqua: Adventure in Popular Education" (typescript in Chautauqua Institution Archives, no date).

18. J. H. Vincent, *Movement*, 4, 5–6. The principles of education amounted to ethical standards for what today might be called a justly ordered capitalist and democratic society, at least for those included within its cultural purview. "Popular education must tend to a better understanding between the classes of society, causing the poor to honor wealth won by honest ways of work, by skill and economy; to despise wealth and winners of wealth, when greed and trickery gather the gold; to honor knowledge and a taste for knowledge, whether it be clad in fine linen or in linsey-woolsey; to hate with resolute and righteous hatred all sham and shoddy, all arrogance and pretentiousness; to avoid struggles between capital and labor, and to promote, in all possible ways, the glorious brotherhood of honesty, sympathy and culture, a culture that addresses itself to all sides of a man's nature." J. H. Vincent, *Movement*, 9.

19. Lester Vogel, *To See a Promised Land: Americans and the Holy Land in the Nineteenth Century* (University Park: Pennsylvania State University Press, 1993).

20. Troy Messenger, *Holy Leisure: Recreation and Religion in God's Square Mile* (Minneapolis: University of Minnesota Press, 1999). One of Vincent's contemporaries made a superficial comparison between the two camp meeting sites: Warren, *Chautauqua Sketches*, 7.

21. The entire speech is reprinted verbatim in J. H. Vincent, *Movement*, 301–308.

22. Hurlbut, *Story of Chautauqua*, 198–99.

23. Racial categories infused with judgments of value and status were widely accepted at the time, and reinforced by standard instructional works such as Heinrich Kiepert, *A Manual of Ancient Geography* (London: Macmillan, 1881). Kiepert drew upon the Bible to delineate the cultural and physiognomic branches of human "stock," the Hamitic, Semitic, and Aryan. Kiepert believed that the last-named "family," though the youngest, excelled "all the rest not only in the early maturity of its language, but also in historical importance. Since the palmy days of Greece and Rome it has been the most active promoter of the advance of human culture, as in modern times it is the only one that is always progressing and expanding" (11).

24. All quotations from J. H. Vincent, *Movement*, 303–308.

25. Hurlbut, *Story of Chautauqua*, 199.

26. Ibid.

27. Ibid., 201–202.

28. See John Davis, *The Landscape of Belief: Encountering the Holy Land in Nineteenth-Century American Art and Culture* (Princeton, N.J.: Princeton University Press, 1996), 53–72.

29. Westgate, *Official Report*, 124.

30. All quotations are from "Perrine's Landscape Views of Palestine," *Chautauqua Assembly Daily Herald* 4, no. 14 (August 16, 1879): 1.

31. Hurlbut, *Story of Chautauqua*, 66–67. See "Lessons in Orientalism," *Chautauqua Assembly Daily Herald* 5, no. 17 (August 17, 1880): 1. Another news article noted Ostrander's "distinction of teaching the first classes in Biblical geography at Chautauqua" (Adelaide L. Westcott, *Chautauqua Scrapbook*, vol. 2, 1888–1895 [Chautauqua Institution Archives], 94). This is one of three paste-up albums of mementos collected beginning in 1877, the year that Ms. Westcott first attended the Chautauqua Assembly.

32. "Lessons in Orientalism," 1. See William Brown, *The Tabernacle and Its Priests and Services Described and Considered in Relation to Christ and the Church* (Edinburgh: W. Oliphant, 1871). This work was so popular that it went through three editions, each revised and enlarged, between 1871 and 1874.

33. J. H. Vincent, *Movement*, 267.

34. From the *Chautauqua Assembly Daily Herald* of 1876, reprinted in Wythe's obituary, *Chautauquan Weekly* 1, no. 15 (December 6, 1906): 1.

35. Vincent recorded such lecture titles as "Illustrations of Biblical Life," "Oriental Illustrations," and "Bible Manners and Customs Illustrated" during the first years of the Chautauqua Assembly (J. H. Vincent, *Movement*, 274, 278, 280). For similar theatrical presentations at the Ocean Grove camp meetings, see Messenger, *Holy Leisure*, 114–20.

36. "Lessons in Orientalism," 1.

37. Vogel, *Promised Land*, stresses this discord between expectations and actual experiences in Palestine. Mark Twain gave a characteristically wry and insightful account in *The Innocents Abroad; or, The New Pilgrim's Progress* (Hartford, Conn.: American Publishing Co., 1869; reprint, New York: New American Library, 1966).

38. A notice of her appearance at Chautauqua in 1891 called her "an old Chautauqua favorite" who had most recently lectured there in 1889. *Chautauqua Assembly Daily Herald* 16, no. 17 (August 10, 1891): 1.

39. Quoted from the *Melbourne Argus* and reprinted in Lydia (Mary Olive) Mamreoff von Finkelstein Mountford, *The Life Sketch of Lydia (Mamreoff) von Finkelstein* (New York, 1908), 48.

40. Apparently privately published, with some photographs taken by the famous Mormon artist Charles E. Johnson, Mountford's *Life Sketch* was a theatrical piece in its own right. It was self-promoting and self-effacing, imbued with moralisms, hagiology, and passionate Christian evangelism. Of course, it announced the author's availability for lectures. See also "Madame Lydia von F. Mountford," *Relief Society Magazine*, February 1, 1921, 71–77, a report which offers some additional biographical details and recalls her 1897 and 1898 lectures among the Mormons in Utah (and incidentally, her baptism into the Church of Jesus Christ of Latter-Day Saints). See also "Madam

Mountford," *Latter-Day Saints' Millennial Star*, February 17, 1898, 105–107. Madame Mountford died in 1917, alone and practically penniless, though still lecturing before church audiences in Lakeland, Florida. An obituary was published in the *Lakeland Evening Telegram*, Wednesday, March 22, 1917.

41. *Ocean Grove Record*, August 16, 1884, 2. Quoted in Messenger, *Holy Leisure*, 116.

42. Messenger, *Holy Leisure*, 120.

43. Lydia Mamreoff von Finkelstein Mountford, *Jesus Christ in His Homeland*, Lectures Stenographically Recorded (Cincinnati: Jennings and Graham, 1911), 7. See also Mountford, *The King of the Shepherds and His Psalm*, Lecture Stenographically Recorded (Cincinnati: Abingdon, 1914).

44. Westcott, *Chautauqua Scrapbook*, vol. 3, *1896–1907*, 86.

45. Mountford, *Jesus Christ in His Homeland*, 15–17, 60.

46. Westcott, *Scrapbook*, vol. 1, *1874–1887*, 1.

47. "Oriental Life," *Chautauqua Assembly Daily Herald* 4, no. 11 (August 13, 1879): 7.

48. J. H. Vincent, *Movement*, 275. See Westgate, *Official Report*, 124.

49. "Fair Point Gleanings," *Chautauqua Assembly Daily Herald* 12 (August 8, 1876): 1.

50. Westcott, *Scrapbook*, vol. 1, 4.

51. Westcott, *Scrapbook*, vol. 1, 1.

52. Hurlbut, *Story of Chautauqua*, 66.

53. An advertisement in the *Chautauqua Assembly Daily Herald* 10, no. 13 (August 15, 1885): 8, offered the services of an "Oriental Bureau" to Chautauquans who wanted to secure "novel lectures and choice entertainments."

54. See Gerald Ackerman, *American Orientalists* (Paris: ACR, 1994); Edward Said, *Orientalism* (New York: Vintage, 1978); Dorsey R. Kleitz, "Orientalism and the American Romantic Imagination" (Ph.D. diss., University of New Hampshire, 1988); Sharra L. Vostral, "Imperialism on Display: The Philippine Exhibition at the 1904 World's Fair," *Gateway Heritage* 13, no. 4 (1993): 18–31.

55. In introducing an elegant book of pressed flowers (Harvey B. Green, *Wild Flowers from Palestine* [Lowell, Mass.: Dumas, 1900]), Selah Merrill, a pioneering archaeologist and the American consul in Jerusalem, declared that despite Palestine's being in ruins, its recurrent crop of wildflowers were nevertheless redolent of the "living Christ." Profiting from such sentiments, businessman Robert Morris successfully sold hundreds of "Holy Land Cabinets" filled with geomemorabilia—bits of wood, stone, earth, shells, coins, flowers, flasks of water, seeds, and other holy objects made to speak "good and comfortable words." Robert Morris, *Catalogue of Holy Land Cabinets* (Chicago: Hazlitt and Reed, 1868).

56. Davis, *Landscape of Belief*, 94.

57. "Oriental Life," 5.

58. "Palestine Park Tour: A Unique Presentation of the Bible Story in Three Dimensions," brochure, c. 1995, courtesy of Mrs. Noel (Cynthia Ann) Calhoun, Jr.

59. *Chautauquan Daily* (weekend edition, July 9–10, 1994): 7.

60. In 1879, Wythe constructed a second model of Jerusalem and presented it to the Methodist camp meeting at Ocean Grove, N.J., where he was a resident (Messenger, *Holy Leisure*, 100). The Chautauqua assembly at Round Lake, near Albany, New

York, had its own version of Palestine Park and a Jerusalem model during the 1880s, possibly also built with Wythe's assistance. A *Round Lake Journal* article (whose date is unknown) claimed that the model would give "clearer, stronger, and more accurate impressions of this Holy Land, and enable one to read and study the Gospel History of its cities and villages, and of the country in its entirety, than any map, raised model, or painting" (Chautauqua Institution Archives).

61. Hurlbut, *Story of Chautauqua*, 13–14.

62. Kimball, "Leaves from the Life," 277.

63. Vincent, introduction to Hurlbut, *Biblical Geography*, viii–ix.

64. "Services in the Tabernacle," *Deseret Evening News*, January 10, 1898, courtesy of Lois Archuleta, Salt Lake City Public Library.

65. Vincent, introduction to Hurlbut, *Biblical Geography*, vi.

66. Westgate, *Official Report*, 271–72, reprinted in J. H. Vincent, *Movement*, 264–65. The claim that knowledge of geography and topography gives biblical history its vividness and power was common to various printed guides to Palestine Park and Bible atlases of the time. It still appears in today's much abbreviated guide to the Park.

67. Westgate, *Official Report*, 272.

68. Jesse Lyman Hurlbut, *Guide Book to Palestine Park* (Chautauqua, N.Y.: Chautauqua Institution, 1920; revised and enlarged from the 1907 edition prepared by Alfred E. Barrows).

69. Ibid., 5–6.

70. Ibid., 22–23.

71. See, for example, "Jerusalem Freed from the Moslem Yoke," *Current Opinion* 64 (January 1918): 6–7; John P. Peters, "Jerusalem Redeemed: The Ancient Holy City and Its Place in History," *American Review of Reviews* 57 (January 1918): 47–58. One famous photograph of Allenby's triumphal entry into the city was widely published and sold in sets of stereographs. See "Spiritual Meaning of Jerusalem's Deliverance," *Literary Digest* 36 (February 16, 1918): 30–31, particularly the caption on p. 31: "As the Crusaders did General Allenby leads his victorious forces on foot into the captured city of Jerusalem." See also "Jerusalem the Holy City, Goal of the Crusaders, Rescued For Ever from the Turks," a stereographic view of Jerusalem published by Realistic Travels, London, c. 1918.

72. Until World War II successive editions of the guidebook left these underlying assumptions unchanged. In 1936, David Taylor acknowledged the lessened importance of Palestine Park among Chautauqua's programs, but noted its continued value as a teaching aid and memorial to "the men whose early vision produced it." David Taylor, *Guide Book to Palestine Park* (Chautauqua, N.Y.: Chautauqua Institution, 1936), 5.

73. See Davis, *Landscape of Belief*, 90–92.

74. *Chautauqua Institution, Palestine Park, and Fair Point: Views* (Cleveland, Ohio: Johnson and Mentzel, Photographers, 1875), Chautauqua Institution Archives.

75. Ironically, the publisher did not get his biblical geography right. The crowd covers not Moab, but most of what the model represented as north of the Dead Sea to the slopes of Mt. Hermon, from the Mediterranean in the west, and to the Transjordan in the east.

76. Westcott, *Chautauqua Scrapbook*, vol. 1, 13. See also *Souvenir of Lake Chautauqua: Photo-Gravures* (New York: A. Witteman, 1895).

77. Stereograph published by L. E. Walker, Warsaw, N.Y., c. 1880.

78. "Jerusalem," *Chautauqua Assembly Herald* 4, no. 15 (August 18, 1879): 5.

79. J. H. Vincent, *Movement*, 263.

80. For this dialectical way of considering fantasy and the "real," I am indebted to Roland Boer, *Knockin' on Heaven's Door: The Bible and Popular Culture* (London: Routledge, 1999), 61.

81. Umberto Eco, *Travels in Hyperreality: Essays* (San Diego, Calif.: Harcourt Brace Jovanovich, 1986), 8.

82. "The Children's Pilgrimage," *Chautauqua Assembly Daily Herald* 3 (August 19, 1878): 1.

83. Hurlbut, *Story of Chautauqua*, 47.

84. Mary Frances Bestor Cram, *Chautauqua Salute: A Memoir of the Bestor Years* (Chautauqua, N.Y.: Chautauqua Institution, 1990), 85–92.

85. John Heyl Vincent, introduction to *A Reading Journey through Chautauqua*, by Frank Bray (Chautauqua, N.Y.: Chautauqua Institution, 1905, unpaginated introduction). A map of the Chautauqua grounds marked sites described in the text of the imaginary tour. Biblical Palestine had been so thoroughly integrated into the sense of Chautauqua as a Holy Land tourist destination that it could be represented on Bray's tour simply by "Dead Sea" and "River Jordan" (17).

86. Edwin P. Booth, "A Biography of Dr. Jesse Lyman Hurlbut," transcript of a lecture delivered at the Chautauqua Institution, July 16, 1965, 9 (Chautauqua Institution Archives). At the time, Booth was Professor of Historical Theology Emeritus at the Boston School of Theology.

87. Davis, *Landscape of Belief*, 92.

88. Rachel L. Dithridge, "Upon the Little Hills of Palestine," dedicated to Jesse Lyman Hurlbut, c. 1930 (privately printed). Used by permission of the Chautauqua Institution Archives.

89. Rudyard Kipling, *Abaft the Funnel* (New York: B. W. Dodge, 1909), 188. The passage appeared in an 1890 essay published in the Indian paper *The Pioneer Mail*, and is quoted in Vogel, *Promised Land*, 237.

90. William M. Thomson, *The Land and the Book: or, Biblical Illustrations Drawn from the Manners and Customs, the Scenes and Scenery, of the Holy Land*, vol. 2 (New York: Harper and Brothers, 1859), xv.

91. Booth, "A Biography of Dr. Jesse Lyman Hurlbut," 8–9.

2. Starred and Striped Holy Lands

1. *Prospectus of the Jerusalem Exhibit Company* (St. Louis: The Jerusalem Exhibit Co., 1903). Copy courtesy of Lester Vogel, Library of Congress.

2. Walter B. Stevens, *The Forest City* (St. Louis, Mo.: N. D. Thompson, 1904), 27. A souvenir record of the convention was published as *The Cruise of the Eight Hundred to and through Palestine: Glimpses of Bible Lands* (New York: Christian Herald, 1905).

3. *World's Fair Authentic Guide* (St. Louis, Mo.: Official Guide Co., 1904), 60.

4. The official contemporary accounts are Mark Bennitt, ed., *History of the Louisiana Purchase Exposition* (St. Louis, Mo.: Universal Exposition Publishing Co., 1905); David R. Francis, *The Universal Exposition of 1904* (St. Louis, Mo.: Louisiana

Purchase Exposition Co., 1913). For later treatments, see Robert Rydell, *All the World's a Fair: Visions of Empire at American International Expositions, 1876–1916* (Chicago: University of Chicago Press, 1984); Rydell, *World of Fairs: The Century-of-Progress Expositions* (Chicago: University of Chicago Press, 1993); Sharra L. Vostral, "Imperialism on Display: The Philippine Exhibition at the 1904 World's Fair," *Gateway Heritage* 13, no. 4 (1993): 18–31; Lester Vogel, "Staying Home for the Sights: Surrogate Destinations in America for Holy Land Travel," in *Pilgrims and Travelers to the Holy Land*, Studies in Jewish Civilization 7, ed. Bryan F. Le Beau and Menachem Mor (Omaha, Neb.: Creighton University Press, 1996), 251–67.

5. *World's Fair Authentic Guide*, 7.

6. From President McKinley's last public address, as quoted on the frontispiece of Bennitt, *Louisiana Purchase Exposition*.

7. Bennitt, *Louisiana Purchase Exposition*, xii. In "The World's Fair at St. Louis," a special issue of *World's Work* (vol. 8, no. 4 [August 1904]), essayists celebrated a commonly accepted narrative of innocence. America enjoyed cultural progress by means of science, technology, the arts, education, and territorial expansion, all led by people of a self-evidently superior nation and race which bore the "white man's burden" (5188) to provide uplift for the darker peoples of the world.

8. Martha R. Clevenger, ed., *"Indescribably Grand": Diaries and Letters from the 1904 World's Fair* (St. Louis, Mo.: Missouri Historical Society, 1996), 14.

9. Edmund Clarence Stedman, "Hymn of the West," composed by invitation of the Exposition management, quoted in Bennitt, *Louisiana Purchase Exposition*, 129.

10. Francis, *Universal Exposition*, 600–601.

11. *World's Fair Authentic Guide*, 147–48.

12. *Prospectus*, 23.

13. Ibid., 24.

14. "Pride of the Fair: What to See in Jerusalem," Rare Books and Special Collections, St. Louis Public Library, St. Louis, Mo.

15. Francis, *Universal Exposition*, 600–601. A brochure advertising Heagle's lectures is housed at the Harvard Semitic Museum, according to Ruth Kark, "Jerusalem in New England," *Ariel* 69 (1987): 53.

16. Bennitt, *Louisiana Purchase Exposition*, 720; Francis, *Universal Exposition*, 600–601; George W. Shepherd, "The Oriental Exposition Company's Great Religious Exhibit," *American Illustrated Methodist Magazine* 9 (April 1903): 353–55; Thomas R. MacMechen, *The True and Complete Story of the Pike and Its Attractions* (St. Louis, Mo.: Division of Concession Stand Amusements, Louisiana Purchase Exhibition, 1904), 31–32.

17. John Walker, "The Walled City of Jerusalem—in St. Louis," *Cosmopolitan* 37 (September 1904): 576.

18. *Prospectus*, 27.

19. Ibid., 13.

20. Barbara Kirshenblatt-Gimblett, "A Place in the World: Jews and the Holy Land at World's Fairs," in *Encounters with the 'Holy Land': Place, Past, and Future in American Jewish Culture*, ed. Jeffrey Schandler and Beth S. Wenger (Philadelphia: National Museum of American Jewish Studies; Center for Judaic Studies, University of Pennsylvania; University of Pennsylvania Library, 1997), 74.

21. *Dictionary of American Biography*, vol. 11 (New York: Charles Scribner's Sons, 1933), 111; *National Cyclopaedia of American Biography*, vol. 9 (New York: J. T. White,

1899), 506. See also James W. Lee, *The Geography of Genius* (New York: Fleming H. Revell, 1920), xi–xxiv.

22. John Heyl Vincent, James W. Lee, and R. E. M. Bain, *Earthly Footsteps of the Man of Galilee* (New York: N. D. Thompson, 1894). This book led Lee to write a similar one aimed at young readers, *The Romance of Palestine* (Atlanta, Ga.: D. E. Luther, 1897). He included a memoir of his trip to Palestine in *Geography of Genius*, 15–28. His *The Self-Interpreting Bible* (Boston: J. Q. Adams, 1898) included many of Bain's photographs.

23. "It is only a question of time," Lee wrote, "when Western civilization that has grown out of the Christian religion is destined to take the place of the civilization of Mohammed." Vincent, Lee, and Bain, *Earthly Footsteps*, 177, caption for photograph, "Moslem Ovens, Nazareth."

24. Lee, *Geography of Genius*, xiii.

25. Ibid. Lee's address at the Louis and Clark Exposition in 1905 would be reported as taking "Portland [Oregon] by storm." Ibid., xix.

26. *National Cyclopaedia of American Biography*, vol. 9, 506.

27. Lee, *Geography of Genius*, xiv.

28. Shepherd, "Great Religious Exhibit," 353–55. See also his "Jerusalem at the World's Fair," *American Illustrated Methodist Magazine* 9 (February 1903): 237–40.

29. *Prospectus*, 29–30.

30. Ibid., 6, 10.

31. Ibid., 6–10.

32. Ibid., 13–14.

33. *World's Fair Souvenir Album of Jerusalem Published by Direction of Jerusalem Exhibit Co.* (St. Louis, Mo.: Towers, 1903).

34. "City of Jerusalem. Site Dedicated with Most Unique and Interesting Ceremonial Rites in the Presence of Thousands," *World's Fair Bulletin* 4, no. 10 (August 1903): 34–39. The quotations that follow are taken from transcriptions of speeches as reported in the *Bulletin*.

35. The words are from "It Came upon the Midnight Clear" by Edmund H. Sears (1810–76) and Richard Willis (1819–1900).

36. Clevenger, *"Indescribably Grand,"* 30.

37. Clippings file, Louisiana Purchase Exhibition, microfilm, p. 121, Rare Books and Special Collections, St. Louis Public Library, St. Louis, Mo.

38. Vogel, "Staying Home for the Sights," 261–62.

39. Clippings file, 121–24.

40. Nelson B. Wadsworth, *Set in Stone, Fixed in Glass: The Great Mormon Temple and Its Photographers* (Salt Lake City: Signature, 1992), 308. Johnson's Holy Land prints and negatives, many of which feature Madame Mountford, are housed in Archives and Special Collections, Brigham Young University, Provo, Utah.

41. Lydia Mamreoff von Finkelstein Mountford, *The Life Sketch of Lydia Mamreoff von Finkelstein* (New York: n.p., 1908), 35.

42. Clippings file, 121–24.

43. Clevenger, *"Indescribably Grand,"* 100–101. All quotations from Philibert's diary are taken from Clevenger's transcription.

44. T. W. Ingersoll, "Moorish Street in 'City of Jerusalem,'" in *Views of the Louisiana Purchase Exposition* (St. Paul, Minn.: Published by the artist, 1904).

45. Clevenger, *"Indescribably Grand,"* 33.

46. Ibid., 30.

47. "The Great Passion Play," a brochure published by the Elna M. Smith Foundation, Eureka Springs, Ark. (no date), inside front cover. See also <http://www.greatpassionplay.com> (accessed March 8, 2002).

48. Glenn Jeansonne, *Gerald L. K. Smith: Minister of Hate* (Baton Rouge: Louisiana State University Press, 1988); *American National Biography*, vol. 20 (New York: Oxford University Press, 1999), 186–87; Leo P. Ribuffo, *The Old Christian Right: The Protestant Far Right from the Great Depression to the Cold War* (Philadelphia: Temple University Press, 1983).

49. According to the Arkansas Roadside Travelogue's Web page, the use of National Crusade funds came to light in a 1970 tax audit. See <http://www.aristotle.net/~russjohn/sacpro.html> (accessed March 8, 2002).

50. Charles F. Robertson, "Interesting Story Comes from Statue Completion," *Carroll County Tribune*, November 25, 1981, A9.

51. Elna M. Smith and Charles F. Robertson, eds., *Besieged Patriot: Autobiographical Episodes Exposing Communism, Traitorism, and Zionism from the Life of Gerald L. K. Smith* (Eureka Springs, Ark.: Elna M. Smith Foundation, 1978).

52. "Gerald L. K. Smith Dies at 78," *Arkansas Gazette*, April 16, 1976, 3A.

53. "Berlin Wall Section Unveiled at Great Passion Play," *The Ozarks Mountaineer*, March 1992. Copy in Eureka Springs Historical Museum, Eureka Springs, Arkansas.

54. After Jesus' burial in the play, smoke and devilish red light emanate from the sealed tomb—a sign of Christ's descent into hell. With solemnly stentorian speech, Jesus binds the power of Satan. Later, many in the audience applauded at Jesus' resurrection, and again when he ascended into the heavens. The evening's performance ended with a benediction and a postlude rendering of Handel's "Hallelujah Chorus." One man told me, close to tears, that he felt the "Real Presence" that night.

55. Calvin Trillin, "U.S. Journal: Eureka Springs, Ark., The Sacred Projects," *New Yorker*, July 26, 1969, 76.

56. *The Great Passion Play*, video recording (Eureka Springs, Ark.: The Elna M. Smith Foundation, 1992).

57. *Arkansas Gazette*, May 4, 1991, 8B.

58. Issues of the *Cross and Flag* provide ample evidence of Smith's obsessive battles. The following excerpts are typical. "The Code of the Enemies of Christian America" listed misdeeds of vaguely identified conspirators, including distributors of drugs and pornography; those who "teach millions to hate the Army, the Marines, and the Navy"; those who are "sadistically determined to mongrelize our race" with enforced school integration and classroom sex education; and "every important worldwide Jewish organization [that] has organized a boycott against the portrayal of Christ's last week on earth as presented in Eureka Springs, Arkansas on Mount Oberammergau" (*Cross and Flag* 28, no. 12 [March 1970]: 2 and 21). On Vatican moves to improve Jewish-Christian relations, Smith wrote in the same issue of *Cross and Flag*, "My definition of better relationships between Jews and Christians is for the Christians to call on the Jews to accept the Christ whom their ancestors crucified and whom they still continue to deny" (26). The Reverend Buddy Tucker, whom Smith had personally chosen to preside over his funeral, eulogized Smith as an embattled hero in a cosmic drama. "All issues sink into insignificance," Tucker proclaimed, "compared to the

battle between the Christ and the anti-Christ Jew, and these same forces which nailed our Savior to the cross are now attempting to crucify Him anew by evaporating our civilization which grew out of His Name and His Blood." Quoted on the Arkansas Roadside Travelogue's Web page.

59. Fundraising flyer, Elna Smith Foundation. Archives, Arkansas History Commission, Little Rock, Arkansas. Place File "Eureka Springs," folder "Elna M. Smith Foundation, The Great Passion Play." Cited by Arkansas Roadside Travelogue.

60. The general goals for each of the exhibits reflect policies that have evolved in discussions and practical experience over time, said David Brown, ordained minister in the Four Square Gospel Church and Supervisor of the New Holy Land Tours. The tabernacle, as a written summary stated, should "help everyone see God's eternal plan of salvation." Bethlehem is to "present a more authentic birth place," and the walk with Peter around Galilee, "one of our key areas," needs to be a "strong first person presentation helping our guests find out what life with Jesus was like from Peter's perspective." Golgotha and the Tomb are to clarify the "central truth of the Gospel concerning the substitutionary work of Jesus on the cross." People should be encouraged "to rejoice in the resurrection through song." The last stop, the Mount of Olives, "must be able to tie into the rest of the tour, ending with the hope of Jesus' promised return." Typescript, courtesy of David Brown.

61. Besides the Bible, Mr. Shaw cited as his main source Doug Solsbery, *The Tabernacle: God's Royal Palace—Why?* (published by the author, 1989).

62. Jim Borden and Ken Rank, *The Tabernacle*, video recording (Eureka Springs, Ark.: The Elna M. Smith Foundation, 1994).

63. Unless otherwise indicated, my observations pertain to the video recording. The on-site tours are similar in conceptual content to the video version, but lack some of the made-for-video enhancements, such as simulated animal sacrifice.

64. Later in the tour, Mr. Ludig provided explicit eschatological significance for these white garments. "But you know," he told his visitors, "there's coming a day for each and every one of us like it did for the High Priest. We're going to have to lay aside everything of the world. And all you have left is a garment that Christ gave you on the first day. You're gonna be in that garment on the day of judgment when you step through that veil and stand before the throne of God. My prayer for you and me of course is that all of our robes will be whiter than snow, 'cause if they are, we are glory bound." Giving an impish shrug, clasping his hands together, Ludig gleefully shouted, "Hallelujah!"

65. In the on-site study tour I observed, Christ equivalence was asserted even before visitors passed into the tabernacle's outer court. Summarizing the daily sacrifices that were regularly offered in ancient times, Mr. Ludig—his white-robed arms outstretched in crucifix form—told his audience that at the end of each day, the officiating priest would announce, "It is finished." Then Ludig paused for dramatic emphasis. "That comes from the Talmud," he said. "I seem to recall finding it somewhere else," he added with feigned puzzlement and a knowing glance to his audience.

66. The Messianic (Jewish) Christian connection is strongly attested at the park. The Smith Foundation announces on its Web site Ludig's "Jewish" credentials. During my visit, I witnessed festivities at which a costumed member of the Great Passion Play cast confessed to the crowd that he was a Messianic Jew, a Jew converted to Christ, but still a Jew, a Christian Jew. A few onlookers nearby softly murmured, "Hallelujah." He taught people how to say *shabbat shalom* (it was a Friday evening) and then sounded the

shofar, thoroughly absorbing what was to him an ancient act of Jewish ritual into his newly found evangelical "lifting up the Lord."

67. In live performance of the Great Passion Play, Herod's flamboyant entry into Jerusalem has been cut. But Salomé the archetypal temptress remains. Under Herod's mocking interrogation, Jesus is silent, and Salomé, in a remarkably sexualized scene, tries to arouse some response. Smoothing the tunic collar of Jesus' robe, she places her hand seductively on his chest, fussing with his garments like a flirting lover. "Perhaps he is only shy," she says, gazing intently into his eyes. Jesus doesn't answer her either. He is, after all, stronger than King Herod, woman, or Satan.

3. Parlor Tours of the Holy Land

1. Edwin P. Booth, "A Biography of Dr. Jesse Lyman Hurlbut," transcript of a lecture delivered at the Chautauqua Institution, July 16, 1965, 8 (Chautauqua Institution Archives).

2. *Palestine through the Stereoscope: A Tour Conducted by Jesse Lyman Hurlbut and Charles Foster Kent* (New York: Underwood & Underwood, 1914), xviii. Hurlbut's earlier work carried the title *Traveling in the Holy Land through the Stereoscope* (New York: Underwood & Underwood, 1900; 2nd edition, 1905). Kent might have been drawn to Chautauqua by his teacher, William Rainey Harper. While a professor at Yale College, and later as president of the University of Chicago, Harper was deeply involved in Chautauqua's educational programs. Shailer Mathews, a New Testament scholar from Harper's Chicago faculty, followed suit and by 1912 was director of religious work, a post he held for twenty-one years. At the invitation of Mathews, Kent offered his first course of lectures at Chautauqua in 1914.

3. Harold F. Jenkins, *Two Points of View: The History of the Parlor Stereoscope* (Uniontown, Pa.: E. G. Warman, 1973).

4. Oliver Wendell Holmes, an enthusiastic promoter of the new technology, cited his vicarious tour of Palestine in "Sun-Painting and Sun Sculpture," *Atlantic Monthly* 8 (July 1861): 13–29. A brief history of the stereograph industry is included in Samuel Batzli, "The Visual Voice: 'Armchair Tourism,' Cultural Authority, and the Depiction of the United States in Early Twentieth-Century Stereographs" (Ph.D. diss., University of Illinois at Urbana-Champaign, 1997).

5. Photographic negatives belonging to Underwood & Underwood and its successor, the Keystone View Co., are now part of the Keystone-Mast Collection in the California Museum of Photography, University of California at Riverside.

6. Letter, Kent to William Rainey Harper, January 28, 1892. Harper, Presidents' Papers, 1889–1925, box 51, folder 6, University of Chicago Archives. All subsequent references to Kent's letters draw upon this same archive.

7. The journals were *Hebrew Student* and *Hebraica*, both launched while Harper was a member of the Yale faculty. The first was founded in 1882 to promote the study of biblical languages. In time it would become *Biblical World*. The more technical *Hebraica*, established in 1884, was later continued as the *American Journal of Semitic Languages and Literature*.

8. *Dictionary of American Biography*, vol. 10 (New York: Charles Scribner's Sons, 1932), 343; *National Cyclopaedia of American Biography*, vol. 24 (New York: J. T. White, 1935), 28–29; *American National Biography*, vol. 12 (New York: Oxford University

Press, 1999), 593–94; "Charles Foster Kent, B.A., 1889," *Obituary Record of Graduates of Yale University* 84 (1924–25): 1380–83.

9. A 1901 letterhead of the American Institute of Sacred Literature lists members of the "Council of Seventy," most of whom were leading biblical scholars and members of theological faculties throughout the United States. University of Chicago Archives, Divinity School, Office of the Dean, Records 1890–1942, box 7, folder 2.

10. *Journal of Biblical Literature* 45 (1926): v.

11. *Chautauquan Daily* 39, no. 2 (July 4, 1914): 3; *Chautauqua Quarterly* 24, no. 1 (January 1924): 5.

12. *Dictionary of American Biography*, vol. 10, 343.

13. Edgar J. Goodspeed, "Abroad in the Nineties," chapter 5, p. 1. Typescript. Edgar J. Goodspeed Papers, box 19, folder 1, University of Chicago Archives.

14. Kent to Harper, January 28, 1892.

15. Kent to Harper, May 1, 1892. A member of an expedition led by Robert Morris, mentioned in chapter 1 as the maker and seller of museum-like Holy Land cabinets, made it plain that Western travelers presumed the right to travel unencumbered. "We came to this country to *direct*, not to be directed," he wrote (emphasis in original). "Free men at home, we could little brook the tyranny to which parties are subjected who put themselves into the power of the professional dragoman [who] orders them about with a nonchalance that would be admirable were it not insufferable." Robert Morris, ed., *Bible Witnesses from Bible Lands* (New York: The American Holy-Land Exploration, 1874), 109.

16. Olga Tufnell, "Excavator's Progress. Letters of F. J. Bliss, 1889–1900," *Palestine Exploration Quarterly* 97 (1965): 118.

17. Kent to Harper, March 12, 1892; May 1, 1892.

18. Kent to Harper, May 1, 1892.

19. Kent to Harper, March 12, 1892. At the end of his travels, Kent reflected that "a glorious commentary on the Bible has been this six weeks sojourn in the land of its birth." Kent to Harper, May 1, 1892.

20. Kent to Harper, May 1, 1892. Unless otherwise indicated, all subsequent quotations from Kent's correspondence are taken from this letter.

21. Charles Foster Kent, "Rhythm in Hebrew Life and Literature," *Chautauquan Daily* 39, no. 6 (July 9, 1914): 2.

22. Charles Foster Kent, *Biblical Geography and History* (New York: Charles Scribner's Sons, 1900).

23. Charles Foster Kent, *Descriptions of One Hundred and Forty Places in Bible Lands* (New York: Underwood & Underwood, 1900, rev. 1911). A promotional letter claimed that "at Professor Kent's earnest solicitation," the publisher had sent a photo team along a route mapped out by Kent so that everyone could see "the very places he himself had explored at great expenditure of time, labor, and money." The writer added that the cost of this stereograph tour ($25.00) was "not one hundredth part of what an actual bodily trip would cost." David Lyon Papers, Harvard University Archives, HUG 1541.5.3, folder "U."

24. Kent, *Biblical Geography*, v and vii.

25. Kent, *Biblical Geography*, 22, and *One Hundred and Forty Places*, viewing position 2, "Ruins of ancient Tyre," 16. See also *Biblical Geography*, 250, and *One Hundred and Forty Places*, viewing position 121, "Shattered Remnants of old Chorazin's

buildings," 86, which for Kent confirmed Jesus' prophetic condemnation of the city (Matthew 11:21).

26. Kent, *Biblical Geography*, 240, and *One Hundred and Forty Places*, viewing position 116, "Nazareth, the home of Jesus," 183.

27. Kent, *One Hundred and Forty Places*, viewing position 117, "Ancient Fountain of the Virgin where Mary came for water," 84. See Kent, *Biblical Geography*, 241.

28. Kent, *Biblical Geography*, 243–44, and *One Hundred and Forty Places*, viewing position 118, "Baptizing in the Jordan," 84.

29. Kent, *Biblical Geography*, 259.

30. Ernest Renan, *Vie de Jésus*, 5th ed. (Paris: Callman-Levy, 1863), published in English as *The Life of Jesus*, trans. Charles E. Wilbour (New York: Carleton, M. Levy Freres, 1869).

31. Henry Van Dyke, *Out-of-Doors in the Holy Land: Impressions of Travel in Body and Spirit* (New York: Charles Scribner's Sons, 1908), 6–7.

32. Selah Merrill, *Galilee in the Time of Christ* (Boston: Congregational Publishing, 1881), 134, 94, 74.

33. Kent, *Biblical Geography*, 253. See Kent, *One Hundred and Forty Places*, viewing position 123, "Fishermen mending nets where the Jordan enters the Sea of Galilee," 87. In the 1920s, as theologians put forth Jesus' preaching as a model for social reform in industrialized America, Kent added his voice to public policy debates. Kent stressed changes in the heart as the true foundation for the genuinely "fraternal community" so needed in the stressful times of labor and social unrest. Charles Foster Kent, "Jesus' Social Plan," in *Christianity and Problems of Today*, The Bross Lectures of 1921 (New York: Charles Scribner's Sons, 1922), 29–45.

34. These and other biographical details are drawn from "Dr. Jesse L. Hurlbut," *Chautauquan Weekly* 51 (September 30, 1926): 2; Edwin Booth, "A Biography of Dr. Jesse Lyman Hurlbut," transcript of a lecture delivered at the Chautauqua Institution, July 16, 1965 (Chautauqua Institution Archives); *Dictionary of American Biography*, vol. 9 (New York: Charles Scribner's Sons, 1932), 424–25; *National Cyclopaedia of American Biography*, vol. 11 (New York: J. T. White, 1901), 392.

35. For example, *Outline Normal Lessons* (New York: Hunt and Eaton; Cincinnati: Cranston and Curts, 1885); *Studies in the Four Gospels* (Cincinnati: Jennings and Graham, 1880); *Studies in Old Testament History* (New York: Hunt and Eaton; Cincinnati: Cranston and Curts, 1890); *Revised Normal Lessons* (New York: Hunt and Eaton; Cincinnati: Cranston and Curts, 1893); *Hurlbut's Story of the Bible* (Oakland, Calif.: Smithsonian, 1904); *Hurlbut's Handy Bible Encyclopedia* (Philadelphia: J. C. Winston, 1906); *Teacher Training Lessons* (Nashville: Abingdon, 1908). The *Manual of Biblical Geography: A Text-Book on Bible History* (Chicago: Rand McNally, 1884), like many of Hurlbut's books, was revised and reprinted frequently for many years after his death.

36. Jesse Lyman Hurlbut, *Traveling in the Holy Land through the Stereoscope: A Tour Personally Conducted by Jesse Lyman Hurlbut* (New York: Underwood & Underwood, 1900).

37. Harry Emerson Fosdick, *A Pilgrimage to Palestine* (New York: Macmillan, 1927).

38. Bertha Hurlbut Doughtery, "Jesse Lyman Hurlbut," transcript of a lecture delivered at Hurlbut Memorial Church, Chautauqua Institution, June 28, 1959, 1, Chautauqua Institution Archives.

39. "The Underwood Travel System—What It Is," promotional brochure. Copy in David Lyon Papers, folder "U." See Jenkins, *Two Points of View*.

40. Batzli, "Visual Voice." See also John Davis, *The Landscape of Belief: Encountering the Holy Land in Nineteenth-Century American Art and Culture* (Princeton, N.J.: Princeton University Press, 1996), 74–76.

41. Lester Vogel, *To See a Promised Land: Americans and the Holy Land in the Nineteenth Century* (University Park: Pennsylvania State University Press, 1993), 12.

42. Hurlbut and Kent, *Palestine through the Stereoscope*, 251.

43. Letter, George Barton to his family, April 1, 1903. Bryn Mawr College Archives, Bryn Mawr, Pa.

44. Hurlbut and Kent, *Palestine through the Stereoscope*, 114.

45. Hurlbut and Kent, *Palestine through the Stereoscope*, 293–94. A complete set of the stereographs with commentary is housed in Archives and Manuscripts, Pitts Theology Library, Emory University, Atlanta, Georgia.

46. Davis, *Landscape of Belief*, 75–76.

47. Hurlbut and Kent, *Palestine through the Stereoscope*, xiv, xvi, 3–4. In his *One Hundred and Forty Places*, Kent instructed reader-viewers on the proper use of the stereoscope so as to "lose all consciousness of one's immediate bodily surroundings and to gain a distinct experience of being in the place itself." To achieve this illusion, home viewers were instructed to sit so that a "strong steady light" fell over their shoulders directly onto the image and to hold the hood of the stereoscope "close against the forehead, shutting out all sight of your immediate surroundings" (10). The theory of the stereoscopic experience, repeatedly offered by authors and publishers alike, was early expressed by Oliver Wendell Holmes, the inventor of the hand-held viewer, in "The Stereoscope and the Stereograph," *Atlantic Monthly* 3 (June 1850): 738–48.

48. Hurlbut and Kent, *Palestine through the Stereoscope*, xvii–xviii.

49. Edward Said, *Orientalism* (New York: Vintage, 1978).

50. Hurlbut and Kent, *Palestine through the Stereoscope*, 3–4.

51. Ibid., 27.

52. Ibid. The photograph also appears in Kent, *One Hundred and Forty Places*, viewing position 21, p. 29, with abbreviated commentary. In the previous view, viewing position 20, pp. 28–29, "Mizpah from the southwest, an old centre of Hebrew history," Kent followed a similar strategy, recalling epic events from Samuel to that "valiant Jewish patriot Judas Maccabeus."

53. Hurlbut and Kent, *Palestine through the Stereoscope*, 21–23.

54. Carroll Smith-Rosenberg, *Disorderly Conduct: Visions of Gender in Victorian America* (New York: Alfred A. Knopf, 1985).

55. Hurlbut and Kent, *Palestine through the Stereoscope*, 22.

56. Ibid., viewing position 78, 237–38.

57. Cathy Gutierrez, "Representation and Ideals: The Construction of Women in Travel Literature to the Holy Land," in *Pilgrims and Travelers to the Holy Land*, Studies in Jewish Civilization 7, ed. Bryan F. Le Beau and Menachem Mor (Omaha, Neb.: Creighton University Press, 1996), 187.

58. Mary R. Melendy, *Perfect Womanhood for Maidens—Wives—Mothers: A Book Giving Full Information on all the Mysterious and Complex Matters Pertaining to Women* (Chicago: Monarch Book, 1903), 7, frontispiece, 64.

59. See also viewing position 73, "Gideon's battlefield and Hill of Moriah," Hurlbut and Kent, *Palestine through the Stereoscope*, 225–26, a rather undistinguished photograph of the countryside described as a "miserable group of mud-houses." Hurlbut and Kent sweep it all away to recall "the palaces of King Ahab and his nobles, which stood on this very height. What a view they had!" (225). See, further, viewing position 45, "The plain of the Jordan . . . from the ruins of ancient Jericho," 143–45.

60. Hurlbut and Kent, *Palestine through the Stereoscope*, 176–77.

61. Mark Twain, *The Innocents Abroad or the New Pilgrim's Progress* (New York: New American Library, 1966), 393.

62. Gutierrez, "Ideals and Representation," 186.

63. Hurlbut and Kent, *Palestine through the Stereoscope*, 105–107; Kent, *One Hundred and Forty Places*, viewing position 124, "Bethany, the home of Jesus' friends," 87–88. See Kent, *Biblical Geography*, 251.

64. See Charles Rosen and Henri Zerner, *Romanticism and Realism: The Mythology of Nineteenth-Century Art* (New York: Viking, 1984), 51. See also Barbara Novak, *Nature and Culture: American Landscape and Painting, 1825–1875* (New York: Oxford University Press, 1981); Bert Yaeger, *The Hudson River School* (New York: Smithmark, 1996).

65. Hurlbut and Kent, *Palestine through the Stereoscope*, 2–3.

66. Ibid., 5. See Hurlbut and Kent, *Palestine through the Stereoscope*, viewing position 31, pp. 101–102, overlooking Jerusalem from the Mount of Olives: "If the head of that Arab up here on the balcony were not directly in the way, we might see the Pool of Bethesda, where Jesus cured a cripple" (102).

67. Hurlbut and Kent, *Palestine through the Stereoscope*, 53.

68. Ibid., 143–44.

69. Kent, *One Hundred and Forty Places*, 87–88.

70. Hurlbut and Kent, *Palestine through the Stereoscope*, 105.

71. Ibid., 106; Kent, *One Hundred and Forty Places*, 88.

72. Hurlbut and Kent, *Palestine through the Stereoscope*, 45–47.

73. F. E. Peters, *Jerusalem: The Holy City in the Eyes of Chroniclers, Visitors, Pilgrims, and Prophets from the Days of Abraham to the Beginnings of Modern Times* (Princeton, N.J.: Princeton University Press, 1985).

74. See Hurlbut and Kent, *Palestine through the Stereoscope*, viewing position 16, "Jerusalem, the City of the Great King," 54–56, another view of the "Noble Sanctuary," which evokes the "sacred history that clusters around that rocky hill," none of it having to do with Islam. Also viewing position 17a, "St. Stephen's Gate," 57–58, a photo of a Muslim procession headed for Neby Musa, a place some Muslims believed to be the site of Moses' burial. Hurlbut and Kent delegitimate the ritual by citing Scripture against it. They pass along a widely shared opinion that the ceremony is a late invention designed to compete with Easter. In a final gesture of dismissal, they remark that "Even though a non-Christian procession, it may remind us of the multitudes who went forth on Palm Sunday from the city, perhaps from that gate . . . to meet Jesus" (58).

75. Hurlbut and Kent, *Palestine through the Stereoscope*, 61.

76. Ibid., 62–63; Kent, *One Hundred and Forty Places*, 75.

77. Hurlbut and Kent, *Palestine through the Stereoscope*, 256–58.

78. See ibid., viewing position 95, "Ruins of ancient Tyre—wonderful fulfillment of prophecy," 273–75. Despite its one-time grandeur, "Tyre has been for centuries a

decayed, insignificant, poverty-stricken town, where a handful of fishermen [fishermen are pictured in the stereoptic photo] spread their nets on the ruins of its ancient splendor. . . . What a complete fulfillment of this prophecy [in Ezekiel 27] is seen here today" (274–75).

79. Hurlbut and Kent, *Palestine through the Stereoscope*, 258.

80. Ibid., 75–76.

81. Ibid., 9, 92, 202.

82. Ibid., 258. Independently of Hurlbut, Kent was even harsher in assessing this photographic view. "The unkempt native at the right is sitting on the pedestal of one of the pillars that stood in front of the synagogue. To-day this spot is a scene of absolute loneliness and desolation." Kent, *One Hundred and Forty Places*, viewing position 121, 86.

83. Hurlbut and Kent, *Palestine through the Stereoscope*, 119–21.

84. Ibid., 32–35. See also Kent, *One Hundred and Forty Places*, 52.

85. See Philip J. King, *American Archaeology in the Mideast: A History of the American Schools of Oriental Research* (Philadelphia: American Schools of Oriental Research, 1983).

4. Landscapes of Democracy

1. Philip J. King, *American Archaeology in the Mideast: A History of the American Schools of Oriental Research* (Philadelphia: The American Schools of Oriental Research, 1983), 27–53.

2. Bruce Kuklick, *Puritans in Babylon: The Ancient Near East and American Intellectual Life, 1880–1930* (Princeton, N.J.: Princeton University Press, 1996).

3. J. Henry Thayer, "Presidential Address," *Journal of Biblical Literature* 14 (1895): 16.

4. Neil Asher Silberman, *Digging for God and Country: Exploration, Archeology, and the Secret Struggle for the Holy Land, 1799–1917* (New York: Alfred A. Knopf, 1982).

5. For the larger picture, see Edward L. Queen II, "Ambiguous Pilgrims: American Protestant Travelers to Ottoman Palestine, 1867–1914," in *Pilgrims and Travelers to the Holy Land*, Studies in Jewish Civilization 7, ed. Bryan F. Le Beau and Menachem Mor (Omaha, Neb.: Creighton University Press, 1996), 209–28; Lester Vogel, *To See a Promised Land: Americans and the Holy Land in the Nineteenth Century* (University Park: Pennsylvania State University Press, 1993), 185–211.

6. King, *American Archaeology*, 8–9. For a history of the American Palestine Exploration Society, see Warren J. Moulton, "The American Palestine Exploration Society," *Annual of the American Schools of Oriental Research* 8 (1926–27): 55–78.

7. Compatriot Eli Smith, also cited in Thayer's clarion call, accompanied Robinson on his first journey. Smith had been Robinson's student, was fluent in Arabic and local custom, and was a leading missionary to Beirut and explorer in his own right. Eli Smith, *Researches of the Rev. E. Smith and H. G. O. Dwight in Armenia: Including a Journey through Asia Minor and into Georgia and Persia, with a Visit to the Nestorian and Chaldean Christians of Oormiah and Salmas* (Boston: Crocker & Brewster, 1833).

8. Robinson's ideological conviction was evident when he became a moving force behind the *American Biblical Repository*, a journal of conservative biblical apologetics. Contributing authors, including Robinson, frequently opposed European historical

criticism and its few New England proponents, mostly Unitarians, who were undertaking biblical study with a decidedly non-traditional bent. The *Repository* provided conservative readings of the Bible and reports from missionary travelers and explorers as confirming evidence of orthodox theology and the Bible's historical accuracy.

9. Edward Robinson and Eli Smith, *Biblical Researches in Palestine, Mount Sinai, and Arabia Petraea: A Journal of Travels in the Year 1838*, 3 vols. (Boston: Crocker & Brewster, 1841), published concurrently in England and in Germany. An account of his second journey appeared as Edward Robinson, *Later Biblical Researches in Palestine and in the Adjacent Regions: A Journal of Travels in the Year 1852—Drawn Up from the Original Diaries with Historical Illustrations, with New Maps and Plans* (Boston: Crocker & Brewster, 1856). Subsequent editions removed some of the technical material and compressed the diaries into more manageable proportions.

10. Robinson and Smith, *Biblical Researches*, vol. 1, "Preface to the Original Work," vii. (Citations follow the 3rd ed., published as *Biblical Researches in Palestine and Adjacent Regions: A Journal of Travels in the Year 1838*, 2 vols. [Boston: Crocker & Brewster, 1868].)

11. Robinson and Smith, *Biblical Researches*, vol. 1, "Introductory," 31–32.

12. Silberman, *Digging for God and Country*, 46–47.

13. *Minutes of the New-York Historical Society*, February 8, 1863, cited in Jay G. Williams, *The Life and Times of Edward Robinson: Connecticut Yankee in King Solomon's Court* (Atlanta, Ga.: Society of Biblical Literature, 1999), 332. The main nineteenth-century biographical sources for Robinson are the eulogizing addresses of Henry B. Smith and Roswell D. Hitchcock in their *The Life, Writings, and Character of Edward Robinson, D.D., LL.D.* (New York: Anson D. F. Randolph, 1863). See also Silberman, *Digging for God and Country*, 37–47; *American National Biography*, vol. 18 (New York: Oxford University Press, 1999), 647–49.

14. John E. Smylie, "Protestant Clergymen and American Destiny: Prelude to Imperialism, 1865–1900," *Harvard Theological Review* 56 (1963): 297–311.

15. See chapter 1 above, pp. 39–40. Outselling Robinson and Smith's *Biblical Researches* by far, Thomson's book eventually appeared in over thirty editions. William M. Thomson, *The Land and the Book: or, Biblical Illustrations Drawn from the Manners and Customs, the Scenes and Scenery, of the Holy Land* (New York: Harper and Brothers, 1859).

16. Thomson, *Land and the Book*, vol. 1, 24. Some twenty years earlier, the Archbishop of York had marked the founding of the Palestine Exploration Fund with similar fanfares of British imperial and Christian rule. "This country of Palestine belongs to you and to me, it is essentially ours," he said. "It was given to the father of Israel in the words, 'Walk through the land in the length of it and in the breadth of it, for I will give it unto ye.' We mean to walk through Palestine, in the length and breadth of it, because that land has been given to us. It is the land from which comes news of our redemption. . . . It is the land to which we look with as true a patriotism as we do to this dear old England." *Palestine Exploration Fund Proceedings and Notes* (London, 1865–69), cited in Silberman, *Digging for God and Country*, 86.

17. Lyman Abbott, a nineteenth-century cleric and prolific writer, was typical of many who presumed that the privilege accorded to scientific rationality also justified the uninhibited exploration of Palestine. "We trust that the science of the nineteenth century," Abbott wrote of British excavations in Jerusalem, "may accomplish what the

armed piety of the twelfth century essayed in vain—the recovery of Jerusalem." Lyman Abbott, "The Recovery of Jerusalem," *Harper's New Monthly* 43, no. 254 (July 1871), 206. Nearly a half century later, newspapers, magazines, stereographs, and postcards, not to mention some biblical scholars, routinely celebrated the military capture of Jerusalem near the end of the war as an entirely justifiable restoration of the Holy Land to Christian rule. See, for example, an essay by prominent biblical archaeologist John P. Peters, "Jerusalem Redeemed: The Ancient Holy City and Its Place in History," *American Review of Reviews* 57 (January 1918): 47–58; "Spiritual Meaning of Jerusalem's Deliverance," *Literary Digest* 36 (February 1918): 31–32; and "Inheritors of Canaan," *Asia* 19 (December 1919): 1229–36, a photo essay which portrayed long-suffering biblical peoples witnessing "a dawn of promise" brought by British victory and its prospect of liberal governance. See further John H. Finley, *A Pilgrim in Palestine: Being an Account of Journeys on Foot by the First American Pilgrim after General Allenby's Recovery of the Holy Land* (New York: Charles Scribner's Sons, 1919); Charles W. Whitehair, "An Old Jewel in the Proper Setting: An Eyewitness's Account of the Reconquest of the Holy Land by Twentieth Century Crusaders," *National Geographic Magazine* 33, no. 10 (October 1918): 325–44.

18. "Middle East Diary of Isabel M. C. Church," March 28, 1868. Typescript, Olana State Historic Site, Hudson, New York. Cited by John Davis, *The Landscape of Belief: Encountering the Holy Land in Nineteenth-Century American Art and Culture* (Princeton, N.J.: Princeton University Press, 1996), 33.

19. *Dictionary of American Biography*, vol. 11 (New York: Charles Scribner's Sons, 1933), 524–25. See also *National Cyclopaedia of American Biography*, vol. 13 (New York: James T. White, 1906), 172–73.

20. William F. Lynch, *Narrative of the United States' Expedition to the River Jordan and the Dead Sea* (Philadelphia: Lea and Blanchard, 1849), 13–14. A competing account of the expedition, also seeking public fame for its author, appeared the same year under the editorship of E. P. Montague, *Narrative of the Late Expedition to the Dead Sea, from a Diary by One of the Party* (Philadelphia: Carey and Hart, 1849). Lynch and other early explorers receive colorful treatment in David Finnie, *Pioneers East: The Early American Experience in the Middle East* (Cambridge, Mass.: Harvard University Press, 1967). See also Silberman, *Digging for God and Country*, 51–62.

21. Selah Merrill, *East of the Jordan* (New York: Charles Scribner's Sons, 1881). Further biographical material is in the *Dictionary of American Biography*, vol. 12 (New York: Charles Scribner's Sons, 1933), 564–65; *Appleton's Cyclopaedia of American Biography*, vol. 4 (New York: D. Appleton, 1887–89), 307; *National Cyclopaedia of American Biography*, vol. 13 (New York: J. T. White, 1906), 218. Thayer mentioned a little-known Henry L. Van Dyck, who served as travel assistant and interpreter for Merrill's explorations.

22. Selah Merrill, *Ancient Jerusalem* (1908; reprint, New York: Arno, 1977); Merrill, *Galilee in the Time of Christ* (Boston: Congregational Publishing Society, 1881); Merrill, "Galilee," in *Picturesque Palestine, Sinai, and Egypt: With Numerous Engravings on Steel and Wood from Original Drawings by Harry Fenn and J. D. Woodward*, ed. Sir Charles W. Wilson (New York: D. Appleton, 1881), 287–358. Merrill wrote introductions to a children's book (Susan G. Knight, *Ned Harwood's Visit to Jerusalem* [Boston: Lathrop, 1888]) and a collection of flower specimens (Harvey B. Greene, *Wild Flowers from Palestine* [Lowell, Mass.: Dumas, 1880]).

23. Shalom Goldman, "The Holy Land Appropriated: The Careers of Selah Merrill, Nineteenth Century Christian Hebraist, Palestine Explorer, and U.S. Consul in Jerusalem," *American Jewish History* 85, no. 2 (June 1997): 151–72; Vogel, *Promised Land*, 157–69, 181–83.

24. Ruth Kark, *American Consuls in the Holy Land, 1832–1914* (Jerusalem: Magnes, Hebrew University, 1994), 138.

25. King, *American Archaeology*, 30.

26. Official policy statements may be found in *Journal of Biblical Literature* 20 (1901), iv–v.

27. Gerald P. Fogarty, S.J., *American Catholic Biblical Scholarship: A History from the Early Republic to Vatican II* (New York: Harper and Row, 1989); S. David Sperling, *Students of the Covenant: A History of Jewish Biblical Scholarship in North America* (Atlanta, Ga.: Scholars, 1992).

28. George Barton, *A Year's Wanderings in Bible Lands* (Philadelphia: Ferris and Leach, 1904), 141, 97, 233, 185–86. See also George Barton, *Archaeology and the Bible* (Philadelphia: American Sunday-School Union, 1916), which was published in many editions into the 1930s. Barton's letters, the basis for his book, may be consulted among the Barton Papers, Archives, Library of Bryn Mawr College, Bryn Mawr, Pennsylvania. For additional material, see George Aaron Barton, Papers, 1903–1942, University of Pennsylvania Archives, Philadelphia, Pennsylvania. Biographical sketches may be found in *National Cyclopaedia of American Biography*, current vol. D (New York: James T. White, 1934), 441–42; *Bulletin of the American Schools of Oriental Research* 87 (October 1942): 2–6; *Bryn Mawr Alumni Quarterly* 13, no. 3 (November 1919): 5–17; *American National Biography*, vol. 2 (New York: Oxford University Press, 1999), 291–92.

29. *Bulletin of the American Schools of Oriental Research* (hereafter *BASOR*) 6 (May 1922): 9. In 1911, David Lyon, an accomplished biblical scholar, Assyriologist, and archaeologist-curator of Harvard's Semitic Museum, explicitly acknowledged a common bond between tourist and scholar, both of whom sought "religious quickening" or "confirmation and elucidation of the Scriptures." David Lyon, "Archaeological Explorations of Palestine," *Journal of Biblical Literature* 30 (1911): 4. See also Lyon's undated illustrated lectures "Palestine and the Bible." These handwritten notes, like Hurlbut's and Kent's parlor tours, constructed memories of glorious biblical days in the light of, as a press release noted, "Palestine of today that is a living commentary on the Bible." David Lyon Papers, Harvard University Archives, box 1, folder "Palestine and the Bible." See also David Lyon, "Palestine, the Bible, and Archaeology," a handwritten manuscript later published in the *Boston Evening Transcript* (February 26, 1910), Lyon Papers, box 2. For biographical information, see *Dictionary of American Biography*, vol. 21, supplement 1 (New York: Charles Scribner's Sons, 1944), 518–19; "David Gordon Lyon: In Memoriam," *BASOR* 62 (April 1936): 2–4.

30. *BASOR* 1 (December 1919): 4. See also *BASOR* 2 (February 1920): 9.

31. James A. Montgomery, "The American School of Oriental Research," *Art and Archaeology* 7 (1918): 173. Albright shared Montgomery's desire to assert American primacy in Palestine research, to judge from comments in *BASOR* 11 (October 1923): 4; *BASOR* 12 (December 1923): 11–12. For biographical material on Montgomery, see Ephraim A. Speiser, "James Alan Montgomery (1866–1949)," *BASOR* 115 (October 1949): 4–8; *Dictionary of American Biography*, vol. 24, supplement 4 (New York: Charles Scribner's Sons, 1974), 594–96.

32. Albright had scant sympathy for those he viewed as driven by irrational passion to take up impractical ventures in Palestine. About a year after his arrival in Jerusalem, he reported that he had met a "poor, deluded American religious fanatic" (perhaps typical of the Christian millenarian colonists of the day) who had "sold his farm in Oklahoma and come to Palestine to invest in a fruit-farm!" Noting that economic realties were against the scheme, he concluded, "And still they come, Jews and Christians, following the same bubble which swept millions into eternity in the past." Albright to his mother, Zephine Viola Albright, June 3, 1921, courtesy of Leona Glidden Running.

33. See Leona Glidden Running and David Noel Freedman, *William Foxwell Albright: A Twentieth-Century Genius* (New York: Morgan, 1975); King, *American Archaeology*, 58, 63–84. Further biographical material may be found in David Noel Freedman, *The Published Works of William Foxwell Albright: A Comprehensive Bibliography* (Cambridge, Mass.: American Schools of Oriental Research, 1975), 3–40; "William Foxwell Albright," in *American Spiritual Autobiographies: Fifteen Self-portraits*, ed. Louis Finkelstein (New York: Harper, 1948), 156–81; *American National Biography*, vol. 1 (New York: Oxford University Press, 1999), 227–28.

34. Albright to Zephine Viola Albright, July 13, 1921, courtesy of Leona Glidden Running. However strong the appeal of science without borders might have been, harmonious academic exchange involved national competition, too. Albright responded to that melody as well, and wrote of it a year later in praising C. C. McCown's studies of Arab folk religion. McCown had followed in the path of Samuel Ives Curtis, Albright wrote, "whose pioneering work in this field placed American scholars under an obligation to continue the studies begun by their illustrious compatriot." *BASOR* 4 (September 1921): 4.

35. William Foxwell Albright, "Archaeological Discovery in the Holy Land," *Bibliotheca Sacra* 79 (1922): 402, 412, 418. See also Albright, "How to Study the Archaeology of Palestine," *BASOR* 52 (December 1933): 12–15.

36. William Foxwell Albright, "Rediscovering Ancient Palestine," *Sunday School Times* 65 (1923): 7.

37. William Foxwell Albright, *The Archaeology of Palestine and the Bible* (New York: Fleming H. Revell, 1932), 62.

38. William Foxwell Albright, *From the Stone Age to Christianity: Monotheism and the Historical Process* (Baltimore, Md.: Johns Hopkins Press, 1940; 2nd ed., Garden City, N.Y.: Doubleday, 1957), 32. All citations follow the second edition.

39. William Foxwell Albright, *Archaeology and the Religion of Israel* (Baltimore, Md.: Johns Hopkins Press, 1942; 5th ed., Garden City, N.Y.: Doubleday, 1967), 4.

40. Albright, "Archaeological Discovery," 402–403.

41. James Weinstein, *The Decline of Socialism in America, 1912–1925* (New York: Monthly Review, 1967), 74.

42. For example, Morris Hillquit and John Ryan, "Socialism: Promise or Menace?" *Everybody's Magazine* 29, no. 10 (October 1913): 482–89. The debate was continued in subsequent issues: 29, no. 11 (November 1913): 629–43; 29, no. 12 (December 1913): 816–31; 30, no. 1 (January 1914): 80–101; 30, no. 2 (February 1914): 225–41; 30, no. 3 (March 1914): 369–86; 30, no. 4 (April 1914): 529–42. See Gerald Birney Smith, "Making Christianity Safe for Democracy," *Biblical World*, n.s., 53 (1919): 3–13, 133–45, 245–58, 408–23, 493–507, 628–39.

43. Albright, *Religion of Israel*, 33.

44. "Science and Religion in a Changing World: Historical Religion and Scientific Thought," lecture delivered February 3, 1941. Albright Papers, American Philosophical Society, Philadelphia, Pa.

45. Mark Silk, "Notes on the Judeo-Christian Tradition in America," *American Quarterly* 36, no. 1 (spring 1984): 65–85. See Anthony Rhodes, *Propaganda* (New York: Chelsea House, 1976), for a number of Bible-based Christian images.

46. *Science, Philosophy, and Religion: A Symposium* (New York: Conference on Science, Philosophy, and Religion in Their Relation to the Democratic Way of Life, 1941).

47. Albright, *Stone Age*, 403.

48. Letter, Albright to Zephine Viola Albright, October 3, 1920, courtesy of Leona Glidden Running.

49. McCown had pursued this anthropological interest in local religion, as distinct from theology, during his missionary days in India. See Chester Charlton McCown, "New Year's among the Mohammedans of Calcutta," *Epworth Herald* 23 (1912): 5–7, 23, and "Muslim Shrines in Palestine," *Annual of the American Schools of Oriental Research*, vols. 2 and 3 (Philadelphia: American Schools of Oriental Research, 1923).

50. William Foxwell Albright, "Chester Charlton McCown: An Appreciation," in *An Indexed Bibliography of the Writings of Chester Charlton McCown* (Berkeley, Calif.: Howell-North Press, 1947, unpaginated). For further biographical information, see John Herbert Otwell, "In Memoriam Chester C. McCown," *Pacific School of Religion Bulletin* 37, no. 1 (March 1958): 2; Harland E. Hogue, *Christian Seed in Western Soil: Pacific School of Religion through a Century* (Berkeley, Calif.: Pacific School of Religion, 1965). Note also McCown, "Ninety Years of Faith and Freedom," typescript and audio recording of a lecture celebrating the faculty and history of the Pacific School of Religion. Special Collections, Library of the Graduate Theological Union, Berkeley, California.

51. Compare McCown's *The Genesis of the Social Gospel: The Meaning and Ideals of Jesus in the Light of Their Antecedents* (New York: Alfred A. Knopf, 1929) with Albright's *From the Stone Age to Christianity*. See also McCown, *The Ladder of Progress in Palestine: A Story of Archeological Adventure* (New York: Harper and Brothers, 1943).

52. George Adam Smith, *The Historical Geography of the Holy Land Especially in Relation to the History of Israel and of the Early Church* (London: Hodder and Stoughton, 1894).

53. McCown, letter, September 17, 1920, McCown Papers, Correspondence 1920–21, Archives, Pacific School of Religion, Berkeley, California. McCown called his lightly edited letters "annals" and "chronicles." He sent them from Palestine in 1920–21, 1929–31, and 1936, apparently as a record of his experiences, but they now bear no names of recipients.

54. Meat was scarce, auto transport unreliable or non-existent; drinking water had to be transferred into old petroleum tins, carted five minutes to the American School, and then stored in a large covered jar. The city had no sewage system, food costs, he complained, were very high, and cook Frau Stahel's culinary "German regime"—despite good breakfasts of porridge and soft-boiled eggs—was "enough to wreck any stomach." McCown, letter, October 9, 1920, McCown Papers.

55. McCown, letter, September 28, 1920, McCown Papers. See also the letters of November 6, 1920 (McCown felt repulsed by "gaudy altars and quarreling sects" in

Bethlehem, and preferred the open fields "where David drove his flocks and the shepherds watched on that 'glorious night'"); January 17, 1921 (seeing Nazareth in the moonlight would "make a poet of anyone," but the "next morning we had to come down to Nazareth as she is").

56. "On Foot in the Mountains of Judea," unfinished typescript, c. 1930, McCown Papers. Compare similar travel memoirs by McCown's University of Chicago teachers and colleagues. Shailer Mathews, "A Reading Journey through Palestine: Going Up to Jerusalem," *Chautauquan* 43, no. 6 (August 1903): 493–560; Edgar J. Goodspeed, "From Haifa to Nazareth," *Biblical World* 16 (1900): 407–13; also Edgar Goodspeed's unpublished work "Abroad in the Nineties," Edgar Goodspeed Papers, University of Chicago Archives, box 19, folder 1.

57. See Thomson, *Land and the Book*, and John Heyl Vincent, James W. Lee, and R. E. M. Bain, *Earthly Footsteps of the Man of Galilee* (New York: N. D. Publishing, 1894). For analysis of the latter, see Davis, *Landscape of Belief*, 77–88.

58. Besides Charles William Wilson, ed., *Picturesque Palestine, Sinai, and Egypt*, 2 vols. (New York: D. Appleton, 1881), see John Fulton, *The Beautiful Land, Palestine: Historical, Geographical, and Pictorial, Described As It Was and As It Now Is, along the Lines of Our Saviour's Journeys* (New York: T. Whittaker, 1891), and Edward Wilson, *In Scripture Lands: New Views of Sacred Places* (New York: Charles Scribner's Sons, 1895).

59. McCown, "Things Said and Done 1900 Years Ago," section 3, 19, unpublished typescript, 1952, McCown Papers. Another manuscript, dated 1928, surveyed recent study of Palestine under the rubric "The Fifth Gospel Written in the Dust of the Holy Land." McCown Papers, letter box, section R. See further McCown, "Climate and Religion in Palestine," *Journal of Religion* 7 (1927): 5–6, 520–39; and "The Geographical Conditioning of Religious Experience in Palestine," in *The Story of the Bible Today and Tomorrow*, ed. H. R. Willoughby (Chicago: University of Chicago Press, 1947), 231–46.

60. Henry Van Dyke, *Out-of-Doors in the Holy Land: Impressions of Travel in Body and Spirit* (New York: Charles Scribner's Sons, 1908).

61. McCown, *Genesis of the Social Gospel*, 361–62, 147–48. The last reference is in a chapter entitled "The Dawn of Democracy." See also McCown, *The Promise of His Coming* (New York: Macmillan, 1921).

62. McCown, *Genesis of the Social Gospel*, 156.

63. The political debates carried on in the popular press from the 1890s to the 1930s were fierce, complex, and difficult to summarize. Writers dealt variously with real and imagined threats from anarchism, socialism, Bolshevism, and, after World War I, communism and fascism. The religious press was certainly not univocal. Some writers found socialism attractive, as for example Adam Rosenberg, "Socialism in Ancient Israel," *Arena* 28 (1902): 37–44, and James T. Van Rensselaer, "The Identity of Socialism and Christianity," *Arena* 34 (1905): 39–44. Others linked Christianity in origin and essence with non-collectivist democratic, not socialist, ideals. For example, Lyman Abbott, "Christianity and Democracy," *Outlook* 53 (1896): 97–100, and Chauncey B. Brewster, "The Democratic Ideal and the Christian Church," *North American Review* 191 (1910): 302–10. The First World War gave the edge to democracy in such debates, as interest in socialist philosophies gave way to a wartime posture of, as Woodrow Wilson announced, "making the world safe for democracy." See James Weinstein, *The Decline of Socialism in America, 1912–1925* (New York: Monthly Review, 1967). After the war, some writers, celebrating recent victories and looking toward

rising nationalistic forms of communism and fascism, renewed discussion about "Americanism" and the origin of its clearly superior democratic ideals. Charles Foster Kent (see above, chapter 2) pushed the question beyond the classic Greek and Roman worlds to the "hilltops of Palestine" in "The Birth of Democracy," *Yale Review* 9 (1919–20): 131–42. See also J. L. Gillin, "The Origin of Democracy," *American Journal of Sociology* 24 (1919): 704–14, which includes the Hebrews among other "primitive" peoples who gave birth to democratic forms of polity.

64. McCown, *Genesis of the Social Gospel*, 370–73.

65. McCown, "The Temptation of Jesus Eschatologically and Socially Interpreted," *Biblical World* 53, no. 4 (1919): 402–407. See further McCown, "The Social Gospel," in *The Church Looks Ahead: American Protestant Christianity, an Analysis and Forecast*, ed. Charles E. Schofield (New York: Macmillan, 1933), 161–85; also McCown, *Search for the Real Jesus* (New York: Charles Scribner's Sons, 1940); McCown, "The Kingdom of God and the Life of Today," in *Theology and Modern Life: Essays in Honor of Harris Franklin Rall*, ed. Paul Arthur Schilpp (Chicago: Clark, Willet, 1940), 212–36; McCown, "The Major Emphasis in Preaching—Social," *Christian Advocate* 106 (1940): 54.

66. Writing nearly thirty years later, McCown tenaciously held to the promise he found in the idea of a "Democracy of God." It was a message McCown still felt urgently needed to be accepted in the anxious days of post–World War II America. Jesus' embodiment of the God-commanded "proletarian ethical tradition" (the phrase is remarkable for its delicate traversal of America's Cold War hysteria) marks the way and the truth, despite its being nearly forgotten. McCown, *Man, Morals, and History: Today's Legacy from Ancient Times and Biblical Peoples* (New York: Harper Brothers, 1958), 268, 271, 293.

67. *City Commons Club Bulletin* 21, no. 1 (1949): 1, McCown Papers.

68. Ibid.

69. The trajectory of the "nomadic ideal" from enthusiastic acceptance, through fundamental questioning, to abandonment is nicely reflected in successive reference works. See C. U. Wolf, "Nomadism," in *Interpreter's Dictionary of the Bible*, vol. 3 (Nashville: Abingdon, 1962), 559–60; Norman Gottwald, "Nomadism," in *Interpreter's Dictionary of the Bible, Supplementary Volume* (Nashville: Abingdon, 1976), 629–31; Ernst A. Knauf, "Bedouin and Bedouin States," *Anchor Bible Dictionary*, vol. 1 (New York: Doubleday, 1992), 634–38.

70. McCown, "On Foot in the Mountains of Judea," 26–27, McCown Papers.

71. Max L. Margolis, "The Scope and Methodology of Biblical Philology," *Jewish Quarterly Review*, n.s., 1 (1910–11): 32–33; Margolis, "The Jewish Defense of the Bible," *B'nai B'rith News* (June 1915): 10. For more details, see Leonard Greenspoon, *Max Leopold Margolis: A Scholar's Scholar* (Atlanta, Ga.: Scholars, 1987), 111–33. For other biographical information, see Robert Gordis, ed., *Max Leopold Margolis: Scholar and Teacher* (Philadelphia: Alumni Association of Dropsie College, 1952); Sperling, *Students of the Covenant*, 48–51.

72. Max L. Margolis, *Micah: The Holy Scriptures with Commentary* (Philadelphia: Jewish Publication Society, 1908).

73. Max L. Margolis, "The Central Thought of the Book of Job," in *Papers Presented at the Fifth Annual Session of the Summer Assembly of the Jewish Chautauqua Society* (Philadelphia: Jewish Publication Society, 1902), 56–70. For the scope of Margolis's less technical writings, see Joseph Reider, "Bibliography of the Works of Max Leopold Margolis," in Greenspoon, *Max Leopold Margolis*, 165–78.

74. Max L. Margolis, "Professor Max Margolis a Zionist: An Open Letter Defining His Position, and Offering His Active Co-operation," *Maccabaean* 12, no. 3 (March 1907): 97–99.

75. Max L. Margolis, "A Year in the Holy Land," part 1, *B'nai B'rith Magazine* 39, no. 1 (October 1924): 8. On page 44, Margolis mentions the welcoming (and welcome) deference extended to the special needs of Jews on board the steamship. Reports of his travels appeared serially in the *B'nai B'rith Magazine*: 39, no. 1 (October 1924): 8–10 (part 1), 44–45 (part 2); no. 2 (November 1924): 74, 86 (part 3); no. 3 (December 1924): 106–107 (part 4); and no. 5 (February 1925): 167, 182–83 (part 5).

76. *BASOR* 15 (October 1924): 12.

77. Max L. Margolis, "Oriental Research in Palestine," *Jewish Institute of Religion Bulletin* 3, no. 2 (November 1925): 16.

78. Margolis, "A Year in the Holy Land," part 5, 182. See also Margolis, "Oriental Research," 9–10.

79. Margolis, "Oriental Research," 3.

80. Ibid., 11. Indeed, study of the ancient land was a *mitzvah*, a religious duty. Margolis fully agreed with an early-nineteenth-century Bavarian Jew, Joseph Schwarz, who closely studied the land five years before Edward Robinson began his famous journeys, and felt ashamed that Jews had paid so little attention to topographical details. Ibid., 4.

81. Max L. Margolis, "The Leadership of Herzl," *Maccabaean* 22, no. 8 (August 1917): 23.

82. See Ben Halpern, "The Americanization of Zionism, 1880–1930," *American Jewish History* 69, no. 1 (September 1979): 15–33. See also Arthur Goren, "Spiritual Zionists and Jewish Sovereignty," in *The Americanization of the Jews*, ed. Robert Seltzer and Norman Cohen (New York: New York University Press, 1996), 165–92.

83. Goren, "Spiritual Zionists," 169. See Joshua Bloch, "Max L. Margolis' Contribution to the History and Philosophy of Judaism," in Gordis, ed., *Margolis: Scholar and Teacher*, 53–57.

84. Max L. Margolis, "Zionism and Reform," *Maccabaean* 19, no. 5 (May 1917): 227.

85. Max L. Margolis, "The Message of Moses," *Maccabaean* 12, no. 2 (February 1907): 41–46.

86. Max L. Margolis, *B'nai B'rith News* (September–October 1918): 17, cited in Gordis, ed., *Margolis: Scholar and Teacher*, 53.

87. Margolis, "Oriental Research," 16–17.

88. Margolis, "A Year in the Holy Land," part 3, 74.

89. Margolis, "A Year in the Holy Land," part 4, 106.

90. Margolis, "A Year in the Holy Land," part 5, 167, 182–83. The reference to freedom of choice in schooling comes from Max Margolis and Alexander Marx, *A History of the Jewish People* (Philadelphia: Jewish Publication Society, 1927), 737.

5. Mapmakers and Their Holy Lands

1. A. W. Kayyali, *Palestine: A Modern History* (London: Croom Helm, 1978), 187–227; Michael Cohen, *From Palestine to Israel: From Mandate to Independence* (London: Frank Cass, 1988), 39–67; Tom Segev, *One Palestine, Complete: Jews and Arabs under the British Mandate* (New York: Metropolitan, 2000).

2. *New York Times*, April 29, 1936, 1; May 2, 1936, 5.

3. Postcard published by Greek Convent Press, Jerusalem. From my personal collection.

4. Jack Finegan, *The Archeology of the New Testament: The Life of Jesus and the Beginning of the Early Church*, rev. ed. (Princeton, N.J.: Princeton University Press, 1992), v.

5. Finegan, *Archeology*, 66–67.

6. J. B. Harley, "Maps, Knowledge, and Power," in *The Iconography of Landscape: Essays on the Symbolic Representation, Design, and Use of Past Environments*, ed. Denis Cosgrove and Stephen Daniels (Cambridge: Cambridge University, 1988), 278. The notion of map as manipulated, controlled fiction comes from Phillip C. Muehrcke, *Map Use: Reading, Analysis, and Interpretation* (Madison, Wis.: JP Publications, 1978), 295.

7. The latest summary of these uncertainties is in David Noel Freedman et al., *Anchor Bible Dictionary*, vol. 3 (Garden City, N.Y.: Doubleday, 1992), 608–609.

8. G. Ernest Wright, *Shechem: The Biography of a Biblical City* (New York: McGraw-Hill, 1964).

9. André Parrot, *The Land of Christ: Archaeology, History, Geography* (Philadelphia: Westminster, 1968), 65.

10. Finegan, *Archeology*, 67–71.

11. Michael Avi-Yonah, *The Madaba Mosaic Map* (Jerusalem: Israel Exploration Society, 1954); Kenneth Nebenzahl, *Maps of the Holy Land: Images of Terra Sancta through Two Millennia* (New York: Abbeville, 1986), 8, 24–25.

12. Edward Robinson and Eli Smith, *Biblical Researches in Palestine and Adjacent Regions: A Journal of Travels in the Year 1838*, vol. 2 (Boston: Crocker & Brewster, 1868), 283–86. In 1852, Robinson visited Jacob's Well again. He found nothing new for his geographical researches, but noted afresh the site's overwhelming importance to Christianity. "I was glad," he wrote, "once more to visit this undoubted scene of our Lord's conversation with the Samaritan woman; and to yield myself for the time to the sacred associations of the spot." Edward Robinson and Eli Smith, *Later Biblical Researches in Palestine and Adjacent Regions: A Journal of Travels in the Year 1852* (Boston: Crocker & Brewster, 1871), 132.

13. Heinrich Kiepert, *Maps of Palestine, the Peninsula of Sinai and Arabia Petraea and Plan of Jerusalem* (Berlin: engraved by H. Mahlmann, 1840). Kiepert's maps set a new standard and were reprinted many times.

14. Frederick J. Bliss, "The Church at Jacob's Well," *Palestine Exploration Quarterly Statement*, 1894, 108–13.

15. Harry Emerson Fosdick, *A Pilgrimage to Palestine* (New York: Macmillan, 1927), 19–20, 221. See my discussion of the "out-of-doors Jesus" above, pp. 98–100, 152. In Fosdick's frontispiece map of biblical Palestine, artist Henry J. Soulen noted sites of biblical interest and encoded Fosdick's militant claim to the Holy Land for Protestant sensibilities. Yet, suspended over the Great Sea, Mary, mother of Jesus, knelt in adoration before her child. Vaguely suggestive of Byzantine or medieval Western iconography, Mary presides over the Holy Land like the Virgin of Catholic devotion who refuses to be entirely suppressed by Fosdick's astringent iconoclasm.

16. George Adam Smith, *The Historical Geography of the Holy Land Especially in Relation to the History of Israel and of the Early Church* (London: Hodder and Stoughton, 1894), 120. The quotation is taken from John 4:21–24.

17. Jesse Lyman Hurlbut and Charles Foster Kent, *Palestine through the Stereoscope: A Tour Conducted by Jesse Lyman Hurlbut and Charles Foster Kent* (New York: Underwood & Underwood, 1914), viewing positions 59 and 60, pp. 188–92.

18. Finegan, *Archeology*, pl. 63, p. 72. Note a very similar image in the photo series "Palestine—The Same Yesterday as Today," *The Independent* 77 (February 9, 1914): 198–99. The entirely Scriptural caption suited Christian interests: "A WOMAN OF SAMARIA WHO HAS COME TO JACOB'S WELL TO DRAW WATER. 'Jacob's well was there. Jesus, being wearied with his journey, sat on the well, and there cometh a woman of Samaria to draw water.'" The scene belongs not only to religious culture, but also to the pop culture of commerce and tourism, to judge from countless reproductions in postcards, advertising, and travel mementos. The New Holy Land tour at the Great Passion Play theme park in Eureka Springs, Arkansas, includes a stop at Jacob's Well, too.

19. Denis Wood, *The Power of Maps* (New York: Guilford, 1992), 1, 16.

20. Finegan, *Archeology*, v; see also xiv. Our knowledge of Melito rests on references to his writings by the early-fourth-century church historian Eusebius, a few fragments, and one surviving work interpreting the Passover.

21. Harley, "Maps, Knowledge, and Power," 290–94.

22. Wood, *Power of Maps*, 24.

23. S. W. Boggs, "Cartohypnosis," *Library Journal* 72 (March 15, 1947): 433–35; J. B. Harley, "Historical Geography and the Cartographic Illusion," *Journal of Historical Geography* 15, no. 1 (1989): 80–91. See also a broader treatment by James Flanagan, "Mapping the Biblical World: Perceptions of Space in Ancient Southwestern Asia," a lecture delivered on October 1, 1999, before members of the Humanities Research Group, University of Windsor, Ontario, Canada, published in *Humanities Group Working Papers*, ed. Jacqueline Murray, vol. 5 (Windsor, Ont.: University of Windsor, 2001), 1–18, and available at <http://www.cwru.edu/affil/GAIR/Constructions/xtrapapers 2000.html> (accessed March 8, 2002).

24. A. H. Kellogg, *A Sermon Commemorative of the Life and Character of the Reverend Lyman Coleman* (Easton, Pa.: Lafayette College, 1882). See also *Dictionary of American Biography*, vol. 4 (New York: Charles Scribner's Sons, 1930), 293–94; *National Cyclopaedia of American Biography*, vol. 11 (New York: James White, 1901), 247; obituary in the *New York Times*, March 17, 1882, section 5, p. 2.

25. All quotations are from Lyman Coleman, *An Historical Textbook and Atlas of Biblical Geography* (Philadelphia: J. B. Lippincott, 1854; rev. ed., 1867), 3–6 and 259. Coleman ended his work with a poem or hymn fragment, as though leading his readers, now a congregation of petitioners, to ask for Christian conviction. "Anoint mine eyes / O Holy Dove / That I may prize / This book of love / Break my hard heart / Jesus my Lord / In th'inmost part / Hide thy sweet word" (259). The *Atlas* superseded Coleman's earlier work, *An Historical Geography of the Bible* (Philadelphia: E. H. Butler, 1850).

26. George Adam Smith, *The Historical Geography of the Holy Land Especially in Relation to the History of Israel and of the Early Church* (London: Hodder and Stoughton, 1894). For a contextual study of Smith's work, see Robin A. Butlin, "George Adam Smith and the Historical Geography of the Holy Land," *Journal of Historical Geography* 14, no. 4 (1988): 381–404.

27. Coleman, *Atlas*, 270.

28. Besides Kiepert, *Maps of Palestine*, see Heinrich Kiepert, *Bibel-Atlas nach den Neuesten und Besten Hülfsquellen* (Berlin: Müller, 1851).

29. For primary sources, see Nebenzahl, *Maps*. For descriptive studies, see Robert North, *A History of Biblical Map Making* (Wiesbaden: Ludwig Reichert, 1979); Milka Levy-Rubin and Rehav Rubin, "The Image of the Holy City in Maps and Mapping," in *City of the Great King: Jerusalem from David to the Present*, ed. Nitza Rosovsky (Cambridge, Mass.: Harvard University Press, 1996), 352–79; Robin A. Butlin, *Historical Geography: Through the Gates of Space and Time* (London: Edward Arnold, 1993).

30. See James Ward Smith and A. Leland Jamison, eds., *Religious Perspectives in American Culture* (Princeton, N.J.: Princeton University Press, 1961). The literature of the colonial period is particularly rich in biblical metaphor used by European immigrants to North America. See, among many treatments, two by Perry Miller: *The New England Mind: The Seventeenth Century* (Cambridge, Mass.: Harvard University Press, 1954); and *Errand into the Wilderness* (Cambridge, Mass.: Belknap Press of Harvard University Press, 1956).

31. Coleman, *Atlas*, 98.

32. Ibid., 48–49, quoting Robinson and Smith, *Biblical Researches*.

33. Ibid., "Explanation to Map VI."

34. Ibid., 6.

35. For example, Nebenzahl, *Maps*, 26–27, 33, 40–41, 91. On early Christian ideas about Jerusalem and the Holy Land, see Robert L. Wilken, *The Land Called Holy: Palestine in Christian History and Thought* (New Haven: Yale University Press, 1992).

36. Coleman, *Atlas*, 124–25, 122.

37. See Keith Whitelam, "Constructing Jerusalem," a paper presented at a meeting of the Society of Biblical Literature, November 1998, available at <http://www.cwru.edu/affil/GAIR/Constructions/xtrapapers2000.html> (accessed March 8, 2002).

38. Robin A. Butlin, "Ideological Contexts and the Reconstruction of Biblical Landscapes in the Seventeenth and Early Eighteenth Centuries: Dr. Edward Wells and the Historical Geography of the Holy Land," in *Ideology and Landscape in Historical Perspective: Essays on the Meaning of Some Places in the Past*, ed. Alan Baker and Gideon Biger (Cambridge: Cambridge University Press, 1992), 31–62.

39. *Who's Who in America*, part 1: 1976–77 (Chicago: Marquis Company), 995–96.

40. David Noel Freedman, "G. Ernest Wright: Scholar, Teacher, Christian," *Minutes of the Biblical Colloquium*, 1974, unpublished, courtesy of David Noel Freedman.

41. Burke O. Long, *Planting and Reaping Albright: Politics, Ideology, and Interpreting the Bible* (University Park: Pennsylvania State University Press, 1997).

42. See chapter 4 above, pp. 141–146.

43. Leona Glidden Running and David Noel Freedman, *William Foxwell Albright: A Twentieth-Century Genius* (New York: Morgan, 1975), 187.

44. "George Ernest Wright, In Memoriam," *Newsletter*, American Schools of Oriental Research, 3 (September 1974): 1–8. A memorial tribute to Wright appeared in *Biblical Archaeologist* 50, no. 1 (March 1987): 5–21. See also *American National Biography*, vol. 24 (New York: Oxford University Press, 1999), 21–23.

45. G. Ernest Wright and Floyd Filson, eds., *The Westminster Historical Atlas to the Bible* (Philadelphia: Westminster, 1945; rev. ed., 1956). The editors added considerable material for the revised edition. However, the preface, in which Filson and Wright explain how their *Atlas* relates to both historical geography and theology, was unchanged. Subsequent references are to the 1956 edition.

46. The editors deemed Albright's contributions to the *Atlas* so important that they made a private arrangement with him to share their royalties. Letter, Wright to Albright, July 19, 1943; Filson to Albright, November 22, 1946, Albright Papers, American Philosophical Society, Philadelphia, Pa.

47. George Adam Smith, *Historical Atlas of the Holy Land* (London: Hodder and Stoughton, 1915; rev. ed., 1935). This atlas was a companion to Smith's popular *Historical Geography*. Smith, the modernist, drew upon the British Ordnance Survey, greatly expanded the range and subject matter of Holy Land maps, was suspicious of facile identifications of biblical sites, and downplayed the contribution of geography to confirming the Bible's version of history. Yet, in matters of style and commitment to missionary Christianity, his atlas continued the tradition of the romantic travel narrative. He cited, for example, as indispensable to Holy Land geography, William M. Thomson, *The Land and the Book* (New York: Harper and Brothers, 1859), that astonishingly popular hunt for biblical illustration and confirmation in Palestine. See above, chapter 1, pp. 39–40.

48. Extravagant publications had codified this romanticism of Arcadian Palestine. See Charles William Wilson, ed., *Picturesque Palestine, Sinai, and Egypt*, 2 vols. (New York: D. Appleton, 1881).

49. Wright and Filson, *Atlas*, fig. 46, p. 67; fig. 68, p. 91. See also fig. 6, p. 18, "The Plain of Shechem in the Heart of Samaria," with mention of Jacob's Well; fig. 7, p. 38, "The River Jordan"; fig. 69, p. 92, "The Jerusalem-Jericho Road . . . which has always offered hiding places for robbers (cf. Luke 10:30)."

50. G. Ernest Wright and Floyd Filson, *Atlas historico Westminster de la Biblia* (El Paso, Tex.: Casa Bautista de Publicaciones, 1992).

51. A briefer handbook by Emil G. H. Kraeling (*Rand McNally Historical Atlas of the Holy Land* [Chicago: Rand McNally, 1959]) proved far less popular.

52. Letter, Albright to Wright, July 2, 1956, Albright Papers.

53. Ernest Saunders, *Searching the Scriptures: A History of the Society of Biblical Literature, 1880–1980* (Chico, Calif.: Scholars, 1982), 59. Davis Perkins, president and publisher of the Westminster–John Knox Press, gave me the sales figures for Wright and Filson's *Atlas*. Private communication, October 19, 2001.

54. Coleman, *Atlas*, 5.

55. Wright and Filson, *Atlas*, 5. Wright was especially drawn to theologian Karl Barth's vibrant use of the Old Testament as Christian message, and was worried, as was his mentor Albright, about the bland Jesus-centered "liberalism" that had become popular in theological circles before World War II. Letter, Wright to Albright, August 6, 1942, Albright Papers. See Long, *Planting and Reaping Albright*, 78–79.

56. See Romans 12:2; 1 Corinthians 3:21–23; 7:29–31; 2 Corinthians 10:3; Colossians 2:20–3:11.

57. On the Canaanites, compare Wright and Filson, *Atlas*, 36, with William Foxwell Albright, *From the Stone Age to Christianity: Monotheism and the Historical Process* (Baltimore, Md.: Johns Hopkins Press, 1940; rev. ed., Garden City, N.Y.: Doubleday, 1957), 230–36, 281.

58. Wright and Filson, *Atlas*, 5–6, 26. Note also G. Ernest Wright, *Biblical Archaeology* (Philadelphia, Pa.: Westminster, 1955; rev. ed., 1962), esp. 17–18. Works by Wright and Filson individually articulated more fully the passionate theological vision which animated the *Atlas*. Among those by Wright, see *The Challenge of Israel's*

Faith (Chicago: University of Chicago Press, 1944); *God Who Acts: Biblical Theology as Recital* (London: SCM Press, 1952); and *The Old Testament against Its Environment* (London: SCM Press, 1950). The latter had its counterpart in Floyd Filson, *The New Testament against Its Environment: The Gospel of Christ, the Risen Lord* (London: SCM Press, 1950).

59. See Martin Noth, *Geschichte Israels* (Göttingen: Vandenhoeck and Ruprecht, 1950). The first of many translations and revised printings appeared as *The History of Israel*, trans. Stanley Godman (London: A. and C. Black, 1958). The Albright school, encouraged by Wright, answered Noth's challenges in John Bright, *A History of Israel* (Philadelphia: Westminster, 1959).

60. This and the preceding quotations are from Wright and Filson, *Atlas*, 36–37.

61. Keith W. Whitelam, *The Invention of Ancient Israel: The Silencing of Palestinian History* (London: Routledge, 1996), 119.

62. See above, chapter 4, pp. 145–146.

63. See Mark Silk, "Notes on the Judeo-Christian Tradition in America," *American Quarterly* 36, no. 1 (spring 1984): 65–85.

64. J. Maxwell Miller, "Old Testament History and Archaeology," *Biblical Archaeologist* 50, no. 1 (March 1987): 59.

65. David R. Seely, "Shur," *Anchor Bible Dictionary*, vol. 5 (New York: Doubleday, 1992), 1230. See, in the same volume, Barry Beitzel, "Roads and Highways," 776–82.

66. Coleman, *Atlas*, map 6 and p. 82. Robinson and Smith (*Biblical Researches*, vol. 1, 569–70) were quite disappointed that they could not find a peak that properly fit the geographical descriptions of the biblical narrative.

67. Nebenzahl, *Maps*, 132.

68. David L. Jeffrey, ed., *A Dictionary of Biblical Tradition in English Literature* (Grand Rapids, Mich.: W. B. Eerdmans, 1992), 616–17; Clifton Harby, *The Bible in Art* (New York: Covici Friede, 1936), 65.

69. Frank S. DeHass, *Buried Cities Recovered; or, Explorations in Bible Lands*, 5th ed. (Philadelphia: J. W. Bradley, 1882), 341; George Barton, *A Year's Wandering in Bible Lands* (Philadelphia: Ferris and Leach, 1904), 150–51.

70. Hurlbut and Kent, *Palestine through the Stereoscope*, 159.

71. Wright and Filson, *Atlas*, 39.

72. For a summary, see J. R. Bartlett and Burton McDonald, "Edom," in *Anchor Bible Dictionary*, vol. 2, ed. David Noel Freedman et al. (New York: Doubleday, 1992), 287–301. Similar questions might be raised about the "kingdoms" of Moab and Sihon and what was thought to be known about them as thirteenth-century entities.

73. John Rogerson, "Frontiers and Borders in the Old Testament," in *In Search of True Wisdom: Essays in Old Testament Interpretation in Honour of Ronald E. Clements*, ed. Edward Ball (Sheffield, U.K.: Sheffield Academic Press, 1999), 121.

74. See Keith W. Whitelam, "Transcending the Boundaries: Expanding the Limits," paper presented at a meeting of the Society of Biblical Literature, November 2001, available at <http://www.cwru.edu/affil/GAIR/Constructions/Program2001.html> (accessed March 8, 2002). See also Eric J. Hobsbawm, *Nations and Nationalism since 1780: Programme, Myth, Reality* (Cambridge: Cambridge University Press, 1990).

75. Wright and Filson, *Atlas*, 40.

76. Ibid., 105.

77. Ibid., 94.

78. Smith, *Historical Geography*. In his *Historical Atlas*, 55–56, Smith included a map of modern Jerusalem entitled "Present Political Divisions and Christian Missions." See also George Adam Smith, *Jerusalem: The Topography, Economics, and History from Earliest Times to A.D. 70* (London: Hodder and Stoughton, 1907; reprinted with a critical assessment by Samuel Yeivin, New York: KTAV, 1972).

79. By holding to this theological tradition and adhering to the seventeenth-century notion that historical geography illustrated historical events, Wright and Filson did not adopt the new directions and paradigms for the field that historical geographers at the time were developing. See Butlin, *Historical Geography*.

80. See Yohanan Aharoni and Michael Avi-Yonah, *The Macmillan Bible Atlas* (New York: Macmillan, 1968; 3rd ed., 1993). While marshaling complex evidence and aware of inevitable ambiguities in historical argument, the authors nevertheless assumed the Bible's authority in reconstructing history (they even used biblical quotations as chapter epigraphs). The maps and commentary reiterated, not a Christian foundation story ("Israel" and the Church) as did Wright and Filson's, but a charter narrative of modern Zionism (the "Jewish people"). Even more robust in this regard is Zev Vilnay, *The New Israel Atlas: The Bible to Present Day* (Jerusalem: Israel Universities Press, 1968), a work published to help commemorate the twentieth anniversary of the State of Israel.

Epilogue

1. Letter, G. Ernest Wright to W. F. Albright, June 29, 1956, Albright Papers, American Philosophical Society, Philadelphia, Pa.

2. G. Ernest Wright, "Bringing Old Testament Times to Life," *National Geographic Magazine* 112, no. 12 (December 1957): 833–64. See also Wright, "The Last Thousand Years before Christ," *National Geographic Magazine* 115, no. 12 (December 1960): 813–53.

3. Wright, "Old Testament Times," 833–34, 836.

4. John Dominic Crossan and Jonathan L. Reed, *Excavating Jesus: Beneath the Stones, Behind the Texts* (San Francisco: HarperSanFrancisco, 2001).

5. American Academy of Religion and Society of Biblical Literature, *Program Book: 2001 Annual Meetings*, Denver, Colo., November 17–20, 2001, 196.

6. Ibid., 178.

7. See John Dominic Crossan, *The Historical Jesus: The Life of a Mediterranean Jewish Peasant* (San Francisco: HarperSanFrancisco, 1991); Crossan, *Jesus: A Revolutionary Biography* (San Francisco: HarperSanFrancisco, 1994).

8. Crossan and Reed, *Excavating Jesus*, 248, 16, 36.

9. Ibid., 37 and color inserts following p. 70.

10. Ibid., 126, 88 on the courtyard house. For the Galilean boat, see xvi–xvii, 3, and 85–87. Color renderings follow p. 70.

SELECT BIBLIOGRAPHY

Archival Resources

Albright, William F. Papers. American Philosophical Society. Philadelphia, Pa.

Arkansas History Commission, Archives. Little Rock, Ark.

Barton, George. Papers. Archives, Library of Bryn Mawr College. Bryn Mawr, Pa.

Chautauqua Institution Archives. Chautauqua, N.Y.

Eureka Springs Historical Museum. Eureka Springs, Ark.

Goodspeed, Edgar J. Papers. University of Chicago Archives. Chicago, Ill.

Harper, William Rainey. Presidents' Papers, 1889–1925. University of Chicago Archives. Chicago, Ill.

Lyon, David. Papers. Harvard University Archives. Cambridge, Mass.

McCown, Chester Charlton. Papers. Archives, Pacific School of Religion. Berkeley, Calif.

Missouri Historical Society, Archives. St. Louis, Mo.

St. Louis Public Library, Rare Books and Special Collections. St. Louis, Mo.

Major Works Consulted

Ackerman, Gerald. *American Orientalists*. Paris: ACR, 1994.

Aharoni, Yohanan. *The Land and the Bible*. Philadelphia, Pa.: Westminster, 1967; rev. ed., 1979.

Aharoni, Yohanan, and Michael Avi-Yonah. *The Macmillan Bible Atlas*. New York: Macmillan, 1968; 3rd ed., 1993.

Albright, William Foxwell. "Archaeological Discovery in the Holy Land." *Bibliotheca Sacra* 79 (1922): 401–17.

———. *Archaeology and the Religion of Israel*. Baltimore, Md.: Johns Hopkins Press, 1942; 5th ed., Garden City, N.Y.: Doubleday, 1967.

———. *The Archaeology of Palestine and the Bible*. New York: Fleming H. Revell, 1932.

———. "Chester Charlton McCown: An Appreciation." In *An Indexed Bibliography of the Writings of Chester Charlton McCown*, unpaginated. Berkeley, Calif.: Pacific School of Religion, 1947.

———. *From the Stone Age to Christianity: Monotheism and the Historical Process*. Baltimore, Md.: Johns Hopkins Press, 1940; 2nd ed., Garden City, N.Y.: Doubleday, 1957.

———. "Rediscovering Ancient Palestine." *Sunday School Times* 65 (1923): 7–8.

Avi-Yonah, Michael. *The Madaba Mosaic Map*. Jerusalem: Israel Exploration Society, 1954.

Barton, George. *A Year's Wanderings in Bible Lands*. Philadelphia: Ferris and Leach, 1904.

Batzli, Samuel. "The Visual Voice: 'Armchair Tourism,' Cultural Authority, and the Depiction of the United States in Early Twentieth-Century Stereographs." Ph.D. diss., University of Illinois at Urbana-Champaign, 1997.

ben-Arieh, Yehoshua. *The Rediscovery of the Holy Land in the Nineteenth Century*. Jerusalem: Magnes, 1979.

Bennitt, Mark, ed. *History of the Louisiana Purchase Exposition*. St. Louis, Mo.: Universal Exposition Publishing Co., 1905.

Bliss, Fredrick J. "The Church at Jacob's Well." *Palestine Exploration Quarterly Statement*, 1894, 108–13.

Boggs, S. W. "Cartohypnosis." *Library Journal* 72 (March 15, 1947): 433–35.

Bolton, Sarah Knowles. "The Rev. John H. Vincent, D.D." In *How Success Is Won: Twelve Biographies of Successful Men*. Boston: D. Lothrop, 1885.

Bonnell, Richard Kenneth. "The Chautauqua University: Pioneer University without Walls, 1883–1898." Ph.D. diss., Kent State University, 1988.

Borden, Jim, and Ken Rank. *The Tabernacle*. Video recording. Eureka Springs, Ark.: The Elna M. Smith Foundation, 1994.

Brown, Kenneth O. *Holy Ground: A Study of the American Camp Meeting*. New York: Garland, 1992.

Butlin, Robin A. "George Adam Smith and the Historical Geography of the Holy Land." *Journal of Historical Geography* 14, no. 4 (1988): 381–404.

———. *Historical Geography: Through the Gates of Space and Time*. London: Edward Arnold, 1993.

———. "Ideological Contexts and the Reconstruction of Biblical Landscapes in the Seventeenth and Early Eighteenth Centuries: Dr. Edward Wells and the Historical Geography of the Holy Land." In *Ideology and Landscape in Historical Perspective: Essays on the Meaning of Some Places in the Past*, ed. Alan Baker and Gideon Biger, 31–62. Cambridge: Cambridge University Press, 1992.

"City of Jerusalem. Site Dedicated with Most Unique and Interesting Ceremonial Rites in the Presence of Thousands." *World's Fair Bulletin* 4, no. 10 (August 1903): 34–39.

Clevenger, Martha R., ed. *"Indescribably Grand": Diaries and Letters from the 1904 World's Fair*. St. Louis, Mo.: Missouri Historical Society, 1996.

Cohen, Michael. *From Palestine to Israel: From Mandate to Independence*. London: Frank Cass, 1988.

Coleman, Lyman. *An Historical Geography of the Bible*. Philadelphia: E. H. Butler, 1850.

———. *An Historical Textbook and Atlas of Biblical Geography*. Philadelphia: J. B. Lippincott, 1854; rev. ed., 1867.

Cross, Frank Moore, Jr., et al. *Magnalia Dei: The Mighty Acts of God—Essays in Memory of G. Ernest Wright*. Garden City, N.Y.: Doubleday, 1976.

Crossan, John Dominic. *The Historical Jesus: The Life of a Mediterranean Jewish Peasant*. San Francisco: HarperSanFrancisco, 1991.

———. *Jesus: A Revolutionary Biography*. San Francisco: HarperSanFrancisco, 1994.

Crossan, John Dominic, and Jonathan L. Reed. *Excavating Jesus: Beneath the Stones, Behind the Texts*. San Francisco: HarperSanFrancisco, 2001.

Davis, John. *The Landscape of Belief: Encountering the Holy Land in Nineteenth-Century American Art and Culture*. Princeton, N.J.: Princeton University Press, 1996.

Davis, Moshe. *America and the Holy Land*. With Eyes toward Zion 4. Westport, Conn.: Praeger, 1995.

DeHass, Frank. *Buried Cities Recovered: or, Explorations in Bible Lands*. 5th ed. Philadelphia: J. W. Bradley, 1882.

Dieter, Melvin Easterday. *The Holiness Revival of the Nineteenth Century*. Metuchen, N.J.: Scarecrow, 1980.

Eagleton, Terry. *Ideology: An Introduction*. New York: Verso, 1991.

Filson, Floyd. *The New Testament against Its Environment: The Gospel of Christ, the Risen Lord*. London: SCM Press, 1950.

Finegan, Jack. *The Archeology of the New Testament: The Life of Jesus and the Beginning of the Early Church*. Rev. ed. Princeton N.J.: Princeton University Press, 1992.

Finkelstein, Louis, ed. *American Spiritual Autobiographies*. New York: Harper Brothers, 1948.

Finkelstein, Louis, et al. *Science, Philosophy, and Religion: A Symposium*. New York: Conference on Science, Philosophy, and Religion in their Relation to the Democratic Way of Life, 1941.

Finley, John H. *A Pilgrim in Palestine: Being an Account of Journeys on Foot by the First American Pilgrim after General Allenby's Recovery of the Holy Land*. New York: Charles Scribner's Sons, 1919.

Finnie, David. *Pioneers East: The Early American Experience in the Middle East*. Cambridge, Mass.: Harvard University Press, 1967.

Flanagan, James. "Mapping the Biblical World: Perceptions of Space in Ancient Southwestern Asia." In *Humanities Group Working Papers*, ed. Jacqueline Murray, vol. 5, 1–18. Windsor, Ont.: University of Windsor, 2001. Available at <http://www.cwru.edu/affil/GAIR/Constructions/xtrapapers2000.html> (accessed March 8, 2002).

Flood, Theodore. "Old Chautauqua Days." *Chautauquan* 131, no. 5 (August 1891): 560–93.

Fogarty, Gerald P., S.J. *American Catholic Biblical Scholarship: A History from the Early Republic to Vatican II*. New York: Harper and Row, 1989.

Fosdick, Harry Emerson. *A Pilgrimage to Palestine*. New York: Macmillan, 1927.

Francis, David R. *The Universal Exposition of 1904*. St. Louis, Mo.: Louisiana Purchase Exposition Co., 1913.

Freedman, David Noel. *The Published Works of William Foxwell Albright: A Comprehensive Bibliography.* Cambridge, Mass.: American Schools of Oriental Research, 1975.

Freedman, David Noel, et al. *Anchor Bible Dictionary.* 6 vols. Garden City, N.Y.: Doubleday, 1992.

Fulton, John. *The Beautiful Land, Palestine: Historical, Geographical, and Pictorial, Described As It Was and As It Now Is, along the Lines of Our Saviour's Journeys.* New York: T. Whittaker, 1891.

"George Ernest Wright: In Memoriam." *Newsletter,* American Schools of Oriental Research, 3 (September 1974): 1–8.

Goldman, Shalom. "The Holy Land Appropriated: The Careers of Selah Merrill, Nineteenth Century Christian Hebraist, Palestine Explorer, and U.S. Consul in Jerusalem." *American Jewish History* 85, no. 2 (1997): 151–72.

Goodspeed, Edgar J. "From Haifa to Nazareth." *Biblical World* 16 (1900): 407–13.

Gordis, Robert, ed. *Max Leopold Margolis: Scholar and Teacher.* Philadelphia: Alumni Association of Dropsie College, 1952.

The Great Passion Play. Video recording. Eureka Springs, Ark.: The Elna M. Smith Foundation, 1992.

Greenberg, Gershon. *The Holy Land in American Religious Thought, 1620–1948: The Symbiosis of American Religious Approaches to Scripture's Sacred Territory.* Lanham, Md.: University Press of America, 1994.

Greenspoon, Leonard. *Max Leopold Margolis: A Scholar's Scholar.* Atlanta, Ga.: Scholars, 1987.

Gutierrez, Cathy. "Representation and Ideals: The Construction of Women in Travel Literature to the Holy Land." In *Pilgrims and Travelers to the Holy Land,* Studies in Jewish Civilization 7, ed. Bryan F. Le Beau and Menachem Mor, 181–94. Omaha, Neb.: Creighton University Press, 1996.

Halperin, Samuel. *The Political World of American Zionism.* Detroit: Wayne State University Press, 1961.

Harby, Clifton. *The Bible in Art.* New York: Covici Friede, 1936.

Harley, John B. "Historical Geography and the Cartographic Illusion." *Journal of Historical Geography* 15, no. 1 (1989): 80–91.

———. "Maps, Knowledge, and Power." In *The Iconography of Landscape: Essays on the Symbolic Representation, Design, and Use of Past Environments,* ed. Denis Cosgrove and Stephen Daniels, 277–312. Cambridge: Cambridge University Press, 1988.

Hobsbawm, Eric J. *Nations and Nationalism since 1780: Programme, Myth, Reality.* Cambridge: Cambridge University Press, 1990.

Holmes, Oliver Wendell. "The Stereoscope and the Stereograph." *Atlantic Monthly* 3 (June 1850): 738–48.

Hurlbut, Jesse Lyman. *Guide Book to Palestine Park.* Chautauqua, N.Y.: Chautauqua Institution, 1920. Revised and enlarged from the 1907 edition prepared by Alfred E. Barrows.

———. *Hurlbut's Handy Bible Encyclopedia*. Philadelphia: J. C. Winston, 1906.

———. *Hurlbut's Story of the Bible*. Oakland, Calif.: Smithsonian Co., 1904.

———. *Manual of Biblical Geography: A Text-Book on Bible History*. With an introduction by John Heyl Vincent. Chicago: Rand McNally, 1884.

———. *Outline Normal Lessons*. New York: Hunt and Eaton; Cincinnati: Cranston and Curts, 1885.

———. *Revised Normal Lessons*. New York: Hunt and Eaton; Cincinnati: Cranston and Curts, 1893.

———. *The Story of Chautauqua*. New York: G. P. Putnam's Sons, 1921.

———. *Studies in Old Testament History*. New York: Hunt and Eaton; Cincinnati: Cranston and Curts, 1890.

———. *Studies in the Four Gospels*. Cincinnati: Jennings and Graham, 1880.

———. *Teacher Training Lessons*. Nashville: Abingdon, 1908.

———. *Traveling in the Holy Land through the Stereoscope: A Tour Personally Conducted by Jesse Lyman Hurlbut*. New York: Underwood and Underwood, 1900; 2nd ed., 1905.

Hurlbut, Jesse Lyman, and Charles Foster Kent. *Palestine through the Stereoscope: A Tour Conducted by Jesse Lyman Hurlbut and Charles Foster Kent*. New York: Underwood and Underwood, 1914.

Jeansonne, Glenn. *Gerald L. K. Smith: Minister of Hate*. Baton Rouge: Louisiana State University Press, 1988.

Jeffrey, David L., ed. *A Dictionary of Biblical Tradition in English Literature*. Grand Rapids, Mich.: W. B. Eerdmans, 1992.

Jenkins, Harold F. *Two Points of View: The History of the Parlor Stereoscope*. Uniontown, Pa.: E. G. Warman, 1973.

John Heyl Vincent, February 23, 1832–May 9, 1920. Commemorative exercises, August 1, 1920. Chautauqua, N.Y.: Chautauqua Institution, 1920.

Kark, Ruth, ed. *The Land That Became Israel: Studies in Historical Geography*. New Haven: Yale University Press, 1990.

Kayyali, A. W. *Palestine: A Modern History*. London: Croom Helm, 1978.

Kellogg, A. H. *A Sermon Commemorative of the Life and Character of the Reverend Lyman Coleman*. Easton, Pa.: Lafayette College, 1882.

Kent, Charles Foster. *Biblical Geography and History*. New York: Charles Scribner's Sons, 1900.

———. *Christianity and Problems of To-day*. The Bross Lectures of 1921. New York: Charles Scribner's Sons, 1922.

———. *Descriptions of One Hundred and Forty Places in Bible Lands*. New York: Underwood and Underwood, 1900; rev. ed., 1911.

———. "The Hebrew Lyrics." Part 1, "Hymns of Praise," *Chautauquan Daily* 39, no. 16 (July 21, 1914): 1–2; part 2, "The Prayers of the Psalter," no. 17 (July 22, 1914): 7; part 3, "The Reflective and Didactic Lyrics," no. 19 (July 24, 1914): 6.

———. "Rhythm in Hebrew Life and Literature." *Chautauquan Daily* 39, no. 6 (July 9, 1914): 2–3.

Kiepert, Heinrich. *Bibel-Atlas nach den Neuesten und Besten Hülfsquellen*. Berlin: Müller, 1851.

———. *Maps of Palestine, the Peninsula of Sinai and Arabia Petraea and Plan of Jerusalem*. Berlin: engraved by H. Mahlmann, 1840.

Kimball, Kate F. "Leaves from the Life of Bishop John H. Vincent. I. The Palestine Class: A Unique Experiment in Pedagogy." *Chautauquan* 72, no. 14 (December 6, 1913): 273–77.

King, Philip J. *American Archaeology in the Mideast: A History of the American Schools of Oriental Research*. Philadelphia: American Schools of Oriental Research, 1983.

Kirshenblatt-Gimblett, Barbara. "A Place in the World: Jews and the Holy Land at World's Fairs." In *Encounters with the 'Holy Land': Place, Past, and Future in American Jewish Culture*, ed. Jeffrey Schandler and Beth Wenger, 60–82. Philadelphia: National Museum of American Jewish Studies; Center for Judaic Studies, University of Pennsylvania; University of Pennsylvania Library, 1997.

Kleitz, Dorsey R. "Orientalism and the American Romantic Imagination." Ph.D. diss., University of New Hampshire, 1988.

Kuklick, Bruce. *Puritans in Babylon: The Ancient Near East and American Intellectual Life, 1880–1930*. Princeton, N.J.: Princeton University Press, 1996.

Laundry, Franklin B. *Guide Book for a Walking Tour of Palestine Park*. Chautauqua, N.Y.: Chautauqua Institution, 1985.

Le Beau, Bryan F., and Menachem Mor, eds. *Pilgrims and Travelers to the Holy Land*, Studies in Jewish Civilization 7. Omaha, Neb.: Creighton University Press, 1996.

Levy-Rubin, Milka, and Rehav Rubin. "The Image of the Holy City in Maps and Mapping." In *City of the Great King: Jerusalem from David to the Present*, ed. Nitza Rosovsky, 352–79. Cambridge, Mass.: Harvard University Press, 1996.

Long, Burke O. *Planting and Reaping Albright: Politics, Ideology, and Interpreting the Bible*. University Park: Pennsylvania State University Press, 1997.

Lynch, William F. *Narrative of the United States' Expedition to the River Jordan and the Dead Sea*. Philadelphia: Lea and Blanchard, 1849.

Lyon, David. "Archaeological Explorations of Palestine." *Journal of Biblical Literature* 30 (1911): 1–17.

MacMechen, Thomas R. *The True and Complete Story of the Pike and Its Attractions*. St. Louis, Mo.: Division of Concession Stand Amusements, Louisiana Purchase Exhibition, 1904.

Margolis, Max L. "The Central Thought of the Book of Job." In *Papers Presented at the Fifth Annual Session of the Summer Assembly of the Jewish Chautauqua Society*, 56–70. Philadelphia: Jewish Publication Society, 1902.

———. *Micah: The Holy Scriptures with Commentary*. Philadelphia: Jewish Publication Society, 1908.

———. "A Year in the Holy Land." Parts 1–5. *B'nai B'rith Magazine* 39, no. 1 (October 1924): 8–10, 44–45; no. 2 (November 1924): 74, 86; no. 3 (December 1924): 106–107; no. 5 (February 1925): 167, 182–83.

Mathews, Shailer. "A Reading Journey through Palestine: Going Up to Jerusalem." *Chautauquan* 43, no. 6 (August 1903): 493–560.

McCown, Chester Charlton. *The Genesis of the Social Gospel: The Meaning and Ideals of Jesus in the Light of Their Antecedents*. New York: Alfred A. Knopf, 1929.

———. "The Kingdom of God and the Life of Today." In *Theology and Modern Life: Essays in Honor of Harris Franklin Rall*, ed. Paul Arthur Schilpp, 212–36. Chicago: Clark, Willet, 1940.

———. "The Major Emphasis in Preaching—Social." *Christian Advocate* 106 (1940): 54.

———. *Man, Morals, and History: Today's Legacy from Ancient Times and Biblical Peoples*. New York: Harper Brothers, 1958.

———. *The Promise of His Coming*. New York: Macmillan, 1921.

———. *Search for the Real Jesus*. New York: Charles Scribner's Sons, 1940.

———. "The Social Gospel." In *The Church Looks Ahead: American Protestant Christianity, an Analysis and Forecast*, ed. Charles E. Schofield, 161–85. New York: Macmillan, 1933.

———. "The Temptation of Jesus Eschatologically and Socially Interpreted." *Biblical World* 53, no. 4 (1919): 402–407.

Melendy, Mary R. *Perfect Womanhood for Maidens—Wives—Mothers: A Book Giving Full Information on all the Mysterious and Complex Matters Pertaining to Women*. Chicago: Monarch Book, 1903.

Merrill, Selah. *Ancient Jerusalem*. 1908. Reprint, New York: Arno, 1977.

———. *East of the Jordan*. New York: Charles Scribner's Sons, 1881.

———. "Galilee." In *Picturesque Palestine, Sinai, and Egypt: With Numerous Engravings on Steel and Wood from Original Drawings by Harry Fenn and J. D. Woodward*, ed. Sir Charles W. Wilson. 287–380. New York: D. Appleton, 1881.

———. *Galilee in the Time of Christ*. Boston: Congregational Publishing Society, 1881.

Messenger, Troy. *Holy Leisure: Recreation and Religion in God's Square Mile*. Minneapolis: University of Minnesota Press, 1999.

Miller, J. Maxwell. "Old Testament History and Archaeology." *Biblical Archaeologist* 50, no. 1 (1987): 55–63.

Montague, E. P. *Narrative of the Late Expedition to the Dead Sea, from a Diary by One of the Party*. Philadelphia: Carey and Hart, 1849.

Morris, Robert, ed. *Bible Witnesses from Bible Lands*. New York: The American Holy-Land Exploration, 1874.

Morrison, Theodore. *Chautauqua: A Center for Education, Religion, and the Arts in America*. Chicago: University of Chicago Press, 1974.

Moulton, Warren J. "The American Palestine Exploration Society." *Annual of the American Schools of Oriental Research* 8 (1926–27): 55–78.

Mountford, Lydia Mamreoff von Finkelstein. *Jesus Christ in His Homeland*. Lectures Stenographically Recorded. Cincinnati: Jennings and Graham, 1911.

———. *The King of the Shepherds and His Psalm*. Lecture Stenographically Recorded. Cincinnati: Abingdon, 1914.

———. *The Life Sketch of Lydia Mamreoff von Finkelstein*. New York: n.p., 1908.

Muehrcke, Phillip C. *Map Use: Reading, Analysis, and Interpretation*. Madison, Wis.: JP Publications, 1978.

Nebenzahl, Kenneth. *Maps of the Holy Land: Images of Terra Sancta through Two Millennia*. New York: Abbeville, 1986.

Noble, F. P. "Chautauqua as a New Factor in American Life." *New England Magazine*, n.s., 2 (1890): 90–101.

North, Robert. *A History of Biblical Map Making*. Wiesbaden: Ludwig Reichert, 1979.

Parrot, André. *The Land of Christ: Archaeology, History, Geography*. Philadelphia: Westminster, 1968.

Peters, John P. "Jerusalem Redeemed: The Ancient Holy City and Its Place in History." *American Review of Reviews* 57 (January 1918): 47–58.

Post, D. H. "Chautauqua." *Harper's New Monthly Magazine* 59 (June–November 1879): 350–60.

Prospectus of the Jerusalem Exhibit Company. St. Louis, Mo.: The Jerusalem Exhibit Co., 1903.

Queen, Edward L., II. "Ambiguous Pilgrims: American Protestant Travelers to Ottoman Palestine, 1867–1914." In *Pilgrims and Travelers to the Holy Land*, Studies in Jewish Civilization 7, ed. Bryan F. Le Beau and Menachem Mor, 209–28. Omaha, Neb.: Creighton University Press, 1996.

Reinharz, Jehuda, and Anita Shapira, eds. *Essential Papers on Zionism*. New York: New York University Press, 1996.

Ribuffo, Leo P. *The Old Christian Right: The Protestant Far Right from the Great Depression to the Cold War*. Philadelphia: Temple University Press, 1983.

Robinson, Edward. *Later Biblical Researches in Palestine and in the Adjacent Regions: A Journal of Travels in the Year 1852—Drawn Up from the Original Diaries with Historical Illustrations, with New Maps and Plans*. Boston: Crocker & Brewster, 1856.

Robinson, Edward, and Eli Smith. *Biblical Researches in Palestine and Adjacent Regions: A Journal of Travels in the Year 1838*. 2 vols. 3rd ed. Boston: Crocker & Brewster, 1868.

———. *Later Biblical Researches in Palestine and Adjacent Regions: A Journal of Travels in the Year 1852*. Boston: Crocker & Brewster, 1871.

Rogerson, John. "Frontiers and Borders in the Old Testament." In *In Search of True Wisdom: Essays in Old Testament Interpretation in Honour of Ronald E.*

Clements, ed. Edward Ball, 116–26. Sheffield, U.K.: Sheffield Academic Press, 1999.

Running, Leona Glidden, and David Noel Freedman. *William Foxwell Albright: A Twentieth-Century Genius*. New York: Morgan, 1975.

Rydell, Robert. *All the World's a Fair: Visions of Empire at American International Expositions, 1876–1916*. Chicago: University of Chicago Press, 1984.

————. *World of Fairs: The Century-of-Progress Expositions*. Chicago: University of Chicago Press, 1993.

Said, Edward. *Orientalism*. New York: Vintage, 1978.

Saunders, Ernest. *Searching the Scriptures: A History of the Society of Biblical Literature, 1880–1980*. Chico, Calif.: Scholars, 1982.

Segev, Tom. *One Palestine, Complete: Jews and Arabs under the British Mandate*. New York: Metropolitan, 2000.

Shepherd, George W. "Jerusalem at the World's Fair." *American Illustrated Methodist Magazine* 9 (February 1903): 237–40.

————. "The Oriental Exposition Company's Great Religious Exhibit." *American Illustrated Methodist Magazine* 9 (April 1903): 353–55.

Silberman, Neil Asher. *Digging for God and Country: Exploration, Archeology, and the Secret Struggle for the Holy Land, 1799–1917*. New York: Alfred A. Knopf, 1982.

Silk, Mark. "Notes on the Judeo-Christian Tradition in America." *American Quarterly* 36, no. 1 (1984): 65–85.

Smith, Eli. *Researches of the Rev. E. Smith and H. G. O. Dwight in Armenia: Including a Journey through Asia Minor and into Georgia and Persia, with a Visit to the Nestorian and Chaldean Christians of Oormiah and Salmas*. Boston: Crocker & Brewster, 1833.

Smith, Elna M., and Charles F. Robertson, eds. *Besieged Patriot: Autobiographical Episodes Exposing Communism, Traitorism, and Zionism from the Life of Gerald L. K. Smith*. Eureka Springs, Ark.: Elna M. Smith Foundation, 1978.

Smith, George Adam. *Historical Atlas of the Holy Land*. London: Hodder and Stoughton, 1915; rev. ed., 1935.

————. *The Historical Geography of the Holy Land Especially in Relation to the History of Israel and of the Early Church*. London: Hodder and Stoughton, 1894.

————. *Jerusalem: The Topography, Economics, and History from Earliest Times to A.D. 70*. London: Hodder and Stoughton, 1907. Reprinted with a critical assessment by Samuel Yeivin. New York: KTAV, 1972.

Smith, Henry B., and Roswell D. Hitchcock. *The Life, Writings, and Character of Edward Robinson, D.D., LL.D.* New York: Anson D. F. Randolph, 1863.

Smith-Rosenberg, Carroll. *Disorderly Conduct: Visions of Gender in Victorian America*. New York: Alfred A. Knopf, 1985.

Soja, Edward W. *Thirdspace: Journeys to Los Angeles and Other Real-and-Imagined Places*. Oxford: Blackwell, 1996.

Sperling, S. David. *Students of the Covenant: A History of Jewish Biblical Scholarship in North America.* Atlanta, Ga.: Scholars, 1992.

Stevens, Walter B. *The Forest City.* St. Louis, Mo.: N. D. Thompson, 1904.

Thompson, John. *Studies in the Theory of Ideology.* Berkeley and Los Angeles: University of California Press, 1984.

Thomson, William M. *The Land and the Book: or, Biblical Illustrations Drawn from the Manners and Customs, the Scenes and Scenery, of the Holy Land.* 2 vols. New York: Harper and Brothers, 1859.

Trillin, Calvin. "U.S. Journal: Eureka Springs, Ark., The Sacred Projects." *New Yorker,* July 26, 1969, 69–79.

Trimmer, Edward Albert. "John Heyl Vincent: An Evangelist for Education." Ed.D. diss., Columbia University, 1986.

Tufnell, Olga. "Excavator's Progress. Letters of F. J. Bliss, 1889–1900." *Palestine Exploration Quarterly* 97 (1965): 112–27.

Twain, Mark. *The Innocents Abroad; or, the New Pilgrim's Progress.* Hartford, Conn.: American Publishing Co., 1869. Reprint, New York: New American Library, 1966.

Van Dyke, Henry. *Out-of-Doors in the Holy Land: Impressions of Travel in Body and Spirit.* New York: Charles Scribner's Sons, 1908.

Vilnay, Zev. *The New Israel Atlas: The Bible to Present Day.* Jerusalem: Israel Universities Press, 1968.

Vincent, John Heyl. *The Chautauqua Movement.* With an introduction by Lewis Miller. Boston: Chautauqua, 1886.

Vincent, John H., James W. Lee, and R. E. M. Bain. *Earthly Footsteps of the Man of Galilee.* New York: N. D. Thompson, 1894.

Vincent, Leon H. *John Heyl Vincent: A Biographical Sketch.* New York: Macmillan, 1925.

Vogel, Lester. "Staying Home for the Sights: Surrogate Destinations in America for Holy Land Travel." In *Pilgrims and Travelers to the Holy Land,* Studies in Jewish Civilization 7, ed. Bryan F. Le Beau and Menachem Mor, 251–67. Omaha, Neb.: Creighton University Press, 1996.

———. *To See a Promised Land: Americans and the Holy Land in the Nineteenth Century.* University Park: Pennsylvania State University Press, 1993.

Vostral, Sharra L. "Imperialism on Display: The Philippine Exhibition at the 1904 World's Fair." *Gateway Heritage* 13, no. 4 (1993): 18–31.

Wadsworth, Nelson B. *Set in Stone, Fixed in Glass: The Great Mormon Temple and Its Photographers.* Salt Lake City: Signature, 1992.

Walker, John. "The Walled City of Jerusalem—in St. Louis." *Cosmopolitan* 37 (September 1904): 575–76.

Westgate, G. L. *Official Report of the National Sunday-School Teachers' Assembly, Held at Fair Point, Chautauqua County, N.Y., on the Borders of Chautauqua Lake, August 4–18, 1874.* New York: Sunday School Union, 1875.

Whitehair, Charles W. "An Old Jewel in the Proper Setting: An Eyewitness's Account of the Reconquest of the Holy Land by Twentieth Century Crusaders." *National Geographic Magazine* 33, no. 10 (October 1918): 325–44.

Whitelam, Keith W. "Constructing Jerusalem." Paper presented at a meeting of the Society of Biblical Literature, November 1998. Available at <http://www.cwru.edu/affil/GAIR/Constructions/xtrapapers2000.html > (accessed March 8, 2002).

———. *The Invention of Ancient Israel: The Silencing of Palestinian History.* London: Routledge, 1996.

———. "Transcending the Boundaries: Expanding the Limits." Paper presented at a meeting of the Society of Biblical Literature, November 2001. Available at <http://www.cwru.edu/affil/GAIR/Constructions/Program2001.html> (accessed March 8, 2002).

Wilken, Robert L. *The Land Called Holy: Palestine in Christian History and Thought.* New Haven: Yale University Press, 1992.

Williams, Jay G. *The Life and Times of Edward Robinson: Connecticut Yankee in King Solomon's Court.* Atlanta, Ga.: Society of Biblical Literature, 1999.

Wilson, Charles William, ed. *Picturesque Palestine, Sinai, and Egypt.* 2 vols. New York: D. Appleton, 1881.

Wilson, Edward. *In Scripture Lands: New Views of Sacred Places.* New York: Charles Scribner's Sons, 1895.

Wood, Denis. *The Power of Maps.* New York: Guilford, 1992.

World's Fair Authentic Guide. St. Louis, Mo.: Official Guide Co., 1904.

World's Fair Souvenir Album of Jerusalem, Published by Direction of Jerusalem Exhibit Co. St. Louis, Mo.: Towers, 1903.

Wright, G. Ernest. *Biblical Archaeology.* Philadelphia, Pa.: Westminster, 1955; rev. ed., 1962.

———. "Bringing Old Testament Times to Life." *National Geographic Magazine* 112, no. 12 (December 1957): 833–64.

———. *The Challenge of Israel's Faith.* Chicago: University of Chicago Press, 1944.

———. *God Who Acts: Biblical Theology as Recital.* London: SCM Press, 1952.

———. "The Last Thousand Years before Christ." *National Geographic Magazine* 115, no. 12 (December 1960): 813–53.

———. *The Old Testament against Its Environment.* London: SCM Press, 1950.

———. *Shechem: The Biography of a Biblical City.* New York: McGraw-Hill, 1964.

Wright, G. Ernest, and Floyd Filson, eds. *The Westminster Historical Atlas to the Bible.* Philadelphia: Westminster, 1945; rev. ed., 1956.

INDEX

Page numbers in italics refer to illustrations.

Abbott, Lyman, 226n17, 231n63

Ackerman, Gerald, 213n54

Albright, William Foxwell: American Schools of Oriental Research and, 139–141, 188, 229n34; biblical apologetics and, 139, 143–45; biblical archaeology and, 139, 141–43, 188; biography of, xi, 141, *142*, 229n33; C. C. McCown and, 146–47, 229n34; G. E. Wright and, 187–89 passim, 191, 195, 203, 237nn46,55,57, 238n59; Holy Land colonists and, 229n32; idea of the Holy Land, 141–46, 163; ideological commitments of, 141, 143–46; Max Margolis and, 158–59; political debates and, 144–46, 195; socialism and, 144–45; Zionism and, 159

Albright school, 187–88, 238n59

Allenby, Edmund, 32, 214n71

American Colony (Jerusalem), 137

American Consulate (Jerusalem), 137, *138*

American Institute of Sacred Literature, 91–93, 221n9

American Palestine Exploration Society, 132, 134, 137, 225n6

American Schools of Oriental Research, 129, 131–41, 138, 157, 163. *See also* Albright, William Foxwell; McCown, Chester Charlton; Margolis, Max Leopold; Wright, G. Ernest

Bain, Robert E. M., 53

Balogh, Balage, 206–208 passim

Barth, Karl, 237n55

Barton, George, 103, 138–39, 196, 228n28

Bestor, Mary Frances, 37

Biblical Geography and History (Kent), 97–100, 103, 106

Biblical persons: Abraham, 32, 55, 60, 62, 135, 180, 182; Ahab, 224n59; Anna, 25; Boaz, 127; David, 25, 32, 36, 109, 122, 199, 200; Delilah, 159; Ehud, 127; Elijah, 19; Ezra, 199; Gideon, 127, 224n59; Herod, 75, 84, 200, 220n67; Hezekiah, 200; Isaac, 32, 60, 62; Isaiah, 199; Jacob, 32, 55, 95, 169; Jeremiah, 199; John the Baptist, 98, 168; Joseph, 32, 161, 169; Judas, 67, 69; Judas Maccabeus, 223n52; Laban, 95; Martha, 119; Mary, 25, 69, 111, *112*, 116, 222n27; Moses, 161, 179, 196–98 passim, 206; Nehemiah, 199; Noah, 161; Othniel, 127; Paul, 15, 104, 122, 183; Peter, *117*, 125; Pontius Pilate, 75;

Ruth, 127; Salomé, 84, 220n67; Samson, 159; Samuel, 32, 108, 139, 223n52; Saul (King), 32, 108, 139; Sihon, 238n72; Solomon, 25, 32, 56, 60, 122, 199, 200; Stephen, 60; Zerubbabel, 56. *See also* Jesus

Biblical places: Akeldama (Aceldama), 36; Baal-Zephon, 195; Bashan, 19; Beersheba, 135; Bethany, 116, *117*, 118–20, 179, 224n63; Bethlehem, 15, 25, 28, 36, 125; Bethpage, 179; Caanan, 1, 12, 31, 135, 155, 191, 196; Calvary, 62; Capernaum (Chorazin), 122–25, *124*, 206, 207–208, 221n25; Carmel, 19; Chesalon, 159; Damascus, 15, 103, *104*; Dan, 135; Dead Sea, 28, 33, 36–37, 136; Eden, 184; Egypt, 11; Emmaus, 109, *110*, 111–13; Galilee, 19, 95, 98–100, 137, 152, 168; Gethsemane, 122, 200; Gibeah, 139; Gilead, 19; Golgotha, 74; Hill of Evil Council, 36; Holy Sepulchre, 15, 122, 200, 206; house of Joseph of Arimathea, 69; house of Peter, 120, 206; Jacob's Well, 31, 165–76 passim, *166*, *167* (map), *174*, 202, 234n12, 235n18, 237n49; Joppa (Jaffa), 103, 116, *117*; Jericho, 118, 224n59, 237n49; Jordan River, 19, 28, 30, 31, 33, 34, 37, 98, 136–37, 222nn28,33, 224n59, 237n49; Judea, 30, 36, 40, 168; Mar Elyas, 36; Mizpah, 108, 139, 223n52; Moab, 33, 36, 238n72; Mount Ebal, 31, 168, 172; Mount Gerizim, 31, *166*, 168, 173; Mount Hermon, 28, 30, 33, 37, 40; Mount Moriah, 60, 122, *123*, 224n59; Mount of Offence, 36; Mount of Olives (Olivet), 36, 74, 109, 116, 122, 179, 224n66; Mount Scopus, 162; Mount Sinai (Horeb), 15, 183; Mount Tabor, 15; Nazareth, 25, 98, 99, 111–12, *111*, 206–207, 222n26; Pithom, 195; Plain of Gennesaret, 189; Plain of Rephaim, 36; Red Sea, 11–12; Samaria, 19, 168, 237n49; Sea of Galilee, 15, 28, 33, 40, 122–25 passim, 189, 222n33; Seir, 159; Shechem, 168–69, 237n49; Shur, 195; Succoth, 98, 99, 111–11, 206–209; Sychar, 168–69, 173; tomb of Lazarus, 120, 150, *151*; Tyre, 98, 224n78; Valley of Hinnom, 36; Via Dolorosa, 60, 69; Zion, 14, 36, 65, 161–62. *See also* Holy Land map sites; Jerusalem

253

Index

Burke O. Long is the William R. Kenan Professor of Religion
Emeritus at Bowdoin College and author of a number of studies of
the Bible and biblical scholarship, including most recently *Planting and Reaping Albright: Politics, Ideology, and Interpreting the Bible*.